Christian Metal

BLOOMSBURY STUDIES IN RELIGION AND POPULAR MUSIC

Series editors: Christopher Partridge and Sara Cohen

Religion's relationship to popular music has ranged from opposition to 'the Devil's music' to an embracing of modern styles and subcultures in order to communicate its ideas and defend its values. Similarly, from jazz to reggae, gospel to heavy metal, and bhangra to qawwali, there are few genres of contemporary popular music that have not dealt with ideas and themes related to religion, spiritual and the paranormal. Whether we think of Satanism or Sufism, the liberal use of drugs or disciplined abstinence, the history of the quest for transcendence within popular music and its subcultures raises important issues for anyone interested in contemporary religion, culture and society. *Bloomsbury Studies in Religion and Popular Music* is a multi-disciplinary series that aims to contribute to a comprehensive understanding of these issues and the relationships between religion and popular music.

Sacred and Secular Musics, Virinda Kalra

Religion in Hip Hop, Monica R. Miller, Anthony B. Pinn, Bernard 'Bun B' Freeman

Christian Metal

History, Ideology, Scene

MARCUS MOBERG

Bloomsbury Academic
An imprint of Bloomsbury Publishing Plc

B L O O M S B U R Y
LONDON · NEW DELHI · NEW YORK · SYDNEY

Bloomsbury Academic
An imprint of Bloomsbury Publishing Plc

50 Bedford Square, London, WC1B 3DP, UK
1385 Broadway, New York, NY 10018, USA
29 Earlsfort Terrace, Dublin 2, Ireland

www.bloomsbury.com

BLOOMSBURY and the Diana logo are trademarks of Bloomsbury Publishing Plc

First published 2015

© Marcus Moberg, 2015

Marcus Moberg has asserted his right under the Copyright, Designs and Patents Act, 1988, to be identified as Author of this work.

All rights reserved. No part of this publication may be reproduced or transmitted in any form or by any means, electronic or mechanical, including photocopying, recording, or any information storage or retrieval system, without prior permission in writing from the publishers.

No responsibility for loss caused to any individual or organization acting on or refraining from action as a result of the material in this publication can be accepted by Bloomsbury or the author.

British Library Cataloguing-in-Publication Data
A catalogue record for this book is available from the British Library.

ISBN: HB: 978-1-4725-7984-3
PB: 978-1-4725-7983-6
ePDF: 978-1-4725-7985-0
ePub: 978-1-4725-7986-7

Library of Congress Cataloging-in-Publication Data
Moberg, Marcus, 1978- author.
Christian metal : history, ideology, scene / Marcus Moberg.
pages cm. – (Bloomsbury studies in religion and popular music)
Includes bibliographical references and index.
ISBN 978-1-4725-7983-6 (pbk.) – ISBN 978-1-4725-7984-3 (hardback)
1. Contemporary Christian music–History and criticism.
2. Heavy metal (Music)–History and criticism. I. Title.
ML3187.5.M62 2015
782.25'166–dc23
2014044637

Series: Bloomsbury Studies in Religion and Popular Music

Typeset by Integra Software Services Pvt. Ltd

Contents

List of Illustrations   vii

Preface   ix

Permission Page   xi

1 Introduction   1

2 Christian Metal: Origins, Definition and Historical Development   33

3 Verbal, Visual and Aesthetic Traits   53

4 The Experiential, Sensory and Bodily Dimensions   67

5 The Contemporary Transnational Scene   83

6 Main Ideological and Discursive Traits   121

7 Concluding Remarks: Christian Metal, Alternative Religious Expression and Identity   151

Notes   156

Bibliography   173

Index   183

List of Illustrations

Figure 3.1 Christian metal style. Photo: Marcus Moberg (2008) — 62

Figure 3.2 Album cover for War of Ages' *Arise and Conquer*. Reproduced with the kind permission of Facedown Records — 64

Figure 3.3 Album cover for Impending Doom's *There Will be Violence*. Reproduced with the kind permission of Facedown Records — 65

Figure 4.1 'One way'. Crowd at *Immortal Metal Fest*, Finland, 2008. Photo: Marcus Moberg — 77

Figure 4.2 Entrance at *Immortal Metal Fest*, Finland, 2008. Photo: Marcus Moberg — 80

Figure 5.1 Cover for *Heaven's Metal*, issue 88, July–August, 2011. Reproduced with the kind permission of *HM: The Hard Music Magazine* — 106

Figure 5.2 Cover for *HM: The Hard Music Magazine*, July, 2013. Reproduced with the kind permission of *HM: The Hard Music Magazine* — 107

Figure 5.3 Cover for *Extreme Brutal Death*, issue 2, 2013. Reproduced with the kind permission of *Extreme Records* — 108

| **Figure 5.4** | Front page of *The Metal for Jesus Page*. Reproduced with the kind permission of Johannes Jonsson | 109 |
| **Figure 5.5** | Front page of *Angelic Warlord.com*. Reproduced with the kind permission of *Angelic Warlord.com* | 110 |

Preface

My interest in Christian metal started back in early 2004 after having received my Master's degree at the Department of Comparative Religion at Åbo Akademi University in Turku, Finland. Intent on continuing by pursuing a doctoral degree in religious studies, I was pondering different topics relating to the present-day intersection of religion and popular culture. I had played with the idea of somehow researching the relationship between religion and metal in general for a while, but when I by chance found out that a vibrant Christian metal scene actually existed in my own country I knew I had found my topic. If I did not write my thesis on this topic no one else would, I thought. This led me on the research path that I am still partly walking today. Since the completion of my doctoral thesis in 2009, I continued to research the Christian metal scene from different angles. I have tried to include all of the most important things I have to say about Christian metal in this book. I certainly do not wish this book to be the last word on Christian metal, but it is *my* final word. I wish to thank Professor Christopher Partridge at the Department for Politics, Philosophy and Religion at Lancaster University, UK, for giving me the opportunity to write this book.

This book draws together all of my previous work on Christian metal. As such, it includes a large amount of work that has already been published elsewhere and is reproduced here with the kind permission of Taylor & Francis, Equinox Publishing, Sheffield Phoenix Press and The Finnish Society for the Study of Religion. Parts previously published as 'The "Double Controversy" of Christian Metal' (in *Popular Music History* 6/1–2, 2012, Equinox Publishing) are included in Chapters 1 and 2. Parts previously published as 'Portrayals of the End Times, the Apocalypse and the Last Judgment in Christian Metal Music' (in *Anthems of Apocalypse: Popular Music and Apocalyptic Thought*, Sheffield Phoenix Press, 2012) are included in Chapters 1, 2 and 3. Parts previously published as 'Religion in Popular Music or Popular Music as Religion? A Critical Review of Scholarly Writing on the Place of Religion in Metal Music and Culture' (in *Popular Music and Society* 35/1, 2012, Taylor & Francis, http://www.tandfonline.com/loi/rpms20#.U8X5O_mSxyI) are included in Chapter 1. Parts previously published as 'Religious Popular Music: Between the Instrumental, Transcendent and

Transgressive', co-authored with Keith Kahn-Harris (in *Temenos: Nordic Journal of Comparative Religion* 48/1, 2012) are included in Chapters 4 and 7. Parts previously published as 'First-, Second-, and Third-Level Discourse Analytic Approaches in the Study of Religion: Moving from Meta-Theoretical Reflection to Implementation in Practice' (in *Religion* 43/1, 2013, Taylor & Francis, http://www.tandfonline.com/loi/rrel20#.U8X5ofmSxyI) are included in Chapter 6. Parts previously published as 'The Concept of Scene and its Applicability in Empirically Grounded Research on the Intersection of Religion/Spirituality and Popular Music' (in *Journal of Contemporary Religion* 26/3, 2011, http://www.tandfonline.com/loi/cjcr20#.U8X6P_mSxyI) are included in Chapter 5.

All chapters include parts previously published as *Faster for the Master! Exploring Issues of Religious Expression and Alternative Christian Identity within the Finnish Christian Metal Music Scene* (Åbo Akademi University Press, 2009).

Permission Page

The following extracts, lyrics and images were reproduced with kind permission. The author has made every effort to trace copyright holders and to obtain permission to reproduce these materials. This has not been possible in every case, however, any omissions brought to our attention will be remedied in future editions.

Angelic Warlord.com http://www.angelicwarlord.com/ [accessed 13 July 2014].

Deliverance. 'No Time'. *Deliverance* (artist – Deliverance, by Jimmy P. Brown II) ℗&©1989 Intense Records (Broken Songs, a div of Meis Music Group div of Meis Music Group).

Extreme Brutal Death, 2005/1 © Extreme Brutal Death.

Heaven's Metal #88, July/Aug 2011 © HM Magazine.

HM Magazine, July 2013 © HM Magazine.

Impending Doom, 'There Will Be Violence'. *There Will Be Violence* (Facedown Records, 2010).

Metal for Jesus Page http://www.metalforjesus.org [accessed 11 July 2014].

Moberg, M., 'First-, Second-, and Third-Level Discourse Analytic Approaches in the Study of Religion: Moving from Meta-Theoretical Reflection to Implementation in Practice', *Religion* 43 (2013), pp. 4–25. www.tandfonline.com

Moberg, M., 'Religion in Popular Music or Popular Music as Religion? A Critical Review of Scholarly Writing on the Place of Religion in Metal Music and Culture', *Popular Music and Society* 35:1 (2012), pp. 113–130, www.tandfonline.com

Moberg, M. 'The "Double Controversy" of Christian Metal', *Popular Music History* 6:1–2 (2012), pp. 85–99, © Equinox Publishing.

Moberg, M., 'The Concept of Scene and Its Applicability in Empirically Grounded Research on the Intersection of Religion/Spirituality and Popular Music', *Journal of Contemporary Religion* 26:3 (2011), pp. 403–417, www.tandfonline.com

Kahn-Harris, K. and Moberg, M. 'Religious Popular Music: Between the Instrumental, Transcendent and Transgressive', *Temenos: Nordic Journal of Comparative Religion* 48:1 (2012), pp. 87–106.

Moberg, M., 'Portrayals of the End Times, the Apocalypse and the Last Judgment in Christian Metal Music', in C. Partridge (ed.), *Anthems of Apocalypse: Popular Music and Apocalyptic Thought*, Sheffield: Sheffield Phoenix Press, 2012.

Saint. 'Crime Scene Earth'. *Crime Scene Earth* (Armor Records, 2008).

Saint. 'Primed and Ready'. *Time's End* (Pure Metal, 1986).

Saint, *The Mark* (Armor Records, 2006).

War of Ages, 'Salvation'. *Arise and Conquer* (Facedown Records, 2008).

War of Ages, *Arise and Conquer* (Facedown Records, 2008).

1

Introduction

During recent decades, scholars of religion have increasingly started to draw attention to the role being played by *popular culture* within the overall context of religious change and transformation in the West. Popular culture, it is argued, not only reflects these changes but, in turn, also provides important sources of inspiration for the construction of religious identities and the transformation of religious and spiritual practices for increasing numbers of people today.

The growing need for many Christian groups to compete on the contemporary religious marketplace has increasingly come to entail some form of engagement with popular culture. This book explores how popular music has evolved into an ever more natural and self-evident resource for the renewal of traditional Christianity through the lens of the phenomenon of *Christian metal music*. Christian metal – that is metal music that conveys a Christian message and is principally produced both by and for Christians, provides a particularly good example of this. In addition to the music, Christian metal has rather unreservedly adopted most other aspects of its 'secular', 'not-explicitly Christian' counterpart, such as its uncompromising attitude and rhetoric, its distinctive style and deliberately provocative aesthetic.

Since its initial emergence in the early 1980s, Christian metal music has developed into a distinct transnational Christian popular musical phenomenon in its own right. It has developed its own and highly independent means of production, distribution, media and festivals. As such, it has developed into a distinct transnational space in which Christians from a number of countries, with a range of different Christian backgrounds and affiliations, and a passion for metal music, can meet. Although it remains firmly embedded in evangelical Protestantism, the Christian metal scene is not directly controlled by any Christian institution or group and it advocates no particular denominational creed.

The contemporary Christian metal scene can thus be seen as an example of a space in which Christianity and a distinct and highly controversial form of popular music and its culture have met and merged. Having said that, Christian metal music has simultaneously also always been at least partly defined in opposition to its secular counterpart. Following from its appropriation of all central aspects of metal music and culture and its efforts to rework these through a Christian frame, Christian metal has always been precariously located on the borderline between the worlds of evangelical Christianity and metal music and culture. Compared to the world of secular metal and its global reach, Christian metal has remained a marginal phenomenon. Yet, through the untiring evangelistic efforts of Christian metal bands such as Stryper, Bloodgood, Barren Cross and Mortification, the phenomenon of Christian metal has become widely known and often fiercely contested in the secular metal community and, as such, fairly widely known among the general public as well. That said, there are still plenty of people who are not aware that such a thing as Christian metal even exists. Partly following from its marginal status, the phenomenon of Christian metal has so far received only a very limited degree of scholarly attention.

This book aims to provide a comprehensive guide to the phenomenon of Christian metal music, its history, main characteristics, development, diversification and key ideological traits from its formative years in the early 1980s to the present day. This book situates Christian metal in a wider international evangelical cultural environment, accounts for its diffusion on a transnational scale and explores what religious meanings and functions Christian metal holds for its own musicians and followers. As part of this, the book also aims to explore the ways in which the contemporary Christian metal scene provides its members with resources for the shaping of a consciously and pronounced alternative way of expressing and 'doing' religion. These issues will be explored in relation to an understanding of the contemporary Christian metal scene as a distinct space that is popular cultural in form but religious in outlook. Last but certainly not least, in doing this, this book aims to provide an account of Christian metal that is fair and recognizable to its own creators and followers.

The structure of the book

In this introduction we will set the stage for subsequent chapters by providing a general account of the historical development, diversification and main musical, verbal and aesthetic characteristics of metal music and culture on the whole. Particular attention will be devoted to metal's relationship with religion since that is key to an adequate understanding of the development of Christian metal. In this introduction, we will also situate the development of Christian metal within a wider contemporary historical, social, cultural and religious context through highlighting how its emergence and development necessarily needs to be understood in connection to the broader phenomenon of 'evangelical popular culture'.

Chapter 2 provides a general account of the origins, historical development and musical diversification of Christian metal since its initial emergence in the early 1980s and discusses notable developments in Christian metal history. This chapter also discusses the ways in which Christian metal typically is defined by its own followers. Building on the general account of metal music and culture provided in the Introduction, Chapter 2 concludes with a discussion of the controversies that Christian metal engendered in evangelical and conservative Christian circles during its formative years of development in the 1980s.

Chapter 3 turns to a discussion of Christian metal's main verbal, visual and aesthetic dimensions as expressed through song lyrics, album cover artwork, the design of Christian metal webpages and so on. The main aim of this chapter is thus largely descriptive. It is intended to provide readers with a general idea of what Christian metal 'sounds' and 'looks like' through addressing questions such as: What are the main lyrical themes of Christian metal and how do these relate to the main lyrical conventions and rhetorical traits of metal music on the whole? What are the stylistic and aesthetic characteristics of Christian metal and how do they relate to metal style and aesthetics in a wider sense? Particular focus is directed at the ways in which Christian metal reworks secular metal's verbal, visual and aesthetic traits through a Christian frame while simultaneously striving to conform to metal's main genre conventions.

Chapter 4 discusses the experiential, sensory and bodily dimensions of Christian metal, particularly as experienced in the context of the live Christian metal concert setting. While Christian metal on the whole often positions itself in binary opposition to secular metal's main transgressive elements (as outlined in earlier chapters), it nevertheless clearly stands out from most other forms of Christian popular music through its rather unreserved appropriation of metal's energetic sensory and bodily practices. The chapter starts out on a more critical tone through a discussion of how the experiential categories of the 'transcendent', 'transgressive' and 'instrumental' may be of help in approaching and understanding the appropriation of popular music for religious purposes. The chapter then goes on to explore the ways in which Christian metal concert practices involve a conscious combination of typical metal practices with a range of recognizably religious or 'church-like' practices and modes of bodily behaviours. This chapter thus highlights how such a mixing of metal and religious 'repertoires' contributes to the construction of Christian metal live concerts as events that are equally characterized by religious worship and expression as they are by collective musical appreciation, release and entertainment. The chapter thus aims to explain how live Christian metal concerts provide participants with a temporal space that is consciously designed to foster a sense of community and shared religious experience via and through the particular musical expression and bodily practices of metal.

Chapter 5 outlines Christian metal's diffusion on a transnational scale. Utilizing the methodological framework of *scene*, this chapter focuses on Christian metal culture as a distinct transnational religious-popular cultural space and maps its core regions and structure on a transnational level. This chapter accounts for how Christian metal musicians and followers around the world have formed their own transnationally dispersed independent infrastructure of production and distributions outlets, different print and online Christian metal media and different gatherings and festivals. The chapter also briefly discusses how Christian metal has spread to predominantly Catholic countries with significant Protestant minorities such as Brazil and Mexico. The principal aim of the chapter is to provide a general account of how the contemporary transnational Christian metal scene, although it consists of a web of national and regional scenes of various sizes which display their own peculiarities, still needs to be viewed as a distinct religious-cultural phenomenon that transcends national and regional borders.

Chapter 6 explores the central ideological traits of Christian metal through focusing on the ways in which Christian metal musicians and followers themselves discursively construct Christian metal as a particular type of phenomenon that serves a certain set of main functions and purposes. Through employing a discourse-analytic approach, the chapter thus highlights what specific meanings and functions Christian metal is ascribed by its own creators and followers. This is done through looking at the ways in which Christian metal is talked about and represented in different forms of Christian metal media in particular. Four key discourses are identified and discussed that still dominate the discursive construction of the phenomenon of Christian metal on a transnational level and continue to affect the ways in which Christian metal typically is both represented and understood among its own creators and followers.

Chapter 7, finally, offers some general concluding observations about the functions that Christian metal culture fills in the everyday religious lives of its followers; how it provides its followers with alternative modes of religious expression, an alternative way of 'doing' religion and important resources for the construction of alternative Christian identities.

Metal music and culture: A general overview

Metal is no doubt one of the most aggressive, extreme, controversial and debated forms of popular music of our time. Its history stretches back to the emergence of the heavy metal rock-genre in the late 1960s and early 1970s. Since then, heavy metal has developed, evolved and diversified in a number of different directions. These days, the term 'metal' is commonly used as a general term, coupling together a large amount of varyingly related subgenres and styles that have developed through the years and that share some distinctive musical and aesthetic traits (some commentators also use the term 'heavy metal' itself as a general term).

With a history spanning around four and a half decades, metal has also proven exceptionally enduring and long-lived in the context of a global, rapidly changing and increasingly fluid world of popular musical production and consumption. As such, it has exerted considerable influence on the development of many other forms of popular music.[1] Together with the tribal-type popular music culture that has constituted an inseparable and central component of it since its early days, metal has also spread on a global scale far beyond what is usually seen as the Western cultural sphere. Vibrant metal scenes can nowadays be found across the globe, from Latin America and South East Asia to the Middle East and Northern Africa.[2] In some countries, most notably Nordic countries such as Finland, Sweden and Norway, metal has since long entered the popular musical mainstream. The extreme character of the music and its corresponding use of provocative and often radical lyrical themes and aesthetics have also sparked a great deal of controversy and debate and made metal a highly polarizing form of music that is as dearly loved, appreciated and defended among its fans as it is detested and reviled among its detractors.[3] This chapter provides a general overview and discussion of the history and key musical, verbal, visual and aesthetic characteristics of metal music and culture. However, because of the huge range and scope of the subject, this account does by no means aim to be comprehensive or exhaustive. The story of metal has already been told in detail in several excellent studies.[4] In the following, we will direct most of our attention at the verbal dimension of metal and particularly the inspiration it always has drawn from different forms of, often subversive, religious themes and imagery.

Studying metal music and culture

Compared to the interest directed at most other major and long-lived popular music genres, scholarly work on metal used to be scarce. This might seem strange considering the exceptional longevity of metal as a genre, the many often 'Satanism'-related controversies and moral panics that have surrounded it, and the fact that it has long ago developed into a truly global popular music culture that continuously attracts new and ardent followers all over the world. As Brown has argued, earlier scholarly disregard of metal music and culture (especially within youth subcultural research) is perhaps best explained by metal culture's general disinterest in matters related to cultural politics.[5] As a consequence of this, scholars interested in exploring popular music 'subcultures' as sites of 'counter hegemonic resistance' in the late 1970s and early 1980s instead turned their investigating eye to more obviously politically oriented popular music cultures such as punk.[6]

Although the field of metal studies long remained a small, marginal area of study, there has nevertheless been an uneven flow of scholarly explorations of metal music and culture since the early 1990s. These include book-length works such as Weinstein's seminal work *Heavy Metal: A Cultural Sociology* (and its later edition *Heavy Metal: The Music and Its Culture*), Walser's *Running with the Devil: Power, Gender, and Madness in Heavy Metal Music*, Arnett's *Metalheads: Heavy Metal Music and Adolescent Alienation*,[7] Berger's *Metal, Rock and Jazz: Perception and the Phenomenology of Musical Experience*,[8] and Keith Kahn-Harris's *Extreme Metal: Music and Culture on the Edge*.[9]

Through primarily concentrating on the various forms of relationships that exist between heavy metal artists, fans and specialized media, Weinstein's work aims to offer a broad yet comprehensive account of all central aspects of metal music and culture by understanding them as forming a cultural bricolage. Weinstein's study also directs particular focus at the various ways in which heavy metal music and culture serves to empower its supposedly disenfranchised fans and audiences. This focus on empowerment, as Kahn-Harris points out, has always constituted 'a key theme in studies of metal'.[10] However, since Weinstein's analysis mainly concentrates on the 'classic' heavy metal of the 1980s, its value for an understanding of the later development of other forms of metal is limited.

Walser's study offers a largely similar account of heavy metal culture as providing disenfranchised youth with a vehicle to, as Kahn-Harris puts it, 'escape the oppressive confines of deindustrialized capitalism'.[11] One notable virtue of Walser's study is that it combines an account of heavy metal's history with a musicological analysis of its purely musical qualities and characteristics. Like Weinstein, however, Walser concentrates almost exclusively on the heavy metal of the 1980s. In spite of these limitations, Weinstein's and Walser's pioneering work has been hugely influential in the study of metal by setting the stage for subsequent research and providing it with much to build on. Combined, their studies offer a comprehensive and valuable account of heavy metal music and culture, particularly that of the 1980s.

The interpretation of metal as empowering its audience by providing a sense of meaning and community first developed and elaborated in these studies has been of particular importance since it highlights the need for metal to be understood within broader social and cultural contexts, particularly those of late modern post-industrial societies.[12] Arnett's study explores the issue of empowerment in a rather different light, arguing that the popularity of metal is best explained by American society's incapability or failure to 'properly' socialize its youth and adolescents.[13]

All of the studies of metal mentioned so far also share the widespread notion of metal fans being young, 'predominantly white, male, heterosexual and working class', a notion that 'has been taken as fact by many researchers and applied indiscriminately to all metal genres' even though there exists only 'very limited data' to support it.[14] Although there are some merits to some parts of this commonly held notion, one should nevertheless be cautious in drawing any more specific conclusions about metal fans on the basis of these, often both unsubstantiated and presumed, general demographics.

Kahn-Harris' study differs significantly from those of Weinstein's, Walser's and Arnett's through its focus on the highly significant but often ignored so-called *extreme metal* sub-genres. Kahn-Harris also introduces a new approach to the study of metal based on the framework of *scene* – an approach that will also be employed in this book. Kahn-Harris directs particular attention at the various forms of interrelationships that exist between different elements of the global extreme metal scene, offering an interpretation of it as being sustained through a delicate balance between its 'transgressive' and 'mundane' elements, reflected in scene member's accumulation of transgressive and mundane subcultural capital. In addition to offering a detailed examination of extreme metal music and culture, Kahn-Harris' differently theorized study also offers an alternative approach to the study of metal as such that is more sensitive to the peculiarities of the wider global metal culture of today.

Building on the abovementioned foundational studies, the past decade has witnessed a veritable upsurge in academic interest in metal music and culture. Today, one can find a large number of thorough and detailed article-length analyses of a range of different aspects and issues related to metal music and culture from a variety of different perspectives, including (but far from limited to) such things as gender issues,[15] politics,[16] moral panic,[17] and metal music and culture in post-colonial contexts.[18] More recently published edited volumes such as *Heavy Metal Music in Britain*,[19] *Metal*

Rules the Globe,[20] and *Heavy Metal: Controversies and Countercultures*[21] all attest to the growing interest in metal music and culture across different academic disciplines during recent years.

The first ever global academic conference on metal, organized by UK-based Interdisciplinary.net, was held in Salzburg, Austria, in November of 2008, paving the way for a larger number of subsequent academic conferences on different aspects of metal music and culture. The field of metal studies also reached an important benchmark through the establishment of the academic journal *Metal Music Studies* in 2013.

Over the years, a larger number of popular books on the history of metal or analyses of its particular sub-genres have also been produced.[22] It is important to note, therefore, that metal has been approached and studied from a number of different perspectives. However, although metal studies has gradually developed into a more clearly marketed independent field of research, the field still remains quite fragmented and lacking in any coherent terminology.[23] Moreover, wider awareness of both earlier and more recent contributions to this field, as well as general knowledgeability about metal music and culture on the whole, sometimes vary considerably between individual commentators.

Most researchers of metal music and culture view it in a positive light. Indeed, most of the researchers discussed above are themselves professed metal fans. This is worth noting when studying a popular music culture such as metal which itself has a long-standing tradition of 'fan-scholarship',[24] that is, analyses of metal produced by people in the capacity of fans rather than academic researchers. In aiming to present an account of metal music and culture that is as adequate and nuanced as possible, both academic and fan-work needs to be combined. Naturally, researchers of metal commonly draw on a wide range of sources produced within metal culture itself. However, when subjected to rigorous academic theorizing, methodology and terminology, the picture inevitably becomes quite different from that of fan-scholarly accounts. Hence, researchers and fans typically disagree on specific points and interpret them in different ways (as is often illustrated by the reviews that academic accounts of metal tend to receive within various forms of metal media).

In the following, we shall approach metal music and culture through focusing on its key musical, visual and verbal elements. This account will proceed in relation to a general account of the historical development of metal and a description of its distinct sub-genres and styles. Due to its exceptionally high degree of internal diversity, one easily gets confused in metal's jungle of different sub-genres. The term *genre* thus requires some clarification here at the outset.

Genre

In her seminal work on heavy metal music and culture, drawing on the work of Byrnside,[25] Weinstein[26] argues that popular music genres tend to develop through a certain pattern of stages. During an initial stage of 'formation', the differences between a new form of music and the existing ones from which it develops is unclear. This is followed by a period of 'crystallization' in which a new form of music starts to be recognized, and starts to recognize itself, as a distinct style or form of music. This stage is characterized by numerous small shifts and changes, the setting of boundaries to other genres and the development of distinct general musical and aesthetic traits. This stage may either include or be followed by one of 'fragmentation' in which the genre is divided into different sub-genres. Finally, a popular music genre may enter a stage of 'decay' in which it becomes too predictable for audiences to maintain interest. Thus far, metal has shown no signs of decay.

Popular music genres in this perspective also consist of three interrelated main dimensions, a sound/musical dimension, a visual dimension and a verbal dimension. It is primarily in relation to these dimensions that particular meanings are attached to particular genres. In some genres, one dimension may dominate and be regarded as more important that others, but all three play a part in the construction of a genre and the meanings that are attached to it. In relation to these dimensions, a genre develops a certain 'code' that encapsulates its most distinct and characteristic musical, verbal, visual and aesthetic traits. Genre-codes are not systematic or absolute. However, they are normally sufficiently coherent to enable a largely objective identification of a certain core of music as belonging to a certain genre. As we will see, metal has developed a highly distinctive code that allows people to relatively easily and clearly identify certain songs, bands and visual aspects as belonging to the genre.[27]

Heavy metal: Formation and early development

Heavy metal music first emerged in the late 1960s through the fusion of blues-based hard rock and elements of psychedelic rock. At this time, the counterculture of the 1960s, characterized by its ethos of peace, love and tolerance – most commonly expressed through a widespread belief in the possibility of changing the world through social and political activism – was beginning to fragment and break down. At the turn of the decade, the previously widespread countercultural notion of youth-cultural unity was replaced with a fragmentation into distinct and separate youth cultures. According to Weinstein,[28] the development of heavy metal should be understood in the light of this particular historical, social and cultural context. Although heavy metal never was countercultural in the sense usually understood by that term, it nevertheless did emerge in close enough connection to that environment so as to become considerably influenced by it, especially during its initial stage of development. Weinstein argues that heavy metal did indeed adopt some characteristics typical of the 'Woodstock generation'. Much in line with the countercultural ideology of this time, early heavy metal also came to reflect a deep distrust for social, cultural and political authorities, a view of popular music as a serious form of artistic expression and an emphasis on musical authenticity.

In heavy metal, however, these elements were also transformed in important ways. The most important stylistic element adopted was long hair for men, which has since then remained one of the primary stylistic characteristic of heavy metal culture. Apart from the hair, though, heavy metal also developed its own distinctive style of dress in the form of denim, leather and chains. Only marginally interested in social and political activism, heavy metal eschewed such typical 1960s countercultural concerns. Instead, in heavy metal lyrics and imagery, key elements of the countercultural ethos such as tolerance, peace and love were often replaced with their opposites, evil, death and destruction.

Heavy metal went through its stage of formation in the 1970s. The initial development towards more specific musical, verbal, visual and aesthetic characteristics, or a heavy metal 'code', was at first expressed in particular songs, then by particular groups such as British Led Zeppelin and Deep Purple who further developed 1960s hard rock in a new, more heavy and aggressive direction.[29] These groups produced a great deal of material containing almost all of the musical elements which were later to become typical of heavy metal. However, the British group Black Sabbath is most commonly regarded as having been the first to fully employ the musical, visual and verbal dimensions that later would become the hallmark of heavy metal and is thus widely regarded as the first full-fledged heavy metal group. It is, however, important to note that this has been a constantly debated issue within metal culture since its early days.

Irrespective of whether one chooses to regard groups like Led Zeppelin or Deep Purple as heavy metal in the full sense of the term or not, their influence on the genre can hardly be overstated. Nonetheless, many would argue that even the most casual observer would notice the decidedly heavier and gloomier quality inherent in the music of Black Sabbath. Black Sabbath not only developed the musical elements in a more heavy and aggressive direction but also, from the very start, set the standard for the types of lyrical themes that subsequently were to become a distinctive feature of heavy metal on the whole, such as the battle between good and evil, war and religion.

Heavy metal began to 'crystallize' as a distinct genre in the late 1970s through continuing musical, visual and verbal development by Black Sabbath as well as a number of new groups, particularly Judas Priest from Britain, both of which are still active at the time of writing. The 1970s also witnessed a number of groups on the borderline between hard rock and heavy metal, such as KISS and AC/DC, achieving worldwide success. According to Weinstein, the boundaries of the genre became increasingly clear and fixed at this stage as heavy metal developed into 'full being'[30] and developed a code that 'demarcated a core of music that could be called, indisputably, heavy metal'.[31] It also began to develop its own view on rock music 'as a sensual vitalizing power that only heavy metal brings to its highest pitch, its perfection'.[32] The heavy metal of the 1970s is often regarded as constituting a form of 'proto-metal' and the principal source for all subsequently developed metal sub-genres.

Lastly, it is important to note that the heavy metal audience, most commonly referred to as 'metalheads', 'metallers' or 'headbangers', has always been characterized by its high degree of commitment and sense of community. Heavy metal audiences are generally not casual but highly active consumers of their music, commonly displaying exclusivist rather than eclectic tastes.[33]

The musical dimension

During much of the 1970s, heavy metal's musical dimension was, as mentioned above, particularly influenced by earlier and contemporary blues-based hard rock groups such as The Yardbirds, Cream and The Jimi Hendrix Experience and, arguably, to a lesser extent also by 1960s psychedelic rock groups such as The Grateful Dead and Jefferson Airplane. The distinction between the two was always fluid, with artists like Jimi Hendrix freely incorporating elements from both. Influences from both blues-based hard rock and psychedelic rock are clearly at evidence in the early production of pioneering heavy metal groups such as Black Sabbath and Judas Priest. In addition, as discussed in detail by Walser,[34] elements of classical music, particularly inspired by 'heavier' composers such as Bach and Wagner or virtuoso player-composers such as Paganini, also became common within the genre at an early stage.

The sound of heavy metal is essentially created through considerable amplification of the overdriven distorted electric guitar, loud bass, drums and intense vocals. Synthesizers and keyboards were at first added only occasionally but they later became important instruments for many groups. In heavy metal, no single instrument is assigned a clearly dominating role. Instead, all instruments, including the vocals, collaborate in creating a single whole. Thus, rather than subduing any one instrument, all are instead simultaneously brought to the fore, creating what Weinstein calls a powerful, energetic and intense 'onslaught of sound'.[35]

Usually created by a four- or five-piece group, heavy metal is generally more complex and technically demanding than most other forms of rock. Considerable technical ability is thus required in all instruments. This is further expressed in a common stress on musical virtuosity, particularly on the guitar. The most recognizable feature of heavy metal guitar is the extensive use of the power chord; an interval of a perfect fourth or fifth played on a heavily distorted electric guitar enhanced by feedback, overtones and resultant tones.[36] Typically arranged in repeated sequences of 'riffs', they are often played in staccato-style, using so-called 'palm-muting' techniques. When played on heavily distorted electric guitars, this style produces a thick and crunching sound. A contrast is provided through the use of complex scales and harmonies in solos. Heavy metal is also characterized by its powerful and intense rhythm section. A particularly intense and fierce style of drumming, found almost exclusively in metal, also developed at an early stage. Lastly, the vocal style of classic heavy metal emphasizes intensity and emotion and is usually, although not always, sung in a clear and high pitched voice carrying long notes at the time.[37]

In the late 1970s, a number of new British groups emerged with a faster and more aggressive style of heavy metal. This movement became known as the *New Wave of British Heavy Metal* (NWOBHM). Finding much inspiration in the directness, anger and attitude of punk rock, groups like Iron Maiden, Saxon and Def Leppard left the blues roots of earlier heavy metal behind, 'took their primary inspiration from metal itself',[38] and put greater emphasis on aggressiveness, speed, musicianship, musical complexity and melody. NWOBHM revitalized and upgraded heavy metal but also steered it in a more aggressive direction. At this stage, the genre had fully developed a set of highly distinctive musical, visual and verbal characteristics.

The visual dimension

Heavy metal's visual dimension is expressed in a number of different ways: in group logos and group photos, on album covers, clothing merchandise, in concert outfits, in the use of visual effects in live performances and music videos etc. Generally speaking, the visual dimension of heavy metal elevates the fantastic, exaggerated and shocking. Groups typically develop own identifiable band logos to express an association with a certain attitude or image. These are used on album covers and all forms of group-merchandise such as t-shirts, caps and pins. Album and merchandise artwork commonly display menacing, threatening and grotesque motifs inspired by horror films and literature, heroic fantasy, science fiction and, most conspicuously, mythology and religion.

Heavy metal also adopted biker-culture style at an early stage. In the 1970s and early 1980s, a distinctive heavy metal style had developed, mostly consisting of jeans, leather, studded belts, chains, jewellery, band t-shirts and tattoos. However, as already noted, the most identifiable way for heavy metal fans to express their affiliation with heavy metal culture was, and largely remains, to grow their hair long. These basic stylistic characteristics have changed very little over time although some sub-genres have developed some more distinctive stylistic elements of their own. These basic stylistic elements have given rise to a highly recognizable, and since long globally spread, 'metal uniform' through which metal audiences distinguish themselves as members of metal culture.[39]

Finally, metal has also created some of its own distinctive bodily practices, most of which become actualized in the context of the live metal concert setting. The most central of these are 'headbanging' and 'moshing' (a practice also common in hardcore punk). While the former denotes the practice of swinging one's head up and down in sync with the beat of the music, the latter refers to the practice whereby a larger group of audience members (sometimes up to hundreds of people) form a temporary area called a 'mosh-pit' in front of the stage in which they slam into each other in seemingly violent and totally uncontrolled ways (although, in reality, moshing is a controlled practice with a set of shared implicit rules).

The verbal dimension

Heavy metal's musical and visual dimensions are in many ways informed by its verbal dimension. Although metal lyrics have never been dominated by any one specific theme, as Weinstein has observed in relation to the 'classic' metal (heavy metal) of the 1970s and 1980s, one can nevertheless discern a 'significant core of thematic complexes'.[40] According to Weinstein, metal's verbal dimension can be divided into two main categories, the 'dionysian' and the 'chaotic', which are, in some respects, contradictory. While the dionysian category primarily includes themes such as ecstasy, sex, intoxication, youthful vitality, male potency and power, the category of the 'chaotic', by contrast, includes themes such as chaos, war, violence, struggle, alienation, madness, evil and death. Indeed, metal has become particularly known for its exploration of these types of chaotic themes, and it is within this thematic category that one also finds frequent references and allusions to the figure of Satan and the apocalyptic visions of the Bible.

Heavy metal's fascination with the Devil can ultimately be traced back to its roots in the blues. However, regarding explicit references to Satan or the Devil in heavy metal, Walser argues that, 'as with other transgressive icons, the Devil is used to signify and evoke in particular social contexts; he is not simply conjured up to be worshipped'.[41] As noted above, such themes may be interpreted as constituting an inversion of the central themes of 1960s counterculture and 'an act of metaphysical rebellion against the pieties and platitudes of normal society'.[42] As Weinstein observes, not only has the Bible always provided metal bands with a host of narratives and themes to draw upon but also provided a broad range of religious symbols and a rich religious terminology.[43] In addition to the Bible, metal bands have also typically drawn inspiration from themes and ideas found in various strands of occultism, esotericism, Paganism and Satanism, as well as in the world of legend and myth, especially as found Germanic, Norse and Celtic traditions. Different bands have, however, explored such themes in varying depth and in varyingly sophisticated ways.

Metal thus stands out from most other forms of contemporary popular music through its highly conspicuous use of religion and the supernatural as a primary source of lyrical and aesthetic inspiration. Indeed, one could even go so far as to argue that religious themes and imagery in general have developed into an integral component of metal's lyrical and aesthetic conventions on the whole. When metal bands have drawn on themes inspired by the world of religion, and biblical eschatology and apocalypticism in particular, they have also typically used them in combination with other key 'chaotic' themes such as war, chaos and madness.

Later development and diversification

In the early 1980s, metal music and culture started to diversify and fragment as it became divided up into the two contrasting main sub-genres of *glam* and *thrash* metal. While the glam metal movement represented a turn towards 'lighter' sounds and a much greater emphasis on 'pop' sensibility, the largely underground thrash metal movement, strongly inspired as it was by the emergence of punk in the late 1970s, largely developed in the opposite direction as bands such as Metallica, Megadeth and Slayer created a decidedly more fierce form of metal 'characterized by speed, aggression and an austere seriousness'.[44] For the purposes of this discussion, it is of particular import to note that the thrash metal movement also was characterized by its almost exclusive emphasis on metal's 'chaotic' themes, particularly the destruction of the world as a consequence of (often nuclear) war and environmental disaster.[45]

Thrash metal also laid the foundation for the subsequent development of so-called extreme metal-styles such as *death* and *black* metal in the mid-1980s and early 1990s. As Kahn-Harris writes, extreme metal sub-genres 'all share a musical radicalism that marks them out as different from other forms of heavy metal'.[46] The creation of death metal by groups such as Death, Possessed and Morbid Angel in the mid-1980s once again changed the way metal was made and experienced, by taking the already powerful music to its outermost extremes with raging tempos, extensive use of extremely fast so-called 'blast-beat' drumming, unconventional song-structures, innovative guitar riffing and guttural or growled vocals. Death metal generally combines typical metal themes such as death, violence and war with extensive use of various types of Satanic and occult themes. In addition, 'the destruction of the body', typically expressed through explicit and graphic descriptions of rotting, mutilated corpses, torture and murder, also became an important source of lyrical and aesthetic inspiration.[47]

In the beginning of the 1990s, inspired by the earlier work of explicitly 'Satanic' groups such as Venom and Bathory, black metal was developed into a distinctive sub-genre by Norwegian groups such as Mayhem, Emperor and Darkthrone. Favouring a raw and unsophisticated sound, black metal was principally created through very fast tempos, bright and heavily distorted guitars and high-pitched, screaming or shrieking vocals.[48] Some groups, such as Dimmu Borgir and Cradle of Filth, later developed a more melodic variant of black metal characterized by much higher production values. Above all, this sub-genre has become particularly known for its radical lyrical themes. Black metal, writes Kahn-Harris 'embraced satanism wholeheartedly' and developed a radical anti-Christian ideology as expressed in the black metal slogan 'support the war against Christianity!'[49] Combined with elements of Norse paganism (e.g. Odinism and Ásatrú), this particular brand of anti-Christian sentiment was essentially based on a loosely defined 'black metal ideology' which advocated a revitalization of Norse pagan heritage and a return to a pre-Christian culture and society untarnished by the perceived hypocrisy and herd mentality both engendered and ingrained by a historically imposed Christianity.[50] Some bands also started incorporating national socialist themes and discourses into their lyrics and imagery. This eventually led to the development of a separate and highly marginal sub-genre called *National Socialist Black Metal* (NSBM).

As part of a 'self-conscious attempt to explore the radical potential of metal', extreme metal sub-genres became increasingly occupied not only with different forms of 'sonic transgression'[51] but different forms of 'discursive transgression'[52] as well. Elaborating on extreme metal discourse, Kahn-Harris writes: 'Extreme metal discourse represents a departure from heavy metal discourse in that the fantasies it explores are less obviously "fantastic". Heavy metal discourses are generally lurid, theatrical, baroque and often satirical. Extreme metal discourses are detailed, repetitive and apparently serious.'[53]

Although the development of extreme metal sub-genres brought with them a more sustained engagement with esoteric, Pagan, Satanist and anti-Christian themes,[54] *biblical apocalypticism* has also remained a frequently tapped resource of lyrical and aesthetic inspiration within most extreme metal sub-genres.[55] Bands typically draw on narratives found in Revelation in order to convey a general sense of chaos and impending doom. As Weinstein observes, in this context biblical themes provide 'resonance, a cultural frame of reference, for the imagery of chaos itself'.[56] Extreme metal's emphasis on war and chaos is also vividly reflected in the extreme metal aesthetic with its characteristic portrayals of dystopian futures and the often violent depiction of the end of the world.

Apart from the development of extreme metal styles, metal diversified further in the 1990s through the mixing and fusing of metal with elements from other popular music genres. The mid-1990s saw the development of so-called *nu-metal* by groups such as Korn, Limp Bizkit and P.O.D. from the United States. Nu-metal groups incorporated elements from hardcore punk, funk and hip-hop music, thereby creating a new form of metal that in many ways constituted a break with many of its traditional musical and stylistic conventions, particularly through extensive use of funk beats and rapping vocals. Overall, metal has become increasingly musically diverse since the late 1980s with new sub-genres and styles, and hybrids of sub-genres and styles, constantly being developed. In addition to those already discussed above, a few that could be mentioned include *doom metal, grindcore, metalcore, alternative metal, progressive metal, funk metal, industrial metal, gothic metal, sludge metal, stoner metal* and *symphonic metal*. In addition, it is not unusual for bands to experiment with and move between styles. Hence, much contemporary metal defies neat and clear classification. The further diversification of metal, spearheaded by bands such as Children of Bodom, Slipknot and Mastodon from the mid-2000s onward clearly attests to this. As metal continues to diversify in a number of directions, a general fascination for religious themes remains a central and defining lyrical and aesthetic characteristic of the genre as a whole.

Metal and religion

Throughout the years, metal has engendered a great deal of controversy, perhaps more than any other contemporary genre of popular music.[57] Following its ever growing popularity and commercial success, critical debates surrounding metal reached a peak in relation to the concentrated campaign against popular music's perceived negative moral influence on youth spearheaded by the Parents Music Resource Center (PMRC) (in cooperation with other groups such as the Parent-Teacher Association (PTA)) in the United States in 1985. This particular campaign successfully managed to cement the association of metal with the promotion of violence, self-destructive behaviour, suicide, sexual promiscuity and perversion, extreme rebellion, juvenile delinquency and the 'occult' in wider public discourse.[58] Indeed, the key concerns of this campaign – the preservation of traditional 'family values', parental authority and the morality of youth – have historically often stood at the very centre of wider critical public conversations about popular culture.[59]

These types of concerns were, however, not the sole property of secular parental lobbying groups such as the PMRC and the PTA. For slightly different reasons, they were also very much shared by many Protestant conservative Christian, evangelical and fundamentalist groups alike. Conservative Christians of various strands were quick to join the wider crusade against immorality in popular music (often believed to have become epitomized in metal) that was gaining momentum in the mid-1980s. Through their engagement in these wider debates, the issue of 'Satanism' also started figuring ever more frequently in critical debates on metal. As a consequence, metal now also became accused of being anti-Christian and of actively promoting Satanism and outright Devil-worship[60] – an accusation that would also develop into a recurring theme in the contemporary 'Satanic panic' writing.[61] Indeed, the Satanism charge has proven particularly enduring and also assumed a life of its own within wider popular cultural discourse.[62]

Criticism and rejection of dominant social and cultural authorities constitutes a central component of many popular music cultures, and metal is no exception in this regard. However, metal has often been interpreted as presenting a critique of a society and culture that is viewed as false and hollow by consciously and deliberately transgressing the boundaries of the socially and culturally acceptable.[63] As noted above, the apparent seriousness and sincerity of extreme metal discourse and aesthetics in particular is greatly fuelled by the use of various types of subversive religious themes and imagery.

In the beginning of the 1990s, the Norwegian black metal scene attracted worldwide attention in connection to a large number of scene-related, both successful and attempted, church arsons, a few notable instances of extreme violence and even some cases of murder.[64] These extraordinary events have been documented in several books and documentaries.[65] Although it has lost most of its earlier violent aspects, the radical anti-Christian sentiments held by some members of the infamous early 1990s Norwegian black metal scene have been carried on by several contemporary acts. It is, however, equally important to keep in mind that these types of radical ideas are marginal within metal culture on the whole. It is important to note that, although metal music and culture in general remains characterized by a conscious elevation of the 'extreme', it has also always contained a very healthy dose of playfulness, humour, self-irony, a self-conscious fondness for exaggeration, spectacle and over the top theatrics. One should thereby always be wary of taking metal band's exploration of subversive religious themes as reflecting the actual attitudes of musicians and fans themselves.[66]

Metal's relationship to religion remains a somewhat contested issue. In their seminal work, both Weinstein and Walser offer more detailed accounts of the religious themes that most commonly appeared in the 'classic' heavy metal of the 1970s and 1980s in particular. As we will return to shortly, Weinstein also makes some more specific arguments. Arnett's brief discussion of religion in relation to the heavy metal culture of the 1980s and early 1990s is different in this regard as it approaches religion as one of many 'sources of alienation' and concentrates on the actual attitudes towards religion found among a sample of American metalheads. Indeed, Arnett concludes that, when viewed in the context of an increasingly individualized general North American religious landscape in which religious socialization has long been progressively weakening, young American metalheads appear to be even more dismissive of organized religion that their peers.[67] Kahn-Harris has mainly discussed issues related to religion in relation to his exploration of the practices of 'discursive transgression' that constitutes a central feature of extreme metal culture on the whole. As he argues, in contrast to most 'classic' heavy metal, the extreme metal scene is marked by its own consciously extreme discourse characterized by its 'active suppression of reflexivity' or 'reflexive- anti-reflexivity'.[68] This essentially means that extreme metal discourse typically, so to speak, consciously ignores the often negative effects of expressing such things as anti-religious, racist or anti-Semitic sentiment in insensitive and inconsiderate ways.

A handful of notable chapter and article length accounts focused on highlighting how the pervasive religious themes within metal culture provide its followers with important *resources of inspiration* for the construction of worldviews and religious/spiritual identities have also been produced during recent years. The majority of these accounts have directed particular attention at metal's interest in what is variably referred to as 'Satanism', the 'Satanic' or the 'figure of Satan'. Because of this, most of them have focused on the 'Satanic' black metal sub-genre in particular.[69]

Although to very different degrees, there is a tendency in all of this work to, in some way or other, raise the issue of youth rebellion when pondering the sincerity with which metal bands and audiences explore and engage with Satanist/Satanic themes and ideas in particular. Indeed, the Satanist/Satanic element in metal should certainly not be exaggerated or overstated. But, on the other hand, should it automatically be reduced to merely an unimaginative falsetto cry of adolescent rebellion? Although many metal bands have indeed dabbled with Satanism/the Satanic and other types of subversive religious themes in obviously instrumental ways in order to enhance the shock value of their music, one also finds cases of such themes and ideas being explored in ways that are marked by much higher degrees of ideological substance, sophistication and apparent seriousness.[70]

Notably, the issue of rebellion has always constituted a central theme in the scholarship on metal and been interpreted both as a symptom of metal audiences' general alienation towards dominant Western society and culture as well as a means of empowerment. However, as already noted, detailed empirical/ethnographic information on metal audiences has always been in very short supply indeed, and this has undoubtedly had its consequences for how scholars have approached and dealt with the issue of rebellion as well.[71] Indeed, clearer specifications of what is actually meant by terms such as 'youth' or 'adolescent rebellion', what such rebellion actually consist of, who exactly it is that such terms are meant to apply to and how issues related to rebellion play out across different social and cultural contexts have too often been lacking. Future work could usefully examine more critically how issues of rebellion actually surface in the everyday lives and practices of contemporary metal musicians and audiences themselves as well as how this relates (or does not relate) to their explorations of subversive religious themes and ideas. This is to say, therefore, that, although the issue of rebellion remains a legitimate focus of metal studies, it is an issue that needs to be investigated on a firm empirical basis.

Metal as *religion?*

In addition to highlighting the ways in which religious themes and symbolism appear in metal lyrics, imagery and aesthetics more generally or how metal might function as a source of religious inspiration, some commentators have also suggested that the popular music culture of metal itself can be seen as functioning *as* a religion for its most devoted followers. In a very general form, thoughts of this kind are present already in the seminal work of Weinstein. In this view, metal culture is taken to provide its most devoted followers with a particular worldview and way of interpreting their place in society, a cultural identity, collective rituals and a sense of community and belonging – all typical traits of classical *functionalist* understandings of religion. Popular music cultures undoubtedly do indeed provide their followers with important resources for the construction of personal and cultural identities and also significantly serve to foster a sense of community and togetherness among them, and metal can well be viewed as a very good example of this. However, to argue that this equals 'religion' raises many problems pertaining to conceptual clarity and sensitiveness to the lived experiences of metal audiences themselves.

When approached from a functionalist perspective, religion is basically understood in terms of a 'socio-cultural system which binds people into a particular set of social identifications, values and beliefs'.[72] Religious ideas and practices are seen to be oriented towards the 'sacred' and set apart from the ordinary or the 'profane'. In this view a shared understanding of the 'sacred' serves to bind people together within a single moral universe and thereby to underpin and strengthen social cohesion.[73] Functionalist understandings thus highlight the social and communal function of religion, emphasizing the ways in which it offers people structures for everyday life, sources for the construction of identities and a sense of purpose and meaning with life as a whole.[74] In some cases, functionalist understandings have also been combined with phenomenological so-called *sui generis* understandings of religion which argue for the 'uniqueness' of religious experience as such and its 'irreducibility' to sociological, psychological or any other factors. Sometimes such understandings also presume the actual existence of some form of transcendental force which individuals are able to 'experience' in various ways. Here it is enough to note that *sui generis* approaches have long been widely contested within the broader study of religion since they are not only ahistorical and context-insensitive but also 'untestable, and thus unproveable'.[75]

Substantive understandings have provided another way in which the concept of religion has long been approached and understood. While functionalist understandings primarily concentrate on what religion 'does' or on how it 'works', substantive understandings instead focus on what religion 'is' as they strive to outline sets of 'externally observable' generic or 'substantive' elements to serve as a basis on which to determine when a socio-cultural system may 'count' as a religion.[76] The respective virtues and weaknesses of functionalist and substantive approaches continue to be the subject of much debate.

The first functionalist argument about the 'religious' dimension of metal was most probably presented by Weinstein. Discussing the intense and overwhelming 'sensory overload'[77] spectacle of the heavy metal concert, Weinstein argues that 'From a sociological perspective, the ideal heavy metal concert bears a striking resemblance to the celebrations, festivals and ceremonies that characterize religions around the world.'[78] She bases this view on the classical thoughts on the social function of religion offered by Durkheim and Eliade – both influential early developers of functionalist perspectives on religion (and in the case of Eliade phenomenological perspectives as well). As she argues, the traditional heavy metal concert setting in which 'audience and artist encounter one another directly in a ritual-experience, is itself the peak experience, the summum bonum, the fullest realization of the subculture'.[79] Elaborating further on this idea, Weinstein then comes close to explicitly equating the heavy metal concert with a religious event when she writes that 'ideal metal concerts can be described as hierophanies [a term developed by Eliade] in which something sacred is revealed. They are experienced as sacred in contrast to the profane, everyday world.'[80]

It is important to note here that these observations are made through drawing parallels between the heavy metal concert experience and that which is deemed to be particularly characteristic of religion according to a functionalist view. Notably, the 'religious' dimensions of metal are represented as surfacing most clearly when metal fans gather in large numbers to appreciate their music collectively. More generally, this line of argument also connects with a longstanding body of scholarship on the 'ritual' and quasi-religious dimensions of different forms of media reception and appreciation.[81] However, in Weinstein's case, it does appear that the religion parable is employed primarily for the purposes of illustrating the intense atmosphere that undoubtedly does characterize large metal concerts. It thus remains unclear as to whether the intention really was to argue that metal should be interpreted as a religion or as providing its followers with 'religious' functions.

One exceptionally good example of functionalist arguments being driven much further can be found in Sylvan's *Traces of the Spirit: The Religious Dimensions of Popular Music*.[82] In this book, Sylvan explores what he regards to be the essentially 'religious' functions or dimensions of popular music as such in the light of a few distinct popular music cultures, including metal. Notably, Sylvan also adds a strong phenomenological *sui generis* element to his understanding of religion as he postulates the existence of an undefined 'numinous' which is the subject of what is claimed to be humanity's 'religious impulse'[83] and which also functions as the 'ordering structure for human beings'.[84] In applying this functional-phenomenological understanding of religion to metal music and culture, Sylvan directs particular focus at the collective musical experience.

Drawing heavily on Weinstein, he writes of metal concerts as 'the key ritual form which brings metalheads together as a community'.[85] Moreover, he claims, 'It is not only the music, however, but an entire meaning system and way of looking at the world, a surrogate of religiosity if you will, that explains the enduring power of heavy metal.'[86] However, he then also paradoxically goes on to state that 'the specifically spiritual and religious implications of the musical experience in heavy metal are often not so explicitly recognized and consciously articulated by metalheads'.[87] Even so, following from his presumption that metal provides its followers with a vehicle to experience the 'numinous', this does not hinder him from continuing to argue that '[n]evertheless, there is strong evidence from their testimonials that metalheads do have such experiences, and that these experiences are also very powerful and lifechanging'.[88] It needs to be noted that Sylvan does indeed include a few excerpts from interviews with metalheads who invoke the term 'religion' when they describe the musical experience of metal and the sense of community they experience during concerts.[89] However, as noted just above, Sylvan openly acknowledges that it is uncommon for metalheads to invoke the term 'religion' in this regard. What metalheads actually mean when they do use the term religion as well as how this relates to their attitudes towards the category of 'religion' more broadly are also questions left unexplained. Sylvan further adds to the confusion regarding this as he simultaneously also bases his argument on the 'religious' dimensions of metal on interview excerpts in which metalheads simply state that metal concerts provide them with powerful experiences or express their appreciation of metal culture more generally.[90] Sylvan's highly functionalist-phenomenological understanding of religion thus easily runs the risk of itself producing 'evidence' of metal fans experiencing their music in essentially 'religious' ways. The many criticisms that can be levelled against Sylvan's *sui generis* understanding of religion aside, his argument illustrates with all clarity the many problems and ambiguities that easily arise if academics make generalizing arguments about the lived meanings of popular music culture participants regarding such a sensitive issue as religion on the basis of theoretical presumptions which grant them the authority effectively to ignore or arbitrarily interpret the expressed views of these very participants themselves.[91]

Clearly, if functionalist arguments are to be made convincingly in relation to metal's presumed 'religious' dimensions, they need to be empirically substantiated and work from the 'bottom up' rather than the other way around so that individual academics are neither intentionally nor inadvertently invested with the authority to decide on their behalf what 'religious' functions metal culture provides its followers with purely on the basis of unsubstantiated theoretical assumptions.

As has been pointed out in many studies of metal, although metal culture generally displays an obvious fascination with dark and subversive religious themes and ideas, it is also characterized by a broadly defined individualist ethos. Indeed, the complex relationship between these two components has only rarely been explored in direct relation to what thoughts and views metalheads actually express regarding religious institutions and the category of 'religion' as such (with the exception of the short examination provided by Arnett). When metal's individualist outlook is viewed in direct relation to its fascination for (or indeed love-hate relationship) with religion, this would perhaps suggest that more thought-out views on religion in general would be relatively common among wider metal audiences. However, as virtually no information exists on this, it is a question that remains to be empirically investigated. The most central point to note for the purposes of our discussion in this book is that metal's often-controversial exploration of subversive religious themes has had a profound effect on the very self-understanding of Christian metal as a whole. As we shall see in upcoming chapters, to no small degree, Christian metal has always defined itself in contrast and often in outright opposition to its secular equivalent precisely because of its long-standing and enduring interest in these types of themes.

Studying religion and popular culture

Contemporary intersections of religion, media and mass-mediated popular culture are having an increasingly formative impact on religion and religious life and practice worldwide. Our present-day mass-mediated popular cultural environment in the form of film, television series, popular music, computer games and so on has evolved into an increasingly important resource and arena for the exploration of religious ideas and the construction of religious identities and worldviews.[92]

This has happened as part of a set of more general and closely interconnected processes of general social, cultural and religious change in the West. Accelerating globalization has brought about increasing religious pluralism and diversity and aided the global flow and crisscrossing of religious populations and ideas. The continuous and rapid development of 'technologies, institutional arrangements, circulatory systems, and shifting modalities of reception' that may be collectively referred to as 'media' have also to an ever greater extent come to affect how religious communities of virtually all strands self-organize, interact and communicate their messages in ways that previous generations would have found difficult to imagine.[93] Moreover, the definitive establishment of consumerism as the dominant cultural ethos of late-modernity[94] has had a decisive impact on religion and religious life across the globe, making it increasingly important to view ongoing processes of religious change against the background of a more 'recent shaping of culture by economics'.[95]

As argued by a large group of influential social theorists, such processes of general, macro-level social and cultural change have brought about a general shift from a traditional to a post-traditional society, leading to an ever stronger general cultural celebration of and impetus towards expressive individualism.[96] In the field of religion, this has translated into an increasing general subjectivization and privatization of religion and religious life across the Western world in particular. Coupled with a general dissolution of traditional modes of authority, the post 1950s era has also witnessed notable changes in understandings of family, community, gender and gender roles.[97] These developments all constitute central areas of enquiry in the sociological study of religion, but they fall beyond the scope of this book.

The study of the relationship between religion and mass-mediated popular culture has grown exponentially during the last two decades as part of the broader field of 'religion, media and culture'[98] and increasingly started to attract the attention of scholars from a range of different academic fields, leading to the development of an extensive and constantly growing academic literature on the subject.[99]

As many researchers of popular culture have observed, those who claim to study 'popular culture' do not always agree upon the meaning of the concept.[100] The many ways in which the concept of popular culture has been employed in studies of popular culture thus calls for some clarification. Scholars of religion and popular culture generally tend to reject hierarchical-typological understandings of popular culture that make value-laden distinctions between, for example, 'high', 'folk', 'mass' and 'popular' culture and instead favour broader definitions that view popular culture 'as the shared environment, practices, and resources of everyday life in a given society'[101] or 'as a "way of life" for particular people in particular contexts'.[102] Approaching popular culture in this way, therefore, 'involves looking at the wider structures, relationships, patterns, and meanings of everyday life within which popular cultural texts are produced and "consumed"'.[103] In this way, then, popular culture, should not be viewed as 'a straightforward object'[104] that simply 'exists' independently of people's various forms of engagements with it. Rather, as Partridge points out, 'popular culture is both an expression of the cultural milieu from which it emerges and formative of that culture, in that it contributes to the formation of worldviews and, in so doing, influences what people accept as plausible'.[105]

To put this in simpler terms, we might therefore regard the 'popular' in 'popular culture' as something that is never fixed and always open to negotiation and continuous cultural construction. As a category of analysis, however, 'popular culture' can usefully be viewed as encompassing those forms and types of culture that are most clearly and closely related to and implicated in various forms of mass-production and which are most commonly engaged with through various forms of consumption. The term 'mass-mediated popular culture' can in turn be taken to denote forms of popular culture which are primarily disseminated through various types of modern communication technologies, such as film, television, popular music, computer games etc.[106] Indeed, as Hoover writes from the perspective of religion and media studies: 'On a more pervasive level...the "common culture" represented by the media has today become determinative of the contexts, extents, limits, languages, and symbols available to religious and spiritual discourse.'[107] As he goes on to point out, these developments have also made it increasingly important to account for the ways in which people's actual religious beliefs are reflected in various forms of media and mass-mediated popular culture as they are used by individuals and specific religious groups and, moreover, to explore the different ways and degrees to which media may become *formative* and *determinative* of those individuals and groups.[108]

These observations are highly significant for any study of Christian metal. Not only does this group express its Christian faith through a popular cultural form, but that popular cultural form is itself highly formative and determinative of that group. As Lynch points out, when attempting to gain a deeper understanding of how contemporary broader transformations of the general Western religious landscape affects more traditional and institutional religious communities, such as evangelical Christianity for example, it becomes crucial to investigate more closely how the survival and persistence of such communities is 'related to their ability to generate subcultural worlds of media and popular culture through which adherents feel part of a wider collective, learn and maintain particular sensory and aesthetic regimes for encountering their vision of the sacred, and find reinforcement for particular ways of seeing and acting in the world'.[109]

This brings us to actual ways of studying various intersections of religion and popular culture. Forbes' by now classic typology of different approaches to the study of religion and popular culture has proven continually useful as a way to navigate between the principal ways in which religion and popular culture has been studied thus far. Forbes distinguishes between four main areas of inquiry within the study of religion and popular culture on the whole: 'religion in popular culture', 'popular culture in religion', 'popular culture as religion' and 'religion and popular culture in dialogue'.[110] These categories of studies, which simultaneously represent both main areas of inquiry and commonly used approaches within the field, frequently intersect and overlap and should therefore not be understood separately from one another. While the 'religion in popular culture'-category mainly comprises studies concentrating on the both explicit and implicit appearance of religious, spiritual and existential themes, subject matter, imagery, symbols, language etc. within the wider popular cultural mainstream, studies falling within the category 'popular culture as religion' are instead primarily distinguished from studies within the other three categories through their functionalist approach. This is because studies within this category typically have argued that various popular cultural forms (e.g. film, popular music cultures, sport) themselves increasingly have begun to take on functions previously performed by traditional religion and started to function as 'surrogates' or 'substitutions' of religiosity for increasing numbers of people today. The nowadays increasingly redundant category of 'religion and popular culture in dialogue' designates an area of study focused on how religious institutions and groups themselves engage in and relate to wider debates on popular culture within society in either an accommodating or confrontational spirit. Lastly, and most importantly for our discussion here, directing their attention away from the secular popular cultural mainstream, studies within the 'popular culture in religion' category instead look to the appropriation of various popular cultural forms by religious groups themselves. Studies within this category have been comparatively few, with most having concentrated on the phenomenon of 'Christian popular culture' and the *evangelical popular culture* industry in a North American context, which also constitutes the subject of our exploration here.

Evangelical popular culture

Terms such as 'Christian popular culture industry', 'evangelical popular culture', 'Christian media', or some variation thereof, are often used interchangeably to denote a wide array of Christian 'appropriations' of popular cultural forms that are bound to certain industrial and organizational structures and produced and chiefly consumed by evangelical or so-called 'born again' Christians. Henceforth, the term 'evangelical popular culture' will be used.

As evangelical Protestantism in its many forms has spread on a global scale,[111] some slightly different understandings of what evangelicalism 'is' or who exactly counts as an 'evangelical' Christian have also emerged. As Hendershot points out, 'evangelicals tend to see themselves not as a type of Christian but as the only true Christians'.[112] Yet, irrespective of whether people who self-identify as 'evangelicals' would agree or not, the term 'evangelical' is actually most commonly used to denote precisely a certain type of Protestant Christian who espouses a more particular set of beliefs and understandings of what a Christian life is supposed to be all about.[113] According to Clark, people who self-identify as 'evangelicals' tend to espouse the following four 'key beliefs' in particular: (1) the belief in the inherent sinfulness of humanity and the need for personal salvation; (2) the belief that all 'true' Christians should adhere to the biblical Great Commission and aim to spread their faith to others; (3) the belief that the Bible is literally true, infallible and inspired by God; (4) and the belief in the *rapture* and the imminent Second Coming of Christ.[114] For evangelicals, then, faith is essentially a matter of developing a personal and unique relationship with God. Such a relationship starts with a personal choice to accept Christ as one's personal saviour and become 'born again' in him.[115] Evangelicals also stress the importance of spreading the Christian message to others, often through *testimonies* of their own conversion experiences highlighting the wonderfulness of their new lives in Christ as opposed to their earlier sinful and unhappy lives as unbelievers.[116] As Hendershot points out, in evangelical contexts, the telling of conversion stories (or giving testimonies) serves to 'maintain a sense of community, of shared experience'.[117] The importance attached to the giving of testimonies is also reflected in many forms of evangelical popular culture. As we shall see in later chapters, this is also the case within Christian metal, in which testimonies also typically highlight the role of metal music in itself.

For present purposes it is of particular importance to note that, just as evangelicals tend to regard the Bible as the literally true and infallible word of God, they also tend to take 'a more literal approach' to the interpretation of biblical eschatology and prophecy.[118] However, since biblical prophecy, and especially the Book of Revelation, is notoriously difficult to interpret and decipher, evangelicals can turn to a wide array of evangelical popular cultural products designed to provide guidance on these issues.[119] Particularly in North America, evangelical understandings of the biblical foretelling of the Parousia have been profoundly influenced by so-called *dispensationalist* teachings initially developed within the Plymouth Brethren movement in Ireland and Britain in the nineteenth century. At the risk of simplifying matters somewhat, dispensationalist teachings are based on the dividing up of history into (usually seven) different successive periods (i.e. dispensations) marked by different relationships between God and humanity. The belief in the so-called *rapture* occupies a central position in these teachings. Among many slightly different versions, this is essentially the belief that all 'true' Christians will be 'lifted' or 'brought up' (i.e. 'raptured') from earth to heaven either sometime before, during or at the end of a seven year period of 'tribulation' – a time marked by immense hardships and the rise to power of the Antichrist – that is to precede the Second Coming of Christ.[120] Indeed, as a key feature of North American Evangelicalism, this particular belief has become central to evangelical popular culture and sparked the development of what has become varyingly referred to as 'apocalyptic fiction',[121] 'apocalyptic media'[122] or 'prophecy fiction'.[123] A strong interest in apocalyptic themes and other topics dealing with the perceived 'reality of evil in the world'[124] is thus a main characteristic of evangelical popular culture on the whole.[125]

Evangelical popular culture, then, is often interpreted, and indeed often presented, as a 'counter-media' that offers 'Christianized' or more 'sound' versions of various popular cultural forms. The initial establishment in the late 1970s of what later became known as the 'evangelical popular culture industry' essentially remains based on the notion of the neutrality and transformability of popular cultural forms in themselves. Whilst this has involved a rejection of the perceived immorality and lack of constructive 'family values' found in the secular popular cultural mainstream on the one hand, it has also involved the creation of a 'morally sound' or 'family friendly' Christian alternative on the other which, in most respects, emulates secular popular culture in outlook and industrial organization. The phenomenon of evangelical popular culture as a whole is intimately connected to the view still held by many evangelicals that the wider contemporary popular cultural environment constitutes an important battleground over the proper (i.e. Christian) socialization of youth.[126] As such, evangelical popular culture has typically been represented as an attempt at changing or influencing secular popular culture from *within*. Consequently, mirroring a broader longstanding strategy commonly employed by US conservative and evangelical Christians in their efforts to increase their cultural and societal influence, the tactic preferred by many producers of evangelical popular culture has been that of engagement and *infiltration*. That is producers of evangelical popular culture tend to hold the view that, in order for them to be able to bring popular culture more into alignment with 'Christian values' and make it more 'moral' and less indecent, the wider contemporary popular cultural environment needs to be actively engaged within its own vernacular and, partly, on its own terms.[127]

Several studies have explored the ways in which evangelical Christianity may be said to have been influenced, transformed, or even become trivialized or diluted by its appropriation of popular cultural forms.[128] Although such critical arguments may certainly often be warranted, it is also important to recognize how the evangelical movement is particularly characterized by a typically Protestant openness to culture and different forms of media.[129] In relation to this it also becomes of particular importance to note that evangelicalism in general has been experiencing profound changes during recent decades – changes that the phenomenon of evangelical popular culture needs to be understood as part of. On a more general note, commenting on the effects of an increasing general cultural emphasis on expressive individualism and subjectivization, Hunter has argued that 'absorbed in it rather than being (spiritually) repelled by it, modern Evangelicals have accorded the self a level of attention and legitimacy unknown in previous generations'.[130] Similar lines of thought have also been presented by Miller who, focusing on the so-called 'new paradigm' churches in the United States, has highlighted how an ever stronger emphasis on personal and embodied experience increasingly has come to eclipse issues regarding theology and doctrinal purity, essentially rendering such issues secondary to subjective experience.[131] Some very similar observations, especially regarding the cultural influence that the counterculture of the 1960s and today's consumer-oriented marketplace has had on the general character of modern evangelicalism have also been presented by Luhr.[132] These studies all highlight the changing face of evangelicalism and Protestant Christianity (particularly in the United States) in general and as such describe the broader religious-cultural backdrop against which the phenomenon of evangelical popular culture needs to be understood. Most importantly for present purposes, they all draw particular attention to the ways in which evangelicalism as a whole has become increasingly occupied with the self and subjective experience, gradually moved away from traditional and institutional organizational structures and embraced a wide range of new media and popular cultural forms in order to develop new forms of religious expression and practice.

Indeed, returning now to evangelical popular culture specifically, as Hendershot points out, 'if today's thriving Christian cultural products industry illustrates anything, it is that evangelicals continue to spread their messages using the "newest thing", be it film, video, or the Web'.[133] However, as she goes on to highlight: 'contemporary Christian media are incredibly uneven in the degree to which they overtly proclaim their faith'.[134] But as already noted, the aim of evangelical popular culture is not just to 'poach' on secular popular culture but to transform it by means of a Christian direction from within; 'if evangelical media producers and consumers constitute a "subculture", it is one that aspires to lose its "sub" status'.[135]

Hence, evangelical popular culture is primarily concerned, not with popular cultural forms as such, but with their *content*. However, as evangelical popular culture has come to closely mirror secular popular culture in outlook, organization and management style and when a considerable portion of its products only hint at religious beliefs and values, distinguishing between 'Christian' and 'secular' popular culture often becomes a difficult task.[136] However, as Hendershot argues, there is little evidence to suggest that evangelical appropriations of popular culture or the increasing co-option of evangelical popular culture by large secular companies has led to a dilution of evangelical faith as such:

> In their appropriation of secular forms such as science fiction, heavy metal, or hip-hop, evangelicals seem to say that these forms are not inherently secular but, rather, neutral forms that can be used to meet evangelical needs. Such appropriation elides the historical specificity of popular forms…. Evangelical media producers often take styles and genres that nonevangelical youth might use to articulate 'resistant identities', (themselves heavily commodified) and respin that resistance in previously unimagined ways.[137]

Nowhere is this and the ways in which evangelical popular cultural products often vary in 'spiritual intensity'[138] more evident than in *Contemporary Christian Music* (henceforth referred to as CCM) – the fastest growing segment of the evangelical popular culture industry. As explored in detail by Howard and Streck,[139] CCM initially emerged in the United States in close connection to the evangelical *Jesus Movement* of the late 1960s. Primarily still concentrated to the United States, CCM has come to comprise all popular music genres and should thus not be regarded as a genre in itself. Instead, argues Howard and Streck,[140] three non-musical distinctive features – (1) lyrics, (2) artists and (3) organization – function as its primary underlying principles. The music in itself, be it blues, rap or rock, is generally regarded as neutral. The (1) lyrics, however, should deal with Christian themes such as evangelism, praise or moral and social issues from a Christian perspective.

It is also of crucial importance that (2) the artists that create the music themselves are Christians and lead – and are seen to lead – Christian lives. Lastly, (3) the music should be produced on Christian record labels guided by Christian principles and an evangelist agenda and primarily be sold and distributed through Christian networks such as Christian bookstores or Internet-sites.[141] However, these 'requirements', which constitute typical characteristics of evangelical popular culture more generally, are highly debated and frequently contested issues within the world of CCM. For example, issues regarding the relationship between evangelism and commercial profit continue to be the subject of much debate. As Howard and Streck argue: 'Contemporary Christian music is an artistic product that emerges from a nexus of continually negotiated relationships binding certain artists, certain corporations, certain audiences, and certain ideas to one another.'[142] The world of CCM, they argue, should consequently be considered a 'splintered artworld' that is governed by three main types of stance on the combination of Christian faith and evangelism with popular music: 'separational', 'integrational' and 'transformational' CCM. In the transformational stance music is valued for its own sake as art; this, however, is much less common than the separational and integrational stance, both of which are governed by an expressed instrumental view of music as either a form of evangelistic outreach or an acceptable form of 'Christian' entertainment.

The widespread dismissal of Christian popular music among non-religious popular music fans is unfair to the extent that, lyrics aside, the majority of Christian artists are no better or worse than nonreligious artists. Christian music scenes do not always produce 'bad' music and should not be dismissed as such. The lack of aesthetic innovation in religious popular music may also be driven primarily by commercial concerns. But it is nevertheless fair to point out that Christian music scenes are sometimes aesthetically timid and, sometimes openly, parasitic on non-religious popular music. Although Christian artists may be highly proficient in mastering musical conventions, they are sometimes rarely interested in doing much more than that.[143] In CCM, there is often, therefore, an absence of an idea of an aesthetic 'for its own sake' that would drive innovation.

As convincingly demonstrated by Howard and Streck, however, contemporary Christian music should be understood as a multidimensional phenomenon that encompasses multiple and sometimes opposing stances regarding the degree to which the music should serve instrumental purposes. We shall return to the issue of the instrumental use of popular music for religious purposes when we discuss the experiential, bodily and sensory dimensions of Christian metal in Chapter 4.

The aim of this introductory chapter has been to set the stage for subsequent chapters by providing a general overview of the historical development, diversification and main musical, verbal and aesthetic characteristics of metal music and culture, with particular emphasis on its relationship to religion. In this chapter we have also situated the phenomenon of Christian metal in relation to its broader religious and cultural context. It is with these discussions in mind that we now in subsequent chapters proceed to explore the various dimensions of Christian metal music.

2

Christian Metal: Origins, Definition and Historical Development

While the field of metal studies in general has grown exponentially during the past decade, second hand sources on Christian metal remain somewhat difficult to acquire. Academic interest in the phenomenon has also remained very modest indeed. Nevertheless, in most studies of metal, Christian metal is mentioned in passing as a curiosity. In addition to being briefly discussed by Weinstein,[1] and apart from my own work on the subject,[2] Christian metal has so far only constituted the main topic of a handful of studies.[3] More general explorations of evangelical popular culture[4] sometimes mention Christian metal in passing, but they rarely discuss it in any detail, let alone treat it as a distinct Christian music culture in its own right.[5] The scarcity of academic studies of Christian metal is best explained by the fact that Christian metal is such a small phenomenon compared to secular metal and its global scope, with Christian metal fans being counted in the thousands while secular metal fans count in the millions.

Academic explorations of Christian metal have so far almost exclusively focused on mid-1980s and early 1990s Christian metal in the United States. In my own writings I have instead aimed to draw attention to the transnational dimensions of contemporary Christian metal. As I have also argued elsewhere and will continue to argue here, I believe it is important to keep in mind that, despite its religious outlook, regarding most practical aspects, the Christian metal scene functions much like any other popular music scene. In order to gain a fuller, and indeed adequate, understanding of Christian metal, one needs to move beyond lyrical and aesthetic analysis (although that is important too) and also explore Christian metal as a Christian popular music culture in a wider sense. One could even go so far as to argue that some of Christian metal's lyrical and aesthetic dimensions start to make sense only when they are viewed in relation to the workings of Christian metal as a wider Christian musical and discursive space.

Similar to secular metal, Christian metal has also developed its own tradition of 'fan-scholarship'.[6] However, due to the small scale and limited resources of Christian scenes, fan-scholarship on such things as the history and basic tenets of Christian metal have so far largely remained confined to the Internet. Christian musician John J. Thompson's *Raised by Wolves*[7] does, however, contain a quite lengthy section on the history and development of Christian metal in North America. Thompson's account provides a useful complement to the one provided below. Additional information on various Christian metal bands can also be found in Mark Allan Powell's *Encyclopedia of Contemporary Christian Music*.[8]

Perhaps rather surprisingly, the Finnish-language Wikipedia-article 'Kristillinen metallimusiikki' ('Christian metal music') remains the single most comprehensive general fan-scholarly overview of Christian metal's main characteristics and historical development on a transnational level produced to date.[9] Wikipedia also contains a small number of separate articles on the various stages of Christian metal's development and its many styles which, taken together, provide a rich up-to-date resource of general information for anyone interested in the phenomenon. The present chapter draws upon all of them. However, they are all, of course, fan-scholarly accounts and, consequently, all need to be approached critically.

One also finds additional sources on many large Christian metal Internet-sites such as *The Metal for Jesus Page* or *Angelic Warlord.com*, or in magazines such as *Heaven's Metal* and *HM: The Hard Music Magazine*, all of which will be discussed in more detail below. In short, due to the scarcity of resources, any exploration of Christian metal needs to rely on a combination of academic and fan-scholarly accounts as well as a wide range of other sources found across various types of Christian metal media. Ideally, such sources may be further combined with and enriched by material gathered by means of ethnographic research such as in-depth interviews with scene members themselves and participant observations at Christian metal events.

Origins and early development

Christian metal, or *white metal*, as it was also called during its earlier phase of development, started to emerge in the United States in the late 1970s. The musical and ideological foundations for Christian metal had already been laid in the mid-1970s by Christian hard rock bands such as Agape, Resurrection Band and Petra from the United States, Jerusalem from Sweden and Daniel

Band from Canada. In the beginning of the 1980s, however, Christian bands such as Saint, Messiah Prophet and Stryper from the United States, as well as Leviticus from Sweden, appeared with a full-fledged metal sound and look along with an expressed evangelistic agenda. The main missionary efforts of these early seminal bands were expressly directed at spreading the Christian message in the secular metal community. Glam metal act Stryper in particular managed to achieve considerable wider crossover success. Stryper toured extensively with successful secular metal acts and became widely known for their practice of throwing small bibles into the audience. Largely as a result of Stryper's unparalleled success, Christian metal soon started to be noticed in secular metal media such as *Kerrang!* and mainstream popular music media such as *MTV*. Still active at the time of writing, Stryper remains the single most successful and widely known Christian metal band. Their record sales exceed 5 million copies and their 1986 release *To Hell with the Devil*[10] even received a Grammy Award nomination.[11] Christian metal continued to develop and diversify throughout the 1980s, mainly through the efforts of US Christian heavy and glam metal bands such as Whitecross, Sacred Warrior, Holy Soldier, Bride, Barren Cross, Bloodgood, Recon and Rage of Angels – all of which have gained the status of Christian metal classics, and some of which are still active today.[12]

The *Sanctuary* movement

There is one factor that played a particularly crucial role in the initial development of Christian metal in the United States. In 1984, the so-called *Sanctuary*-movement – a temporary 'rock'n' roll refuge' for evangelical Christians who were involved in various rock music scenes but who felt alienated from, bored with and rejected within more conventional and conservative evangelical circles – emerged in Torrance, California. The movement grew fast and soon established its own congregations. *Sanctuary* head-pastor Bob Beeman (or 'Pastor Bob' as he is also called) himself led the way by fully embracing the metal style and look, appearing with long hair, metal-style clothing and tattoos. Indeed, issues regarding style and look constituted an important part of *Sanctuary*'s main aims and efforts as it expressly welcomed anyone into their church regardless of their appearance. It is worth noting here that metal style was certainly far from generally accepted in wider evangelical circles during this time.[13] As against this, *Sanctuary* explicitly encouraged its members to fully opt for the metal style or, as Glanzer puts it: 'The importance of accommodating the heavy metal look became almost a sacred norm at *Sanctuary*.'[14] In addition to also using metal music during its services and encouraging its members to adopt the metal-look, *Sanctuary* also created its own metal-inspired logo, which it also printed on t-shirts and stickers.

By forming an alternative evangelical space, the *Sanctuary* movement can be seen to have offered its members resources for the shaping of an alternative form of religious expression and way of 'doing' religion. As such, *Sanctuary* also provided its members with a space to live out an alternative Christian identity. The church also actively supported Christian bands in their missionary efforts in the secular metal community and invited known Christian metal bands to come and play for the congregation.[15] *Sanctuary*'s emphasis on evangelistic outreach also meant that it offered its members the opportunity to preach the Christian message by playing their own favourite music. While *Sanctuary* rejected what they viewed as metal's 'idolatrous aspects',[16] that is, the 'metal god' image that surrounded many successful secular metal musicians, they instead emphasized the role of Christian metal musicians as 'ministers' or 'missionaries'. Generally speaking, evangelism took precedence over musical creativity. Through its many efforts, *Sanctuary* eventually managed to lend Christian metal some degree of credibility within broader evangelical circles in the United States. Its congregations would come to function as important breeding grounds for US Christian metal bands in the mid- and late 1980s as well as 'centers of socialization by providing a place where other potential band members could meet each other and receive training in reaching the lost youth with their particular brand of ... metal'.[17]

At its peak in the early 1990s, *Sanctuary* had as much as 36 congregations across the United States. In time, as the movement became more known, it also started attracting some degree of outside interest as a curiosity and even tourist attraction. By the end of the 1990s, however, more accepting attitudes towards alternative musical styles had begun to spread within wider evangelical circles and *Sanctuary* therefore decided it had fulfilled its role. With the exception of their San Diego congregation, *Sanctuary* chose to seize its congregational activities and instead transformed itself into an international ministry under the name of *Sanctuary International*. Today, *Sanctuary International* focuses on working with Christian metal scene members and supporting Christian metal all over the world.[18]

Later development and diversification

Apart from a few bands from other countries such as Sweden and Canada, the development of Christian metal in the early and mid-1980s was mainly, although not exclusively, confined to the United States. During its formative period in the mid- to late 1980s, Christian metal did indeed develop more or less in parallel to the North American evangelical popular culture industry, betraying the conspicuous influence of its main aims and aspirations. However, as will be explored in more detail in Chapter 5, although Christian metal still partly continues to be produced under the auspices of the evangelical popular culture industry, it has also increasingly managed to escape such confines through the development of a highly independent transnational scenic infrastructure of record labels, promotion channels, media etc.

The 1980s witnessed the establishment of specialized small Christian metal record labels such as *Pure Metal Records*, *Intense Records* and *R.E.X. Records* in the United States. Some Christian metal bands also managed to obtain contracts with larger secular labels such as *Enigma Records/Capitol* and *Metal Blade Records*. The first Christian metal fanzine *Heaven's Metal* was established in the United States in 1985 by journalist Doug Van Pelt. In 1995, *Heaven's Metal* changed its name to *HM: The Hard Music Magazine*. In 2004, however, *Heaven's Metal* was resurrected by Van Pelt and is now released side by side with *HM*. Other fanzines active during the late 1980s and early 1990s include *Gospel Metal* and *White Throne*.[19]

During the 1980s, Christian metal was mainly distributed through Christian bookstores or small mail order services. During this time, the term 'white metal' also gradually started being replaced by the slightly broader and more inclusive term 'Christian metal'. This shift partly had to do with 'white metal' mostly having been used as a counter-term to the perceived 'satanic' black metal of the early 1980s as represented by bands such as Venom and Mercyful Fate. The term 'white metal' had itself reportedly been invented by the secular metal label *Metal Blade Records* for precisely this purpose. Another reason for the shift also had to do with the word 'white's' potential racist connotations. These days, the term 'white metal' is mostly used within the Latin American Christian metal scenes of Brazil and Mexico while bands in the United States and Europe instead tend to prefer the term 'Christian metal'.[20]

During the second half of the 1980s, Christian metal bands playing more extreme metal styles also started to appear. During this time, Christian thrash metal developed through the efforts of US bands such as Vengeance Rising (initially Vengeance), Deliverance, Believer and Tourniquet. Vengeance Rising's 1988 album *Human Sacrifice* is commonly regarded as an important benchmark in the development of Christian thrash. Tourniquet in particular would go on to achieve considerable success and long-time popularity in the Christian market. In line with the more extreme musical character of thrash, lyrics also took a darker, more solemn and uncompromising turn. Christian thrash metal songs tended to focus on eschatological and apocalyptic themes, the battle between good and evil, 'spiritual warfare' and Christian rebellion against sin.[21] These would all develop into standard themes within the subsequent development of extreme Christian metal styles.[22]

At the end of the 1980s and the beginning of the 1990s, Christian death metal started to develop, mainly through the work of Australian bands Mortification and Vomitorial Corpulence. Mortification's 1992 release *Scrolls of the Megilloth* is widely regarded as having been particularly influential in this regard. The band also managed to achieve wider success in the secular metal community and gain a contract with the major secular metal label *Nuclear Blast Records*. However, the Brazilian band Incubus (later Opprobrium) had already experimented with death metal sounds in the late 1980s. Other Christian death metal bands appearing during this time include Crimson Thorn and Living Sacrifice from the United States as well as Sympathy from Canada. Later influential mid- and late 1990s Christian death metal bands include Extol from Norway, Pantokrator from Sweden, Deuteronomium and Immortal Souls from Finland and Aletheian from the United States.

The emergence of Christian black metal, or 'unblack' as it is more commonly called in Christian metal circles, in the early 1990s further heightened Christian metal's already highly disputed position within the wider metal community. Unblack took off through the release of the Australian one man band Horde's first and only release *Hellig Usvart* ('Holy Unblack') in 1994. Other influential unblack bands appearing during this time include Antestor from Norway and Admonish from Sweden. These early unblack bands tended to fashion their lyrics and activity as a counterweight to the pervasive and sometimes expressed satanic ideology of much of the secular black metal of the time. Later, lyrics started taking a more philosophical turn as more unblack bands started to appear. Some of the most influential include Crimson Moonlight and Sanctifica from Sweden and Vaakevandring, Drottnar and Frosthardr from Norway. Unblack has become one of the most popular Christian metal styles during recent years and become represented by several additional bands such as Light Shall Prevail and Arch of Thorns from the United States, Slechtvalk from the Netherlands and Fire Throne from Poland.

In the late 1990s, updated forms of power metal and progressive metal started gaining popularity anew within the wider metal community. In the late 1980s and early 1990s, Christian power metal had been represented by bands such as Seventh Avenue from Germany and Narnia from Sweden. Later power metal bands include Theocracy from the United States and Harmony, Divinefire and Heartcry from Sweden. Progressive bands include Balance of Power from Britain and Jacobs Dream from the United States. Christian doom metal, which also emerged in the 1990s, was represented by bands such as Veni Domine from Sweden, Paramaecium from Australia and Ashen Mortality from Britain. During the same time, Christian gothic metal also appeared through the work of bands such as Saviour Machine from the United

States, Kohllapse from Australia and Undish from Poland. Around the turn of the millennium, Christian nu metal bands such as P.O.D. (Payable On Death) and Pillar appeared in the United States. P.O.D., which managed to achieve wider crossover success at an early stage, has probably become the most commercially successful Christian metal band after Stryper.

Mirroring the increasing diversification and mixing of styles that has characterized the development of secular metal in the 2000s, the past decade has seen the emergence of several successful new US bands, such as the deathcore band Impending Doom or metalcore bands such as Underoath, Demon Hunter, As I Lay Dying, War of Ages and The Devil Wears Prada.

Christian metal has developed and diversified considerably since the early 1990s, following ever more closely in the footsteps of the overall development of secular metal. Today, Christian metal comprises all metal sub-genres and styles. In line with contemporary general developments in metal, many Christian bands of today frequently experiment with and mix and move between styles and thus defy clear and neat classification into particular sub-genres. In order to distinguish themselves from their secular counterparts, Christian metalheads have also produced some consciously humourous metal-inspired labels of their own. For example, in addition to Christian black metal being referred to as 'unblack', Christian metalcore/hardcore is sometimes referred to as 'Christcore' or 'Godcore' and Christian death/grindcore as 'Goreship' (a play with the word 'worship'). Moreover, Christian metal has also produced some of its own slogans such as 'Faster for the Master!', 'Turn or burn!' and 'Support the war against Satan!'. As the rhetoric of these slogans illustrate, although in a much-transformed sense, Christian metalheads have also created their own ways of expressing the uncompromising attitude that metal has been associated with since its early days.

Christian metal – secular metal: Main similarities and differences

When talking about Christian metal's connections to its secular counterpart, it is important to note at the very outset that Christian metal wholeheartedly embraced the defining musical, rhetorical, aesthetic and stylistic traits of metal in general right from its very inception. Indeed, compared to most other forms of contemporary Christian music, the affinity between Christian and secular metal has always been exceptionally close. Moreover, in a somewhat transformed sense, Christian metal has embraced metal's characteristic uncompromising rhetoric, attitude and lifestyle as well. So, in spite of Christian metal's religious, and more specifically, evangelical underpinnings, it is metal music and culture in general that constitutes the musical and aesthetic backdrop against which Christian metal necessarily needs to be understood.

Hence, although Christian metal constitutes a largely separate and independent metal scene, it should not be regarded as a separate metal subgenre in the sense usually meant by that term. As noted, the differences between Christian and secular metal are primarily of a discursive kind, with the similarities far outweighing the differences. It is worth pointing out once more, though, that when Christian musicians created Christian metal, they did so for *missiological* reasons, the primary aim being to evangelize to secular metal audiences through the genre's styles that were popular at the time. Thus, in a way typical of producers of evangelical popular culture more generally, early Christian metal bands were also very much driven by the idea of 'infiltrating' and transforming secular metal culture from within. But Christian metal musicians did not initially, and have not since, set out to create a separate metal style as such. Rather, their intention was and still remains to express and spread their Christian faith through already existing metal styles.

However, as Christian metal has developed and spread to different countries around the world with different social and cultural environments, not all Christian metal musicians would necessarily accept such a narrow description of their musical aspirations and endeavours. This is because, for many Christian metal musicians and fans today, Christian metal is about much more than merely 'appropriating' or 'borrowing' metal music and style for purposes of evangelistic outreach or the transformation of metal music in a more 'moral' or 'sound' direction from within. Many Christian metal musicians and fans of today consider themselves ordinary metalheads who are Christian and who choose to express their faith in close connection to their cultural sensibilities, that is, through Christian metal understood as an alternative and fully legitimate Christian way of 'doing' religion or, indeed, as a fully legitimate, popular culture-inspired Christian lifestyle. We also need to note here that Christian metal scene members are predominantly young adult males, although women do constitute a clearly visible group within the scene. Most have received a religious upbringing and been involved with a church since childhood. They have also typically come into contact with Christian metal through various evangelical popular cultural channels. Most become more actively involved in the scene in their mid- or late teens and, for many, scenic involvement becomes a lifelong commitment. The majority of scene members also express themselves as metalheads in style and look.

Considering metal's emphasis on power and consciously exaggerated 'machismo' as well as the generally male-dominated nature of the scene, one could perhaps also raise the question of whether Christian metal can be seen to support the construction and expression of traditional masculinities. Indeed, it was not unusual for 1980s US Christian metal bands in particular to write songs that lamented the perceived erosion of traditional family values, gender roles and the increasing acceptability of feminist and gay-rights ideas. Such themes might surely be taken to reflect a more conservative and traditional understanding of gender roles and masculinity, but we also need to point out that this particular subject matter has always been much less common among bands in other parts of the world. In addition, as we will explore in more detail below, Christian metal clearly has an affinity with the notion of the strong male 'warrior of Christ'. However, the macho image in Christian metal also differs from that of secular metal in at least one very important respect; while macho images are generally closely related to celebrations of self-elevating male vitality, potency and power in secular metal, they are clearly more directly connected with the notion of being 'servants of Christ' or a 'higher cause' in Christian metal.

Apart from sharing all basic musical, aesthetic and stylistic tenets, the similarities between Christian and secular metal also extend to a considerable degree of interest in similar types of lyrical themes such as the apocalypse, war and the battle between good and evil.[23] Importantly, apart from the content of song lyrics, it is often virtually impossible to distinguish between Christian and secular metal. The musical dimension of Christian metal is identical to that of secular metal and will thus not be explored any further here. There are, however, some differences in the use of visuals and aesthetics. These differences will be discussed in detail in upcoming chapters. In the following, we shall first explore issues pertaining to the definition of Christian metal.

Defining Christian metal

Looking more closely at how Christian metal is defined also reveals the processes of constant negotiation that combining Christianity with an aggressive and controversial popular cultural form entails. We might begin by noting that, generally speaking, the basic 'requirements' of CCM discussed in the previous chapter largely apply to Christian metal as well. It should also be noted here that the discursive construction of the basic meaning and function of Christian metal (explored in more detail in Chapter 6) also bears many resemblances to the discursive construction of CCM more generally. One can therefore single out three main elements that recurrently surface in accounts of what distinguishes Christian metal as 'Christian' from the perspective of its own musicians and followers.

First, Christian metal is typically defined as metal that somehow conveys some form of Christian content or message. This means that, in some way or other, lyrics should either deal with clearly Christian themes or be based on a Christian worldview. Lyrics may thus deal with explicitly religious topics such as eschatology, apocalypticism or spiritual warfare. But they may also deal with a wide range of other social or everyday issues from a broadly defined 'Christian perspective' or 'Christian point of view'.[24] For example, in the 'Frequently asked questions' section of Sweden-based *The Metal for Jesus Page*, which is one of the oldest, most comprehensive and best known general Christian metal Internet-sites, one can read the following:

> 1) What is Christian Metal?
> Well, Christian Metal is Metal made by Christians with a Christian message.
>
> 2) What is the difference between Christian Metal and Secular Metal?
> Christian Metal is just as brutal and heavy as the Secular when it comes to the music. What differs is the lyrics. Instead of having bad, destructive or meaningless lyrics... the lyrics in Christian Metal are positive. They are bold but positive.[25]

Second, Christian metal is also commonly defined as metal that is made and produced by people who are themselves professed Christians and lead Christian lives. Sometimes, Christian metal may also be defined as being principally produced *for* Christians as well. This view stems from the notion that in order to produce music in a 'truly' Christian spirit with a 'truly' Christian content, it necessarily needs to be grounded in the personal Christian faith of its creators. According to this view, then, a person who is not a Christian can never make truly Christian music. In other words, a non-Christian person may well make music that speaks to or resonates with Christian listeners, but that does not make the music truly Christian in the full sense of the word.

Third, and arguably of lesser importance nowadays, Christian metal is defined as metal that is produced and distributed through various Christian networks guided by 'Christian principles' and an evangelistic agenda. When this element appears in definitions of Christian metal, it usually stems from notions regarding the 'gatekeeping' functions of Christian labels, producers and distributors. These business actors are seen to be in a position in which they, to a certain extent, are able to guarantee that the albums released, produced or distributed convey some form of Christian content and are made by professed Christians who lead Christian lives. Most contemporary Christian metal bands do indeed release their records on Christian labels and mainly rely on various Christian channels for promotion and distribution. These days, however, releasing on secular labels has become increasingly acceptable and desirable, as long as bands that do so do not deviate too much from the other two 'requirements' outlined above. Indeed, releasing on a secular label has increasingly begun to be seen as a sign of wider success since it usually entails at least some degree of wider promotion, distribution and much-desired attention in the wider secular market.

It is important to note that even though these 'requirements' are constantly debated, the overwhelming majority of Christian metal musicians and fans appear to hold the view that, in order to be considered 'truly' Christian, a band would have to meet the second requirement and at least to some degree the first as well. There are, however, a number of bands today who are widely considered Christian although they hardly ever make any clear references to religion in their lyrics. There is thus clearly a sense in which certain bands also may be defined as Christian based solely on the professed Christian faith of their members and what is *not* contained in their lyrics. That said, bands are generally required to convey a Christian message in some form or other. Again, these are much debated issues which surface at all levels of today's transnational scene and they constitute important ingredients of the discursive construction of Christian metal as a distinct form of metal.

Clearly, as Christian metal has developed, diversified and spread to different countries around the world, so have various understandings of its definition, main purposes and aims. Today, it is not unusual for bands to differ widely regarding the degrees to which they explicitly and deliberately proclaim their Christian standpoint. Indeed, the very meanings attached to concepts such as 'Christian standpoint' or 'Christian perspective' in this context have broadened significantly over time and sparked an ongoing debate within today's transnational scene. For one thing, not all Christian metal bands share the same degree of evangelistic fervour. Many who strive to gain wider acceptance within the broader metal community clearly and consciously choose to downplay or 'cloak' their Christian approach in order not to put off secular audiences and hamper their chances of wider success. Although Christian metal continues to be defined as metal that conveys a broadly defined Christian message, as evidenced by internal scenic debates on this issue, it is ultimately up to individual bands to choose for themselves how explicit they want their lyrics to be in this regard. This issue is also related to the manner and style in which lyrics are written. Most Christian metal musicians take the view that lyrics should be written in accordance with metal's genre-conventions, that is written in a way that suits the character of the music. That, in turn, may also affect the choice of lyrical topics to some extent. As one Finnish Christian metal musician interviewed for a previous study commented:

> The difference between Christian and secular metal is maybe that Christian metal has that Christian message, and like, it is a bit differently expressed with different bands so that some say it directly or in the face while others perhaps a bit, maybe say it more metaphorically, but that is probably like the difference. In principle, I have always thought that music is music and as such all neutral and then you can splash any kinds of lyrics you want on it, but of course it will not always work if the contrast is huge.... In my opinion you cannot just splash the kinds of 'Jesus loves you, period' style of thing to death metal, even though some do that.... One is allowed to do that but it is sort of to break with the style a bit. Like, lyrics should be written according to musical style. Things can be said in many different ways.[26]

As seen here, Christian metal is defined as conveying a broadly defined Christian message. But lyrics should nevertheless preferably be written in line with metal's rhetorical conventions. As the musician quoted above went on to state, this is because an important part of making metal, including Christian metal, has to do with 'maximizing heaviness'.

Increasingly, bands have started to avoid using the label 'Christian' metal in the first place, the point of this being that conveying or reflecting a Christian message or worldview should not make a band any less authentic as a metal band. However, considering the rather deeply ingrained verbal conventions, individualistic ethos and broadly defined oppositional ideology of secular metal, this argument has so far not had much impact in the wider secular metal community. This argument can thus also be taken to reflect a certain degree of naivety and refusal on the part of the Christian scene to continue being defined on secular metal's terms.

In addition to functioning as a means of evangelism, however, part of the Christian metal ethos is also about supporting, edifying and inspiring audiences that are already Christian. To illustrate this point we might consider an example of a strongly expressed argument in favour of bands needing to convey their Christian message as clearly as possible. In an interview for *Heaven's Metal* in 2006, Steve Rowe of Mortification, no doubt one of the most respected personas within the wider transnational Christian metal scene, expressed the following views:

> We have always been accepted in the secular market.... We always play with secular bands in Australia. We have sold more than any other metal act from this country. Men who stand for Jesus in their lyrics are the meat of

what is going on. Any band that does not have a strong Christian message should not be sold in Christian bookstores or play at Christian Festivals. The world needs Jesus and the Christian fans need encouragement in their faith and walk with Christ. It is too easy to say you're a Christian and get easy sales in the Christian market.... If you don't have the message you should do the honorable thing and take the hard road like all secular acts do. Don't scam Christians who think they are buying Christian music and get no food. What has happened to the US 'Christian' Rock scene is a disease.[27]

In this excerpt, Rowe clearly states that, in order for Christian metal to be Christian in the full sense of the word, it first of all needs to offer Christians 'encouragement in their faith'. He also appears to state that Christian metal should be produced, not only by Christians but principally *for* Christians as well. In addition, he goes on to emphasize the right of Christian listeners to expect that Christian bands deliver spiritual 'food' in the form of a clear Christian content. Moreover, Christian bands also need to evangelize and cater to the world's 'need for Jesus'. However, even though evangelism is represented as constituting an important part of the activities of bands, Rowe nevertheless appears to regard Christian metal's evangelistic element as secondary to its function as being edifying and providing inspiration. Rowe can thus also be seen to represent Christian metal in terms of a distinct Christian musical culture. He does, however, take a rather exceptionally strong stance in favour of bands needing to convey their message as clearly as possible.

However, this ideology of deliberate separation – that is, the making of categorical distinctions or juxtapositions between Christian and secular or simply 'not-expressly-Christian' metal – has long been a much debated issue within today's wider transnational scene. For one thing, it is evident that separating the two categorically seems quite incompatible with Christian metal's evangelistic aims and general ideology of engagement and infiltration. The views of Christian metal musicians and fans remain divided on this issue as increasing numbers of bands have begun to actively distance themselves from the label 'Christian' and to downplay their religious messages in order to better their chances of wider success and acceptance within the secular metal community on purely musical grounds. As noted above, musicians within the world of CCM (and within evangelical popular culture more generally) have always struggled with this particular issue and the Christian metal scene is no exception in this regard. With this discussion in mind, the Christian metal scene can also be viewed as being rather distinctive from many other Christian or evangelical popular music scenes, in that its internal scenic debates on this issue are so closely bound up with genre-specific notions of authenticity and the closely related predominantly negative and dismissive view of Christian metal found within the broader secular metal community. And yet, as we shall explore in more detail in Chapter 6, an important element of internal scenic discourse centres on distinguishing Christian metal from secular metal, especially regarding the messages that are conveyed through the music.

What makes these issues (i.e. determining what counts as a Christian content and gaining acceptance within the secular metal community) particularly interesting in the case of Christian metal is that they are highly revealing of the ongoing processes of negotiation that go into combining Christian faith with a particular, and highly controversial, popular cultural form. In addition, and perhaps more importantly, they are also highly illustrative of the processes of negotiating and renegotiating that constitute part of legitimating and securing a place for Christian metal within a broader, non-evangelical popular cultural context without making too many compromises regarding its Christian distinctiveness along the way.

Controversy

Christian metal has always occupied a peculiar position within the wider world of metal music. Yet, as has already been noted several times, despite its marginal status, its existence still tends to be widely known and frequently contested among secular metal audiences. In this section, however, we will instead primarily focus on the controversy that Christian metal engendered within conservative Christian circles during its formative years in the mid-1980s – a controversy that would have enduring effects on the very character and self-understanding of Christian metal to this day.

In the mid-1980s, the popularity of metal, particularly in its shock and glam metal variants, had reached unprecedented heights.[28] However, this was also a time during which metal *as a genre* was starting to become the subject of growing controversy, debate and moral panic within the wider context of the US 'culture wars' of the 1980s, which carried on into the 1990s.[29]

Indeed, as has already been noted, the Satanism charges levelled at metal during this time have proven particularly enduring and also assumed a life of its own within wider popular cultural discourse.[30] Considering this, it might seem strange that such a thing as Christian metal ever developed. However, in addition to always having occupied a peculiar position within the wider world of metal music, Christian metal long occupied quite a precarious position within wider conservative and evangelical Christian circles as well. Indeed, it would not be an exaggeration to say that the many controversies that started to surround secular metal in the mid-1980s would come to have a profound and long-lasting effect on the very self-understanding of Christian metal.

As I have already argued elsewhere,[31] Christian metal can be seen to be characterized for what could be called its 'double controversy'. As metal became singled out as a 'prime symbol' and scapegoat for everything that had supposedly gone awry with contemporary youth culture in the United States in the mid-1980s, this served to raise awareness and further reinforce negative attitudes towards metal as a form of music and musical culture *in itself* within many conservative Christian circles.[32] At the same time, many of the accusations levelled at metal during this time gradually also started to become internalized within secular metal culture itself and (often playfully) incorporated into wider discourses about what metal was supposed to be all 'about', making the very idea of 'Christian' metal seem oxymoronic, and therefore controversial, within the wider secular metal community as well.

Thus, in this 'double' sense, within both of these often opposing two camps, Christian metal became ridden with controversy almost from its very inception for reasons that were different yet inextricably interlinked. Moreover, the doubly controversial character of Christian metal has continued to shape contemporary Christian metal discourse and is thus also key to any fuller understanding of the phenomenon of Christian metal on the whole.

Throughout the 1980s, Christian metal became directly implicated in a series of internal Christian debates on proper and permissible forms of Christian engagement with the broader cultural environment.[33] Indeed, according to Luhr, Christian metal provides 'an ideal case study for examining the cultural activism of conservative [and evangelical] Christians' during this time.[34]

As noted above, this period of intensified Christian social and cultural activism can also be viewed in connection to the concept of 'culture wars', initially developed to describe a supposedly deepening divide between liberal and conservative sections of the US population since the early 1980s. Although the concept of culture wars has been repeatedly criticized for having exaggerated the nature of such a supposed divide of US society 'into two polarized, warring camps',[35] for present purposes, it is nevertheless crucial to note that 'culture wars *rhetoric*'[36] has remained a central means through which various religiously and morally motivated social movements alike aim to influence wider public opinion.[37] Indeed, stark culture wars rhetoric, or what Weinstein terms 'discursive terror',[38] constituted a central component of the 'family values'-centred 'movement culture'[39] against popular music's perceived detrimental influence on youth initiated and sustained by the PMRC in collaboration with conservative Christians in the mid-1980s.

As Weinstein observes, in the conservative Christian perspective, the varied notions of metal fostering suicidal tendencies, encouraging rebellion against parental, social and cultural authority and promoting sexual promiscuity/perversion and Satanism among its audiences were all understood to be inextricably intertwined and were intimately connected to metal *as a form of musical culture in itself*.[40] Thus, in the conservative Christian rhetoric of the time, these notions (none of which were questioned) were commonly represented as constituting a unitary assault on 'family values' which had to be met with active resistance.[41] However, it is important to note that wider debates occurring *within* Christian circles during this time also frequently contained various points of disagreement between progressives and conservatives regarding the long-standing Christian predicament of striving to be 'in but not of the world'.[42] Because of its strong musical and aesthetic affinity to its secular counterpart, it is not surprising that Christian metal developed into one such point of disagreement.[43]

One of the debates directly implicating Christian metal concerned metal's connection with *rebellion* against traditional and parental authority. Although usually portrayed in deliberately humouristic ways as exemplified in the music videos of bands such as Twisted Sister, youth rebellion against parental and adult authority did indeed constitute a recurring theme in much of the secular metal of the mid-1980s. However, as argued by Luhr, the evangelistic activities of Christian metal bands from the mid-1980s to the mid-1990s 'confirmed the fluidity of oppositional cultural themes such as "rebellion" and "alienation" '.[44] Turning the 'conventional' understanding of rebellion on its head, Christian bands such as Bloodgood and Barren Cross consciously and directly engaged in wider youth cultural debates through proclaiming that, in late-modern Western society and culture, it was in fact Christian faith and morals that constituted the true and ultimate form of 'rebellion'; 'obedience was the true transgression, and personal morality became the basis for reform'.[45] This may also be taken to reflect wider attempts within evangelical circles, and perhaps within the evangelical popular culture industry in particular, to construct an alternative to 'conventional' forms of rebellion in the form of a 'rebellion against rebellion' during this time.

Sharing the widespread contemporary concern among conservative and evangelical Christians that late-modern society and culture were experiencing a progressive erosion in morals and decency – exemplified by the legalization and increasing acceptability of such things as pornography, abortion and gay and women's rights movements – Christian metal bands thus placed themselves at the forefront of progressive evangelical's efforts to re-conceptualize and 'redefine "rebellion" as resistance to sin and obedience to parental, church, and divine authority'.[46]

Moreover, in order to distinguish themselves as 'warriors of Christ' engaged in 'spiritual warfare' in a hostile cultural environment, Christian metal bands also repeatedly strove to demonize their secular counterparts.[47]

Notably, Christian bands' demonization of secular metal also served as a means to establish and legitimate their own evangelistic mandate – particularly in the face of conservative Christian criticism. This, however, was not something that went unnoticed within the wider secular metal community. Indeed, as a consequence of the untiring evangelistic efforts of many bands, Christian metal increasingly became viewed as a laughing matter and sometimes even met with outright hostility within secular metal settings.[48]

Another issue closely related to that of rebellion which also developed into a point of controversy for Christian metal was that of *appearance* and *style*. This particular issue had already been of central concern to the *Sanctuary* movement discussed above. In particular, Christian metal bands came under attack from conservative Christians for adopting the effeminate and gender-bending style (i.e. of long teased hair, feminine clothes, spandex costumes, makeup etc.) characteristic of 1980s and 1990s glam metal. In the conservative Christian perspective, such appearances posed a direct challenge to traditional gender roles.[49] Christian metal bands, however, emphasized their missiological motivations and argued that styles and appearances constituted 'part of the vernacular of youth culture' and therefore should be regarded as being neutral in themselves.[50]

In addition to the issue of style and appearance, various notions found within more radically conservative Christian circles about the music itself or, more precisely, what types of 'inappropriate' and even dangerous *behaviours* the music supposedly encouraged and instilled among its listeners, also developed into a point of controversy for Christian metal. For example, the very idea of such a thing as 'Christian rock' was categorically rejected in the writing of so-called Christian anti-rock critics such as Jimmy Swaggart[51] and Jeff Godwin.[52] Christian anti-rock critics had long been arguing that rock music in itself served to bring forth primordial sexual urges among its listeners and therefore also served as a catalyst for sexually promiscuous behaviour – a notion that had become fairly widespread within broader conservative Christian circles in the 1980s. What is more, Christian anti-rock writers[53] also tended to locate 'the root of rock's power' in the supernatural force of Satan.[54] Indeed, the world of secular metal, filled as it was with bands like Mötley Crüe and KISS who never missed an opportunity to flaunt their sexual prowess, seemed to support this notion. Following from this, critics also expressed concern about the bodily practices of the 'dionysian'[55] and intense metal concert setting, in which performers and audiences seemed to behave in uncontrolled and morally questionable ways.

Hence, in the conservative Christian view, musical *form* mattered; not every form of music could be 'redeemed' and be used as means for worshipping God. Following on from this, Christian critics of Christian metal thus came to doubt that bands who went out to evangelize among secular audiences would manage to retain their Christian distinctiveness and remain unaffected by the 'immoral', debauchery- and sexual promiscuity-elevating general nature of such environments.[56]

Within broader Christian circles, therefore, Christian metal bands became implicated in wider debates ranging from style and appearance to 'proper' and 'suitable' forms of Christian expression and evangelism. Like many other Christian pop and rock musicians of the time, Christian metal bands turned to the Bible (particularly the book of Psalms) in support of their view that *all* forms of music should be regarded as being neutral in themselves; the underlying intentions and motivations for their use being the only important issue. Even so, while 'lighter' forms of contemporary Christian music already had started to develop into an integral component of the worship practices of the emerging mega-church movement as well as many more progressive charismatic and evangelical congregations,[57] metal was still widely considered inappropriate to be put to such uses.

In addition, albeit for very different reasons, Christian metal bands encountered quite a lot of criticism on musical grounds within the secular metal community as well. In particular, within the world of secular metal, Christian bands were frequently accused of being musically poor and for only copying and mimicking the sound and style of successful secular metal bands. This accusation was, however, not totally unfounded since many Christian bands of the 1980s tended to give precedence to evangelism at the expense of musical capability and innovativeness – an approach also generally shared by the *Sanctuary* movement as discussed above. Even though Christian metal has no doubt become increasingly musically diverse and innovative throughout the years, the view of Christian bands as mere copycats and mimickers has remained widespread throughout the world of secular metal. As a consequence of this, Christian bands continue to be widely discriminated against within the wider secular metal community. We will return to this discussion in more detail in Chapter 6 when we explore the external discursive construction of the Christian metal scene.

Finally, as already briefly discussed above, accusations of metal promoting Satanism among its followers have proven particularly enduring in critical debates on metal. It also needs to be noted that the Satanism charge initially developed in connection with the more commercially successful 'classic' heavy metal and glam metal of the mid-1980s. One can only speculate as to the outcome, had conservative Christian critics of metal, or indeed the members of the PMRC, been more aware of the largely underground development of extreme metal sub-genres such as thrash, death and black metal during largely this same time. In any case, and perhaps somewhat surprisingly, Christian metal bands largely managed to escape this particular charge.

But, as already noted, the Satanism charge nevertheless clearly influenced secular metal in a number of notable ways. For example, one might well argue that, largely due to having become associated with Satanism and the occult in the 1980s and early 1990s, metal's interest in subversive religious themes has steadily intensified over time. As already noted, the black metal-related church arsons in Norway in the early 1990s also spurred the development of unblack metal. The first Christian bands representing this new style, most of which were Swedish and Norwegian, did indeed run into some initial resistance within their own Christian churches. In particular, the controversial issue of style and appearance surfaced anew as some early unblack bands wholeheartedly embraced the black metal aesthetic, including corpse-paint makeup. Although Christian resistance to Christian musicians' appropriation of black metal largely appears to have been confined to some isolated cases, the creation of unblack provoked a much stronger negative response within the secular metal community, in which it immediately became widely viewed as a complete contradiction in terms. The case of the 'anti-Admonish' website, set up in the late 1990s by a secular black metal fan who became outraged by the very existence of Swedish unblack band Admonish, provides a case in point.[58]

Christian criticism of Christian metal has largely ebbed out as attitudes towards alternative musical practices have become increasingly tolerant. Indeed, these days Christian metal musicians commonly have the expressed support of their own churches. Musicians and fans may still, of course, encounter sporadic resistance from individual members of their own churches but, in general, concentrated Christian resistance to or criticism of Christian metal has become rare. Within the secular metal community, however, Christian metal appears to remain as contested as ever.

The interrelated criticism levelled at Christian metal both within conservative Christian circles as well as within the wider secular metal community can thus be viewed as having followed a certain broad trajectory. The increasing controversy and criticism concerning metal music and culture in general in the mid-1980s triggered considerable concern and resistance within many conservative and evangelical Christian circles, making the very idea of 'Christian' metal problematical. At the same time, because of its pronounced and often blatantly evangelistic agenda and its reworking of central metal themes through a Christian frame, the very idea of 'Christian' metal simultaneously also became highly contested within the wider secular metal community. Thus, almost as soon as it first emerged, Christian metal became caught up in struggles over appropriate forms of religious expression and evangelism in many Christian contexts and struggles over genre-specific notions about musical authenticity and ideology in wider secular metal contexts.

Christian metal's precarious and often contested position within both of these contexts could therefore also be understood in terms of a 'dual' controversy although the word 'double' more clearly captures the sense in which Christian metal at once has had to endure a *double dose* of criticism and resistance from two directions during its now over three-decade long balancing act between the often opposing camps of conservative Christianity and secular metal culture.

The reasons for Christian metal's controversiality within Christian circles are quite easily traced as they have been closely linked to a set of more particular internal Christian debates on popular culture. The reasons for Christian metal's controversiality within secular metal settings, however, have essentially revolved around the notion that Christian metal falls short on musical authenticity as it combines the music with an evangelist agenda. As we will continue to explore in more detail in following chapters, Christian metal's 'doubly' controversial character clearly continues to affect the ways in which it is discursively constructed and understood within today's transnational Christian metal scene itself. However, as we shall also continue to explore in more detail in upcoming chapters, Christian metal has not only suffered from its double controversy, it has internalized it and managed to thrive on it as well.

3

Verbal, Visual and Aesthetic Traits

Building on the general account of metal music and culture provided in the introduction, this chapter provides a general, and largely descriptive, account of Christian metal's main verbal (e.g. the content of song lyrics), visual and aesthetic dimensions (e.g. album cover artwork, imagery, symbolism, style). Particular attention will be devoted to Christian metal's verbal dimension since that is most revealing of the ways in which Christian metal differs from its secular counterpart.

The verbal dimension

In addition to always having shared all basic musical and aesthetic tenets, the similarities between Christian and secular metal have also continued to extend to a shared interest in similar types of lyrical subject matter, such as Judaeo-Christian eschatological and apocalyptic themes in particular. Indeed, in contrast to most other forms of contemporary Christian music and their often overly saccharine and upbeat lyrics, Christian metal bands have always preferred a much more straightforward, and sometimes even radical, approach to lyrical style and subject matter. This, however, should not necessarily be interpreted as reflecting the actual views and attitudes of musicians themselves in clear and straightforward ways. This is because writing lyrics in this uncompromising style also has much to do with genre-specific notions of authenticity and adhering to metal's general lyrical conventions.

Although they generally tend to be in line with metal's verbal conventions, Christian metal bands typically choose names that somehow reveal their Christian approach, for example by using biblical references in band names or album titles. Early examples include already mentioned US bands such as Whitecross, Sacred Warrior and Barren Cross. Later examples include Tourniquet, Saviour Machine, Demon Hunter, Holy Blood, Extol, Pantokrator, Sanctifica and Deuteronomium.

Generally speaking, the main lyrical themes of Christian metal can roughly be divided into five main, often closely intertwined and frequently overlapping categories: (1) biblical, apocalyptic and eschatological themes, (2) the crucifixion and sacrificial death of Christ, (3) spiritual warfare, (4) resistance to sin, and (5) everyday social and personal faith-related issues.[1] These categories should by no means be regarded as exhaustive although most Christian metal bands have continued to write according to themes which clearly fit into these categories. In the following, we shall explore these categories in light of a few examples, including lyrics from some of Christian metal's most long-standing and well-known bands. It should be noted that there has been a considerable increase in the number of bands who write lyrics in their own native languages as Christian metal scenes have developed in different parts of the world.

Christian metal's quite strong concentration on stark *biblical, eschatological* and *apocalyptic* themes such as the fall from grace, the rise of the Antichrist or the last judgement do, of course, fit the general lyrical approach of metal well since these types of themes are far from reserved for Christian musicians: they are also long-standing 'metal themes'. Therefore, given its close affinity to its secular counterpart, it comes quite naturally for Christian metal bands to also focus on these types of themes, albeit from their own Christian perspective or point of view. Lyrics in this category frequently deal with the turbulent times prior to the Second Coming of Christ during which the Antichrist is believed to establish a reign of terror on earth. As we saw above in Chapter 1, such themes also continue to occupy a prominent position in much of evangelical popular culture more generally. However, not all biblically inspired lyrics deal with eschatological and apocalyptic themes per se. A range of other particular themes and stories from the Old Testament, mostly inspired by the Books of Moses, are also fairly common.

Many Christian metal bands have developed a special interest in biblical eschatological and apocalyptic themes. Some have even dedicated entire concept albums to the exploration of such themes. More recent examples of this include Swedish unblack band Admonish's *Den yttersta tiden* ('The End Times', 2005) and from Christian metal pioneers, Saint, *The Mark*.[2] Saint's *The Mark* is particularly notable in this regard as the album provides a narrative that takes the listener on a journey through the apocalyptic events depicted in Revelation. The album starts out with songs such as 'The Vision', moves in to songs such as 'The 7th Trumpet', 'The Mark' and 'Bowls Of Wrath' and ends with songs like 'Reaping the Flesh' and 'Alfa & Omega'. The album does not, however, strive to communicate a specifically evangelical interpretation of these prophetic narratives. For the most part, the lyrics instead basically just paraphrase Revelation.

Explicit references to dispensationalist ideas such as the rapture are rare in Christian metal lyrics, and especially so in the lyrics of bands from other countries than North America in which evangelicalism has been less influenced by such teachings. In general, Christian metal bands instead tend to base their exposition of eschatological and apocalyptic themes directly on biblical narratives themselves. Although they typically tend to explore such themes utilizing a type of language and rhetoric that is in line with metal's lyrical conventions in general, it is not all unusual for Christian metal bands to include Bible-references in the liner-notes of their record sleeves in order to underline that their lyrics strive to convey a 'Christian' message.

Moreover, and in quite sharp contrast to secular metal bands, Christian bands also tend to focus on these types of narratives with the aim of illuminating or explaining the Christian understanding of the human condition and the Christian eschatological understanding of time.[3] There is thus often an expressed *educational* aspect to many Christian metal bands' exploration of such themes and narratives. Let us consider some examples. Saint's 'Primed and Ready' contains the following lyrics:

Soon the earth will burn in flames
And wickedness will stake it's claim,
What's to come out from the east
the son of death, the mighty beast,
Sinful men will hear his cry
On judgment day they all will die,
Evils got them by the tail
And with their gods they'll burn in hell

When it all has come to pass
When the first have become last,
When evil's lost the final fight
To the king and all his might,
Memories will fade away
The horrors of forgotten days,
Except the one who's chosen wrath,
He tasting death who's laughing last[4]

Although in a much compressed form, these lyrics basically just retell, and indeed paraphrase, the events prophesized in Revelation. It is also worth noting the uncompromising and blunt style in which these lyrics are written – a style which is not only revivalist in character but also fully in line with metal rhetoric in general or the 'metal-way' of putting things. They do not depart significantly from the original biblical narrative or at least do not make any significant additions to it. However, in addition to these types of general portrayals of the biblical apocalypse and last judgement, one also finds lyrics dealing with these topics that are written in more of a story-like fashion, often in a first-person narrative form. This is also a lyrical form that is quite distinctive to Christian metal as it connects to another central revivalist evangelical theme, namely, the importance of accepting Jesus as personal saviour before it is too late and of living one's life as if Christ might return at any moment. A classic example of this can be found in Deliverance's 'No Time':

> No time, no time
> That's my constant cry
> No time to help those in need
> At last it's time to die
> No time
>
> At last before the Lord I came
> I stood with downcast eyes
> He held a book in His hands
> It was the Book of Life
> He opened up the book and said,
> "Your name I cannot find
> I was once going to write it down
> But I couldn't find the time"[5]

As in the lyrics above, in order to convey the urgency of accepting Christ as personal saviour as soon as possible, Christian metal's first-person lyrical narratives of the last judgement typically take the perspective of the sinner or the damned. These lyrics also tend to be written in a straight-talking style. Indeed, in the final lines of the lyrics quoted above, the band even includes a dark humourous spin. In a sense, these types of lyrics can also, therefore, be viewed in relation to the concept of 'apocalyptic media'[6] discussed above, in that they typically contain direct warnings of consequences faced by those who have not accepted Christ at the Parousia. It is also worth noting that this style is also typical of evangelical revivalist homiletics more generally.[7] Arguably, the 'straight-talking' style of Christian metal lyrics might also be interpreted as connecting to a long-standing particular masculine revivalist culture which laments the 'emasculation of Jesus',[8] celebrates traditional gender roles and elevates the notion of the strong male 'warrior of Christ'. This, of course, also fits well with metal culture's general emphasis on male power and 'machismo'. Lastly, in ways that connect more closely to the other central Christian metal themes of resistance to sin and spiritual warfare, lyrics dealing with dystopian futures and the biblical apocalypse and last judgement sometimes also express a longing for these cosmic events to come about. Such lyrics are, of course, premised on the notion that we are already living in the very end of the end times and that the cosmic battle between good and evil is imminent.

The examples discussed above both constitute examples of apocalyptic themes being dealt with in explicit ways. Sometimes, however, biblical and Christian references appear in lyrics in 'coded' and convert ways. Arguably, in a time marked by institutional religious decline and increasing religious de-traditionalization, these types of coded references might not be as directly recognizable to the 'unchurched' as they are to evangelical audiences. As noted above, the coding of Christian messages is, however, a conscious strategy commonly employed by many Christian bands.

A second main category of lyrics includes lyrics dealing with the suffering, crucifixion and atoning sacrifice of Christ as well as the cosmic and human implications of this event. Such lyrics often make use of central Christian symbolism such as the blood of Christ and Christ as the sacrificial Lamb of God. Although lyrics falling within this category are typically biblically inspired, they still tend to be more detached from particular biblical texts as such. Lyrics in this category often contain direct warnings of the disastrous consequences that follow for those who refuse to accept the call to faith. A good general example of this category of lyrics can be found in Saint's 'Crime Scene Earth':

> With one mans sin we shall die
> The sacrifices pour
> Crime scene Earth
> See the cattails ripping off His flesh
> Crime scene earth
> Where the nails were pound and His side was pierced
> Crime scene earth
> Hear His innocent blood scream forgive
> Crime scene earth
> The prophecies of ancient days
> Have now been complete
> The veil has ripped the serpent crushed
> Pummeled in defeat
> On a cross of shame he hanged
> A sore for eyes to see
> A sacrifice of love to man
> And in the Son you're free[9]

For Christian audiences, these types of lyrics mainly serve edifying and inspirational purposes. But they also offer an alternative way of expressing these central Christian beliefs. For non-Christian audiences, these lyrics are instead mostly aimed at highlighting the importance of accepting Jesus as personal saviour and establishing a personal relationship with God.

In what constitutes a third main category of lyrical themes Christian metal bands also often portray the spiritual battle being fought on a daily basis against the sinfulness of human society and the destructive work of Satan and the forces of evil. The term 'spiritual warfare', which has long been used within many Christian evangelical, Charismatic and Pentecostal traditions, is commonly used as a metaphor for this constantly ongoing struggle. A very similar 'warrior rhetoric'[10] has also constituted a central component of Christian metal's verbal dimension since the very beginning and has remained common to this day.

Christian metal bands have found much inspiration for the notion of spiritual warfare in some particular texts of the Bible. That is, although Christian metal lyrics commonly draw on a wide range of biblical texts, there are also a few particular passages that bands tend to draw upon more frequently than others when dealing with issues of spiritual warfare. These passages are found in 2 Timothy and 6 Ephesians. For example, 2 Timothy: 3–4 provides 'true believers' with the following encouragement: 'Endure hardship with us like a good soldier of Christ Jesus. No one serving as a soldier gets involved in civilian affairs – he wants to please his commanding officer'. Much inspiration has also been found in Ephesians 6: 11–17, which reads:

> Put on the full armor of God so that you can take your stand against the devil's schemes. For our struggle is not against flesh and blood, but against the rulers, against the authorities, against the powers of this dark world and against the spiritual forces of evil in the heavenly realms. Therefore put on the full armor of God, so that when the day of evil comes, you may be able to stand your ground, and after you have done everything, to stand. Stand firm then, with the belt of truth buckled around your waist, with the breastplate of righteousness in place, and with your feet fitted with the readiness that comes from the gospel of peace. In addition to all this, take up the shield of faith, with which you can extinguish all the flaming arrows of the evil one. Take the helmet of salvation and the sword of the Spirit, which is the word of God.[11]

The particular set of war and battle metaphors used in this passage, such as the 'full armor of God', 'the breastplate of righteousness', 'the shield of faith', 'helmet of salvation and the sword of the Spirit', have provided important sources of inspiration for Christian metal lyrics. The notion of spiritual warfare also surfaces in Christian metal album titles such as Stryper's *Soldiers under Command*,[12] Deliverance's *Weapons of our Warfare*[13] and Recon's *Behind Enemy Lines*.[14] However, as bands also tend to emphasize, spiritual warfare is not about actual fighting and violence in the physical world; instead, it is a war waged on a spiritual level though prayer, evangelism and rebellion against the sinfulness of humanity. Examples of this lyrical style are plentiful in Christian metal. One classic example can be found in Recon's song 'Behind Enemy Lines'[15] which, in a style resembling a military-style call to arms, makes direct connections between spiritual warfare and evangelism. As the lyrics for this song explain, taking the Christian message to the unsaved and un-churched, to 'dangerous ground', involves stealth tactics, which demand persistence, determination and courage. The nature of this struggle and the toughness needed in order to prevail is also clearly spelled out in the lyrics for several other classic Christian metal songs such as Deliverance's 'Flesh and Blood'.[16] To take a more recent example of militaristic violent rhetoric, we might consider the following lines from Impending Doom's 'There will be Violence':

> This is violence in its purest form,
> What it is truly made for,
> Love and hatred flow through my throat,
> With this microphone in my hand.
> We are the voice for the voiceless
> Among unholy kingdoms drunk with blasphemy
> We are continents wide and oceans deep,
> The blood of the saints is splashed
> Across the ruins like a holy holocaust
> We will return
> And you will hear an uproar of lost souls
> There will be violence!
> Perverse works are in vain,
> Though the light may now seem dim,
> The whole world chases after Him,
> This is a movement
> Abandoning hate and preaching war[17]

Lyrics of this type also further illustrate the pervasiveness of the eschatological view of history that permeates much of Christian metal lyrics more generally. The militaristic and sometimes aggressive and violent rhetoric often used in Christian metal have indeed sparked some degree of debate in Christian circles. In some cases, such debates have even found their way into Christian metal lyrics themselves, such as in Ultimatum's

'Violence and Bloodshed'.[18] Again, lyrics of the type cited above are obviously not meant to incite actual violence in the real world. Rather, they are most frequently written with the aim of pointing out the radical qualities of the Christian message itself.

Much of the lyrics dealing with spiritual warfare also point out that being 'warriors of God' and engaging in spiritual warfare against evil and sin entails resisting and rebelling against the sinfulness of mankind and human society. Lyrics in this fourth main category highlight contemporary society as fallen and in need of redemption. Consider the following example from War of Age's 'Salvation':

> Ready, I am ready, breathe salvation
> Lord we hear your prayer, bring forth revival
> Rise, oh ancient one, breathe salvation
>
> We failed by the hands of man
> And laid claim to idols
> How selfish are we in the eyes of God
>
> You reject truth and lay claim to idols
> Fearing your demise, breathe salvation
>
> To those of you who hide behind your sorrows
> And cower in your time of need
> We must prepare our hearts for the demise of a nation, which lies in the palm of our hands
>
> Heed the warnings, focus not on what's seen and stand above the weakness,
> for all who know Him stand to gain eternity[19]

Lyrics in this category are also designed to aid, support and inspire Christian listeners in their own everyday struggles of living as Christians in a sinful world. The issue of rebellion against sin is fully compatible with the teachings of most Protestant traditions and it also surfaces at many other levels of the activities of many bands. For example, moving for a moment beyond the content of song lyrics, the official online community of the US band Demon Hunter is called 'The Blessed Resistance' and the official fan community of Mortification is called 'The Infiltration Squad'.[20] Another example can be found on the official webpages of the US band Ultimatum, which include a separate statement by the band on the issue of sin. Under the heading of 'The Ultimatum', visitors can read the following:

> **ULTIMATUM** believes in and trusts in Jehovah God, the Almighty. We are not ashamed of him for He gave himself freely for us. Christianity is the ultimate life on earth and the ultimate life in eternity.

Whom will you serve?

God, the Father loves you and longs to have a RELATIONSHIP with you.... Although God, the Almighty, is the Creator and upholder of the universe He is also our loving Father and He wants to have a personal relationship with all of us.... However, there is one thing that stands in the way of this relationship... **SIN!** Since God is holy and perfect, he cannot and will not have fellowship with sin. Yes, God is a loving God, but he is also a JUST God and sin must be dealt with and we are all sinners!...We guarantee you 100% that Jesus will never leave you if you ask Him to be the Lord of your life. Ask him to forgive you of your sins. He WILL change you life. **This is the ULTIMATUM!**[21]

In short, the issue of rebellion against sin surfaces at many levels of Christian metal culture. This particular theme is also indirectly drawn upon in lyrics dealing with a range of other topics such as evangelism and spiritual warfare in particular.

A fifth and final main category of lyrics focus on everyday social and personal struggles from a Christian perspective. Social injustice and social commentary have long, of course, constituted central themes of popular music lyrics more generally. In Christian metal such issues are, again, typically approached form a broadly defined 'Christian perspective'. For example, social problems and social injustice is often treated in light of notions of humanity and society as inherently sinful or at least in need of deeper spiritual guidance. Following Luhr,[22] a significant subcategory of song lyrics dealing with these types of topics could be called 'issue-based', such as anti-abortion, anti-pornography or anti-gay rights. Reflecting conservative Christian's broader cultural and political engagements and campaigns in the United States, these types of issue-based song lyrics have been particularly common among some US bands. Similar to their secular counterparts, Christian metal bands tend not to shun potentially controversial and disturbing topics. One main purpose of lyrics in this category is therefore to highlight societal ills from a Christian perspective.[23]

The visual and aesthetic dimension

As has already been pointed out numerous times, Christian and secular metal are largely identical when it comes to basic musical, visual, aesthetic and stylistic traits. For example, the appearance of most Christian metalheads is in full accordance with metal styles or variations of the classic 'metal uniform'. Many male Christian metalheads have long hair; most prefer to dress in dark colours, band t-shirts, jeans and leather; they wear chains, band pins, patches and metal-inspired jewellery; some have tattoos etc. Any informed observer would readily identify most of these individuals as metalheads (Figure 3.1).

In all basic respects, Christian metal's visual dimension also conforms to a broadly defined metal aesthetic. It includes typical gloomy metal imagery such as skulls, fire, weapons such as swords and axes, motives of violent battles and death, apocalyptic images of hell and the destruction of worlds and so on. With the exception of overtly anti-Christian motifs, the type of imagery used is largely identical with that of secular metal. Christian bands representing particular metal sub-genres also tend to conform to the particular variations of the general metal aesthetic developed by these particular sub-genres. For example, while Christian thrash metal bands tend to favour the colourful but raw aesthetics of thrash, unblack bands instead tend to adopt typical black metal aesthetics such as Viking-age motifs and mountain and dark forest landscapes. But importantly, Christian metal also makes use of a range of motifs that one would generally not find in secular metal. The ways in which these motifs are presented is fully governed, however, by either the general metal aesthetic or some particular variation thereof.

CCM in general typically makes use of various types of imagery and motifs designed to make either explicit or implicit references to Christianity. These include motifs of crucifixes and crosses, depictions of Jesus himself, angel-like figures, figures or people appearing in various poses of prayer, praise or

FIGURE 3.1 *Christian metal style. Photo: Marcus Moberg (2008).*

worship, churches, altars, stained-glass windows, Bibles and scrolls, grave monuments, beams of light, doves and wine and bread.[24] Of course, these are all considered central and centuries old Christian motifs and symbols that are easily recognizable to most people living in largely Christian cultures. However, not all Christian bands use all of these types of motifs as frequently and some make no use of them at all. When Christian metal bands use central Christian motifs and symbols such as these, they usually tend to espouse the more powerful ones or more powerful ways of depicting them. Some examples would be grim or bloody motifs of crucifixes or the crucified Christ himself, altars, powerful (and often very muscular) angel figures 'doing God's work'[25] and colourful depictions of key Christian biblical, eschatological and apocalyptic events such as the fall from grace or the battle at Armageddon. In short, when combined with the general metal aesthetic, central Christian motifs take on a more specific character as they typically become primarily associated with themes such as war, battle, strife and struggle. Moreover, it may also be noted that Christian metal has also come up with its own variant of the originally biblical symbol '666' or 'number of the beast' commonly used in secular metal aesthetics. In Christian metal aesthetics, the numbers instead read '777'. In Christian metal, therefore, the distinctive general metal aesthetic becomes simultaneously both appropriated and re-worked. As a result of the process of becoming fitted into the particular aesthetic framework of metal, central Christian motifs and symbols go through a *re-aesthetization* and become depicted in as stark and powerful ways as possible.

The employment of the types of imagery outlined above surfaces clearly in Christian metal album cover artwork. To begin with a classic example, the cover for Christian thrash metal band Vengeance Rising's 1988 debut release *Human Sacrifice* depicts a bloody hand roped and nailed to a piece of wood. This, of course, is an obvious reference to the crucifixion of Christ (as is the album title itself). To take another classic example, the artwork of Saint's album *Time's End*[26] is directly inspired by the apocalyptic visions of events to come as related in Revelation. The cover depicts the leopard-like beast with 'a mouth like that of a lion' rising from the sea as related in Rev. 3:12. To take yet another classic example, the cover of Bride's *Show No Mercy*[27] depicts the cosmic battle between the archangel Michael and the dragon or Satan as told in Rev. 12: 7–9.

More recent examples of album artwork portrayals of apocalyptic events directly inspired by these same Revelation themes include War of Age's *Arise and Conquer*, which depicts a knight driving his lance down the throat of a large dragon. The dragon most probably stands for the dragon (i.e. Satan) as related in Rev. 12–20. On the other end of the knight's lance there is a banner with the head of a lion, which is most probably a reference to the 'Lion of Judah' (i.e. Christ) as recounted in Rev. 5: 5–6 – a central symbol of messianic expectation. In line with this interpretation, the knight himself would then be the Archangel Michael who, as told in Rev. 12: 7–9, will fight the dragon in the heavens and hurl him down to earth. Another more recent example of the utilization of apocalyptic motifs in album artwork can be found in Impending Doom's *There Will Be Violence*[28] which depicts the earth from a space-perspective being engulfed in what appears to be some form of 'cosmic' flames. As with the albums of many other Christian metal bands, the apocalyptic references in the artwork for this particular album become even clearer when understood in relation to the album title and the name of the band itself (Figures 3.2 and 3.3).

Lastly, it should be noted that Christian metal album artwork quite frequently also alludes to apocalyptic themes in ways that are not as obviously directly inspired by biblical texts. Stryper's debut EP *The Yellow and Black Attack*[29] provides a classic example of this. The picture on the cover depicts missiles on their way towards earth from space directed by what is presumably the hand of God. Another example can be found in the cover for Mortification's *Post Momentary Affliction*.[30] The surrealistic cover

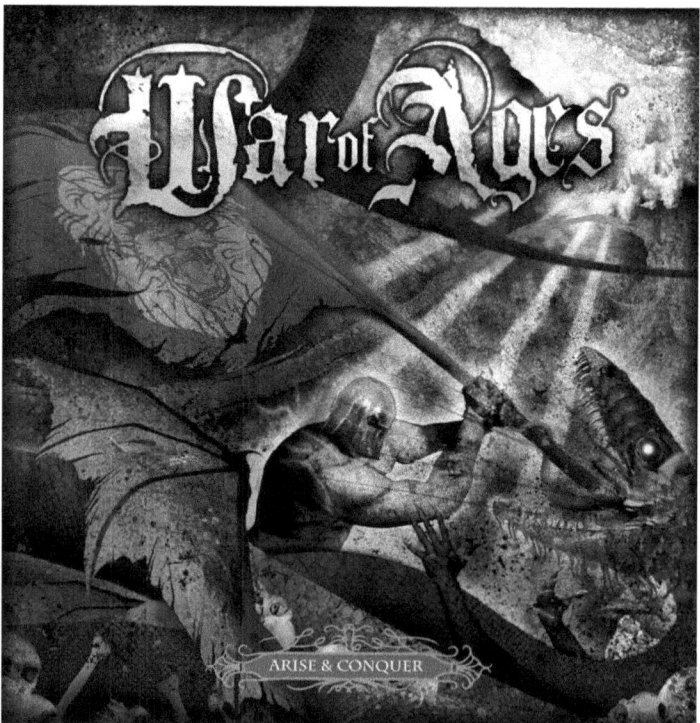

FIGURE 3.2 *Album cover for War of Ages'* Arise and Conquer. *Reproduced with the kind permission of Facedown Records.*

FIGURE 3.3 *Album cover for Impending Doom's* There Will be Violence. *Reproduced with the kind permission of Facedown Records.*

picture depicts white stairs in the midst of a barren landscape leading up to a white throne, against which a large sword is leaning. A human heart (depicted in anatomical detail), bearing what appears to be a crown of thorns, is falling like a bolt of fire from the sky towards the throne while a devilish hand is breaking up through the stony ground below. While it is unclear what precise idea or notion this cover is intended to convey (if it is indeed intended is to convey any precise idea at all), it nevertheless clearly brings the biblical narrative of the cosmic battle between good and evil into mind.

Different types of both explicit and implicit references to Christianity are also sometimes included in the design of the official webpages of bands. Christian metal media, both printed and Internet-based, also tend to include Christian references of various sorts, usually in the form of crosses. All of the central motifs mentioned above may also appear in music videos in which they are usually interspersed with concert-type footage of the band. However, videos by Christian bands need not necessarily employ any such motifs. Notable visual differences between Christian and secular metal also surface in the live concert setting, which is the topic of the following chapter.

4

The Experiential, Sensory and Bodily Dimensions

In this chapter, we will focus on the experiential, sensory and bodily experience of Christian metal, particularly as experienced in the context of the live Christian metal concert setting. With the themes explored in previous chapters in mind, in this chapter we will thus turn to a discussion of Christian metal's appropriation of metal's bodily practices and live concert conventions. Apart from a few notable exceptions – most of which have focused on religion and various types of electronic dance music[1] – the ways in which particular forms of popular music may serve as a basis for the creation of particular alternative religious sensory and bodily regimes has so far not received much attention in the wider scholarly literature on religion and popular music. One main concern when considering various intersections that may exist between religion and popular music has to do with the question of whether, and if so, in what ways and to what extent, different forms of popular music may serve to induce 'religious' or transcendent experiences among their audiences. We will begin our discussion in this chapter on a more philosophical note by considering how the *transcendent*, *transgressive* and *instrumental*, as a conceptual categories, can be used to help understand the experiential dimensions of Christian popular music more generally.

Approaching the transcendent and transgressive

The transcendent is tricky to conceptualize. In large part, the difficulty lies in whether, and if so how, to develop a concept of transcendence that can appreciate both religious conceptions of transcendence as linked to various understandings of the divine and non-religious conceptions of the transcendent as something that, if it exists at all, is ultimately a product of human society and imagination. Religious/theological conceptions of transcendence and the divine consist of everything from treating the divine as totally out of reach of human activity to treating it as immanent to everyday life – with concomitantly different conceptions of the transcendent. Similarly, non-religious or, if you will, 'secular' philosophies range from Hegelian, quasi-mystical notions of 'spirit' to a radically positivist suspicion of anything that is not directly observable – with similarly diverse implications for conceptions of transcendence.

Any expressly *religious* conception of transcendence needs to be considered in close connection to the intimately related, and equally ambiguous, concept of 'religious experience'. This is usually understood as referring primarily, although by no means exclusively, to various types of instances of 'mystical unity' with the divine[2] or more profound individual experiences of something 'wholly other'[3] that is removed from normal everyday existence. It has become increasingly clear, though, that when the concept of transcendence is understood as necessarily standing in some form of binary opposition to everyday material and embodied existence, it also tends to become essentialized and rooted in some unspecified ' "deep" individual feelings' or encounters with an equally unspecified 'numinous' realm – both of which remain ultimately inaccessible and thus ultimately inexplicable, to any outside observer.[4]

Yet most conceptions of transcendence – whether scholarly, theological or some combination of the two – usually retain some sense – of a phenomenological nature or otherwise – that it is an experience that involves *some kind* of perceived sense of separation from everydayness and materiality. Having said that, when the concepts of transcendence and religious experience are used as analytical tools in empirical research, they both need to be approached in terms of 'experiences *deemed* religious',[5] that is, as experiences which gain their particular meanings in particular religious and relational contexts. The anthropologist Birgit Meyer articulates this approach clearly when she asserts that 'religious feelings are not just there, but are made possible and reproducible by certain modes of inducing experiences of the transcendental'.[6]

When considering any given set of notions about experiences deemed religious or transcendent in different religious contexts, we thus have much to gain from striving to identify and learning to recognize recurring ways of encouraging, organizing (including policing) and inducing such experiences – for example through the use of popular music – within such contexts. In doing so, scholars also need to pay attention to the ways in which acceptable and established modes of inducing and attaining such experiences within particular religious settings often tend to stand in some form of more or less clearly articulated *tension* with those practices which are perceived to constitute or encourage transgressions of these accepted modes.

For example, this kind of tension is often in evidence in the search for transcendence within Abrahamic and dualistic religious systems such as Judaism and Christianity, in which the nature of the divine and how to engage with it has always been a subject of debate and controversy. The divine, whether conceived as immanent or as utterly 'other' than or removed from human existence, requires a kind of transcendence to reach.[7] Transcendence could therefore, in a Bourdieusian sense, generally be conceptualized as a kind of experiential 'logic'. In spite of always being grounded in immanence and materiality, transcendence could be understood in terms of a valency, a dynamic along which *people may desire to travel* in order to attempt to experience a kind of 'weightlessness', a sense that everyday reality no longer applies, a sense that there is something greater than oneself and one's immediate environment.[8] Such an understanding is also consonant with non-religious practices that see the temporary achieving of transcendence as a goal, including some forms of musical practice. It might prove fruitful, therefore, to situate transcendence among a cluster of similar, though not identical, logics. The most important of these for our purposes here is the *transgressive*.

Like the concept of the transcendent, the transgressive is similarly knotty. The concept can be used to refer very literally to any activity that breaks a law of some kind, but it also forms the basis for highly theoretical thinking on the experiential limits of human behaviour. Further, the concept of the transgressive has been used to understand a class of activities that, particularly in pre-modern and non-Western societies, temporarily suspend or invert the rules of everyday life. Finally, it is also used to highlight certain forms of art in which social conventions are challenged. It is crucial to note, therefore, that the concepts of transcendence and transgression often overlap, but they are not identical; they also often exist in a kind of tension.

The concept of the transgressive, as developed by theorists such as Bataille[9] and Turner,[10] and as implied in the work of structuralist anthropologists such as Douglas,[11] points towards a form of experience that breaks the boundaries of the everyday. An important point to note is that the *telos* (or perhaps, the *reductio al absurdum*) of attempts at transgression is similar to that of transcendence – the separation of the individual from the world – but that transgression also implies a much stronger, often antagonistic relation to everyday life. Transgression challenges the systems of thought, the boundaries and the power relations through which the world is constructed, treating received and accepted rational, instrumental and economistic forms of reasoning as contingent, as open to challenge.

In structuralist anthropology, the concept of transgression is, moreover, closely allied to that of the 'sacred'. Often, the very experience of the sacred implies or requires a kind of transgression in the first place, a passing from the profane world to another one.[12] The same is true of transcendence, which also implies a kind of movement out of this world. However, although transcendence and transgression may follow similar logics when it comes to attaining or reaching a sense of the sacred, they should by no means be viewed as identical; at certain points they may even be conflictual and contradictory. For example, within some Christian settings the transcendent is frequently expressed through a movement away from corporeality. In contrast, the transgressive is often based on *embodied experience*, its boundaries and limitations, as well as on a fascination with the erotic and with death. As noted above, Keith Kahn-Harris (2007) has insightfully employed the concept of the transgressive to reveal and make sense of the experiential logics that underpin the ideological reproduction of the extreme metal scene.

As we have already discussed in previous chapters, various forms of popular music can be marked out 'Christian' in a number of ways. Such aspects as the content of lyrics, the expressed religious affiliations of the artists themselves and the dissemination of the music through specialized production and distribution outlets are crucial here as possible factors identifying popular music as 'Christian'. While these factors should by no means be disregarded, the aim of the following discussion is to highlight a rarely explored phenomenon that is particularly characteristic and revealing of the dynamics and tensions within Christian popular music and indeed within various types of religious popular music (e.g. Jewish or Islamic) more generally: the instrumental use of popular musical aesthetics for religious purposes. This instrumental use has consequences for the ways in which Christian popular music, including Christian metal, attempts to manage the tension between popular music's transcendent and transgressive potentials.

The instrumental

Opposed to the logics of the transcendent, transgressive and sacred, however, we can identify another cluster of logics, grounded on the everyday and the mundane. In creating the mundane world, logics of the economic, the communal and – most importantly for the argument put forward here – the *instrumental* are paramount. Here we understand instrumentalism in Weberian[13] and Habermasian[14] terms as a form of action that is guided by means-end rationality and that disciplines and governs the bounds of desirable outcomes. Inasmuch as the instrumental, as it is generally understood, aims at producing results in the material world, it is by definition separate from the transcendent and transgressive. Viewed more broadly, however, as a *form of action that intends desirable outcomes*, the relationship to the transcendent and transgressive is much more ambivalent and ironic. This is because there is clearly a sense in which the only way to achieve 'pure' transcendence and transgression appears to be not aiming to consciously achieve it in the first place, making transcendence and transgression almost always implicated in instrumental practice in some way.

Western post-1950s popular music and the scenes that reproduce it are characterized by a complex relationship to everyday life. Popular music is both an integral part of the everyday, perhaps even a source of 'empowerment' within the everyday,[15] but it also facilitates moments of 'liberation' from everyday rationality, for example through producing blissful, quasi-erotic experiences of the body, through which space is carved out from the everyday.[16] In this respect, popular music points towards a transcendence of the everyday. But it is a transcendence that is frequently intimately connected to a logic of transgression that may surpass the transcendent. In its bodily focus and its tendency to challenge boundaries, popular music has often been and often still is a source of transgression. Transcendence was and remains an important aesthetic principle in the Western classical music tradition, although mostly in the form of a transcendence based around a desire to transcend the body in order to reach a 'higher' aesthetic realm.[17]

Through its earthy, bodily focus, and in contrast to notions of transcendence prevalent in most Christian religious contexts, the transcendence of popular music is, however, more firmly rooted within the transgressive. In this respect, popular music's practices often contain a kind of rejection of certain experiential logics. While popular music's logic of transcendence and transgression are more powerfully weighted towards the transgressive, within most forms of Christianity, logics of transcendence and transgression tend to be more strongly weighted towards the transcendent. That is not to say that Christianity cannot be transgressive. Indeed, while the post-enlightenment period has seen the development of rational, formalized, highly disciplined Christian 'mainstreams', it has also seen the development of movements such as charismatic Christianity and Pentecostalism which are rooted in a sustained attempt at reaching the divine through joyous spiritual practices; these are often regarded as transgressive both in their focus on the body and in their marginalization of more ordered forms of religious practice.

A consideration of how different kinds of experiential logics are enabled and restricted helps in understanding the limitations and potentials that arise when religion and popular music encounter each other. As noted, the development of contemporary Christian music in the late 1960s and early 1970s was spurred as much as anything by a desire to make and keep Christianity 'relevant' in a broader social and cultural environment that appeared to be increasingly marked by a general erosion of tradition, decline in traditional forms of religion and an increasing focus on the individual. Even if this has had a sometimes transformative, even liberating impact on religious practice and worship (as for example in many evangelical Christian contexts), the dominant logic clearly remains one of instrumentalism, that is, popular music is employed and used for purposes outside or separate from itself.

As we will explore in more detail later on in this chapter, another distinctive feature of Christian popular music is the ambiguous dividing line between concert and worship. Concerts of contemporary Christian music, which often take place within religious spaces such as churches, frequently feature worship-type practices of various sorts, which are also meant to be recognized as such by participants. Here the tacit injunction to feel spiritually engaged can allow an instrumental logic to enter into an apparently aesthetic practice.

As noted in previous chapters, the contemporary Christian music industry has been particularly successful in creating an entire parallel 'Christianized' popular musical world for Christian youth.[18] Through its reworking of secular popular music styles in an evangelical Christian frame, this is a parallel world largely governed by an instrumental idea of popular musical aesthetics, which also has a bearing on the locations and forms in which the music is performed, received and experienced. As such, it is also a world that is constantly occupied with policing popular music's transgressive potential.

It is not that music has no value in and of itself in most religious theologies – it usually does – but the dominant tendency is to 'use' popular music in certain instrumental ways, as an instrument for certain predetermined 'accepted' purposes. Ironically, a music that is often produced for evangelistic ends frequently has the opposite effect among non-religious audiences.[19] Christian metal's highly contested and controversial place within the world of secular metal provides an as clear as any example of this.

For all the critical implications of what has been said so far, however, the intention here is not to argue that instrumentalization constitutes the entire meaning of Christian metal. It is undoubtedly true that Christian metal can and does facilitate transcendent experiences that participants understand as divine encounters. Instrumental as certain aspects of Christian metal may sometimes be, it may also be an instrumentalism that 'works'.

Christian metal does indeed constitute a very notable example of a form of Christian popular music that goes quite some way in affirming the transgressive potentials of its 'secular' equivalent. Of course, as already discussed in previous chapters, when evangelical musicians appropriated metal music and culture in the early 1980s, they did so for expressly instrumental reasons; the basic idea was to be able to evangelize to secular metal audiences in a way and a language that they were deemed to be more perceptive about and able to relate to and understand. Following its ideological diversification and diffusion on a transnational scale in the early 1990s, however, increasing numbers of bands started to embrace extreme metal styles. As already noted, extreme metal is generally governed by conscious extremes regarding the 'sonic transgression'[20] imbued in the music itself, its often radical lyrical subject matter (such as strongly subversive religious themes), its consciously exaggerated aesthetic and the high degree of intensity and physicality that characterizes its modes of performance and appreciation. In spite of this, as Kahn-Harris[21] has persuasively argued, extreme metal is not appropriately characterized as an entirely 'free', undisciplined cultural form. Rather, although extreme metal music and culture sets out to systematically transgress certain key musical and social conventions; at the same time it also produces its own mundane practices that discipline this transgression.

Like most other forms of Christian popular music, Christian extreme metal also typically engages in the conscious mixing of extreme metal and 'Christian' repertoires through a very deliberate re-working and re-aesthetization of extreme metal themes and imagery through a Christian frame. However, through having developed its own Christian version of the metal style and aesthetic and through its almost unconditional appropriation of bodily practices such as moshing, Christian extreme metal concerts at least open up the possibility of getting 'lost' in the music while simultaneously remaining embedded in a wider context that is expressly delineated as religious.

As such, Christian metal could be viewed an as example of an instrumentalism that 'works'; or at least as an example of religious popular music that, while remaining marked by instrumentalist thinking in many respects, still retains the possibility of transgression, and thereby transcendence, through embodied practices. The dominant logic of transcendence within Christian metal is, however, one that is, at least partly, limited. This is because the instrumentalism of Christian metal (like all other forms of Christian popular music) runs the risk of limiting the capacity of Christian metal to fully 'take off'. Further, its logic largely divorces transcendence from transgression, making it a kind of 'safe' transcendence that actively strives to avoid the more 'dangerous', boundary-crossing, uncontrolled, bodily excess that transgression represents.[22]

The Christian metal live concert setting

Can the Christian metal live concert be regarded a religious event? Do Christian metal live concerts provide Christian metalheads with spaces that aid the attainment of religious experiences, moments of transcendence or 'mystical unity' with the divine? It would surely be a mistake to view Christian metal live concerts as events that, just by the virtue of being 'Christian', automatically would provide its participants with these types of experiences. Nonetheless, as noted above, Christian metalheads have created their own Christian variant of the 'metal lifestyle'. Christian metal culture on the whole can therefore be viewed as forming a simultaneously religious and popular musical 'habitual framework and day-by-day form of life'[23] that underpins the cultural and religious identities of Christian metalheads. Viewed in this light – as events characterized by a deliberate and explicit mixing of 'Christian' and 'metal' repertoires – Christian metal live concerts can be seen to provide participants with temporal environments consciously designed to foster a sense of religious-cultural community and shared religious experience and encourage 'specially intense moments of conviction and commitment'.[24]

It is therefore important to pay close attention to the *particular* religious experiential, sensory and bodily regimes that become actualized and reinforced during Christian metal live concerts. What we need to ask, therefore, is what role the sensory elements, concert practices and bodily behaviours typical of metal music play in the context of the Christian metal concert. Like its secular equivalent, we need to recognize that Christian metal live concerts are consciously designed to exude a high degree of general intensity as well as to directly encourage highly active – and indeed *aggressively active – bodily* participation.

The following analysis will primarily draw on the concept of *sensational forms* as developed by Meyer. As the concept is primarily intended to draw our attention to the ways in which religious practice involves and activates the body and the senses, it provides some intriguing new avenues for a closer analysis of the kinds of creative re-formations and re-configurations of conventional religious sensory and bodily regimes that we find in a phenomenon like Christian metal music. Through its strong emphasis on aggressiveness, intensity and physicality, Christian metal music certainly provides a particularly fruitful case for such analysis. It needs to be noted, though, that Meyer's notion of sensational forms has so far not been applied to cases such as Christian metal which are characterized by a deliberate and intimate merging of conventional evangelical practices with the practices and aesthetics of a specific style of popular music. In addition to this, there is also some un-clarity as to exactly *how* an analysis of sensational forms could proceed or be conducted in actual practice. The analysis that follows will therefore be more suggestive than assertive in character.

Any exploration of sensational forms necessarily needs to build on extensive fieldwork and the careful analysis of fieldwork data. The following discussion is intimately informed by my own ethnographic fieldwork within the vibrant Finnish Christian metal music scene that I carried out during the years 2005–2009.[25]

As already noted above, at first glance, Christian metal seems not to differ from its secular, 'not-expressly-Christian' equivalent to any significant degree. However, at closer inspection a range of noteworthy differences undoubtedly start to appear. For people more comprehensively familiar with metal music and culture, its general, although admittedly multifaceted, aesthetic is usually quite unmistakable. Crudely put, and as has already been discussed in previous chapters, the general metal aesthetic is governed by conscious extremes, associated as it is with motifs such as religion- and mythology-inspired epic and apocalyptic battles, gory images of death, destruction, catastrophe and decay, extreme rebellion and the elevation of male vitality, power and machismo.[26]

As was also discussed in the previous chapter, although generally conforming to the general metal aesthetic, the aesthetics of Christian metal typically contain various types of both direct and covert references to Christianity. The picture is much the same with regard to Christian metal's appropriation and re-working of metal's characteristic sensory dimensions and bodily practices. Again, at first glance, Christian metal live concerts do not appear to differ from secular metal live concerts to any significant degree. On the surface, both performance style and audience reaction resembles secular metal concerts in almost every respect; bands typically aim to execute their musical set as intensely as possible while audiences respond, and are expected to respond, in a correspondingly intense way. As already noted, Christian metal has also incorporated metal concert practices such as headbanging and moshing. Christian metal concerts are thus generally characterized by an equally boisterous atmosphere characteristic of metal live concerts in general. The most notable difference in this regard has to do with the total absence of alcohol consumption, as well as other illegal substances such as marijuana or other drugs, all of which are commonly strictly prohibited at Christian metal events.

As with contemporary Christian music more generally, notable differences to secular metal events usually gradually surface as concerts get underway, although these may be more easily discernible by more experienced observers.

This is because even though the general format of Christian metal concerts is that of the typical metal concert – including all characteristic auditory, sensory and bodily elements – they commonly also contain some quite eye-catching 'church-like' practices and modes of bodily behaviours.[27] These practices and behaviours surface most clearly in the interaction between bands and audiences.

At Christian metal events with a largely, and frequently exclusively, Christian audience, it is not unusual for bands to integrate short prayers, edifying speeches or the reading of a few Bible passages as parts of their very performances. Moreover, musicians sometimes kneel as if in prayer on stage or assume crucifixion or 'praise poses', raising their arms upwards towards the sky or ceiling, thereby indicating that they are engaged in praising God.[28] At Christian metal concerts, praise poses are commonly also taken by members of the audience. Notably, while prayers, edificational speeches and even kneeling on stage all may be viewed as ways of making more unspecified general references to Christian worship practices, the assuming of praise poses has a more direct connection to worship practices prevalent in evangelical, charismatic and Pentecostal settings.

Secular metalheads have long used the so-called 'Il Cornuto' hand sign as a main form of greeting and symbol of metal affiliation. The sign is made through the extension of the index and little fingers from an otherwise clenched fist. This sign is also known as the 'satanic salute' and in some traditions it has also figured as a sign of protection from the 'evil eye'. Throughout the years, the sign has also become widely used as a general symbol for everything having to do with 'metal' and increasingly also for everything having to do with harder styles of rock more generally. While some Christian metalheads view this sign purely as a symbol and form of metal greeting, some indeed abstain from using it. The sign is, nonetheless, commonplace at Christian metal concerts. But Christian rock has also created a hand sign of its own called 'One way' (first developed within the 1960s *Jesus Movement*) which is also commonly used at Christian metal concerts. This sign is made by extending only the index finger from an otherwise clenched fist and raising the arm upwards towards the sky.[29] The sign is meant to symbolize Jesus as the (only) way to God (Figure 4.1).[30]

In relation to Christian metal, in addition to the music itself and its style of performance, characteristic metal live concert practices such as headbanging and moshing would fall within what we could call the 'metal' repertoire. Prayers, edifying speeches, 'one-way' signs, crucifixion- and praise poses, on the other hand, would instead fall within what we could call the 'Christian' repertoire. The main point to note is that Christian metal concerts are characterized by the conscious and very deliberate mixing of these two

FIGURE 4.1 *'One way'. Crowd at* Immortal Metal Fest, *Finland, 2008. Photo: Marcus Moberg.*

repertoires.³¹ This combination of 'metal' and 'Christian' repertoires serves the important function of marking out concerts as not only 'Christian' events but as events where Christianity becomes expressed and experienced *in, via and through* the aesthetical, bodily and musical language of metal. Indeed, when attending Christian metal concerts, there is a clear sense in which the majority of participants directly *expect* such a mixing of repertoires. After all, it is through the inclusion of re-aestheticized Christian elements into the framework of the 'ordinary' metal concert format that these events assume their meaning as *Christian* metal events.

This mixing of repertoires, therefore, contributes to the construction of Christian metal live concerts as events intended just as much for collective musical appreciation, release and entertainment as for religious experience and worship. However, all of these abovementioned practices – prayers, edifying speeches, Bible-readings, kneeling on stage and assuming praise poses – all become totally integrated with typical metal live concert practices and behaviours such as headbanging and moshing, thus somewhat complicating the drawing of any easy distinctions between 'musical' and 'religious' elements. But this mixing of popular musical and Christian repertoires is nevertheless also highly illustrative of the instrumental use of metal in Christian settings, with the 'Christian' repertoire taking on particular importance as the primary means whereby the music is afforded a necessary 'institutional anchoring'[32] as it becomes explicitly connected to institutionalized worship practices found in more conventional evangelical Christian settings. There is a sense, therefore, that attending a Christian metal concert involves something more, or perhaps rather primarily something *else*, than just attending a concert.

For many Christian metal musicians, the concert-setting provides an alternative avenue for religious worship as it allows them to fully assume the role of 'metal ministers'. For example, in my interviews with Finnish Christian metal musicians, some of them stated that they sometimes tangibly feel the presence of the Holy Spirit during their live performances. For audiences, the live concert setting mainly provides a temporal avenue through which to express – both in their minds and through their bodies – their religious beliefs in a way that is fully in line with their own popular cultural sensibilities together with likeminded people. It should be noted, though, that not all musicians and participants report experiencing live concerts in such explicitly religious ways. For some, Christian metal simply constitutes a more 'positive' or 'uplifting' alternative to the perceived potentially destructive messages and practices of secular metal culture.

As noted, the sensory and bodily dimensions of Christian metal live concerts can usefully be viewed in relation to the concept of sensational forms as developed by Meyer. Meyer approaches religion in general as an inherently *mediated* phenomenon or 'as a practice of mediation that organizes the relationship between experiencing subjects and the transcendental via particular sensational forms'.[33] She describes her understanding of the concept of sensational forms as 'relatively fixed, authorized modes of invoking and organizing access to the transcendental, thereby creating and sustaining links between believers in the context of particular religious organizations'.[34] Religious or transcendent experiences, she argues, need to be understood as emerging via and through particular forms of mediation, via particular sensational forms that 'concomitantly tune the senses and induce *specific* sensations, thereby rendering the divine *sense-able*, and triggering *particular* religious experiences'.[35]

The concept of sensational forms is thus primarily intended to denote particular ways of organizing and inducing religious or transcendental experiences within the contexts of particular religious communities. As such, sensational forms should also be understood as being designed to activate the body and the senses in order to induce particular emotions and feelings.[36] Elaborate collective rituals (such as those found in Catholicism or Orthodox Christianity, for example) constitute one obvious example of religious practices where various types of sensational forms become actualized through the employment of religious objects, images, music etc.

Sensational forms become actualized at three main levels. First, there is what could be referred to as the *ontological* level as sensational forms 'organize encounters with an invisible beyond'.[37] Second, there is what could be called a *sensory* or *experiential* level as sensational forms 'address and form people's bodies and senses in distinct ways'.[38] And third, there is what could be termed a *communal* level as sensational forms serve to strengthen aesthetic and stylistic affinities within groups of believers to form 'religious subjects' and thereby to 'underpin a collective religious identity'.[39]

How, then, might these thoughts be applied to the temporal, simultaneously religious and musical setting of the Christian metal live concert? First of all, we need to reiterate that, like their secular equivalents, Christian metal concerts are consciously designed to activate the body and the senses in a range of different ways. Indeed, a high degree of intensity, primarily expressed through the body, is expected at concerts and is therefore also constantly and actively encouraged in a range of ways. As with some other forms of popular music, the quality of a metal concert is commonly measured on the basis of how well musicians and participants are able to create an as intense atmosphere as possible *together*. Musicians (who, we should recall, often act as 'ministers' from stage) typically constantly urge the audience to heighten the intensity of their bodily response to the music while audience members in their turn often strive to compel musicians to take their performance to yet higher levels of aggressiveness and intensity. Therefore, like secular metal concerts, a 'successful' or 'high quality' Christian metal concert needs to be understood as the result of a consciously collective effort by both performers and audience.

When considering the Christian metal concert setting in relation to the concept of sensational forms, we should also pay due attention to the particular ways in which concerts activate the body and the senses in ways that are *distinctive* to this particular type of setting. First of all, however, it is important to note the issue of *place*. It is not uncommon for Christian metal concerts to be held in facilities owned by some church or congregation. However, such concerts are only very rarely held in churches or worship houses themselves and virtually never in the very same spaces where conventional church practice or worship takes place. Concerts may also be held in venues completely disconnected from any type of church or congregation. But irrespective of whether they are held in venues owned by some church or congregation or not, the point to note is that they tend to be held in venues *temporarily converted*, and often to at least some degree specially decorated, for the occasion, serving as temporal alternative spaces of religious-musical activity. This, then, in a sense also serves as a way of *detaching* the Christian metal

FIGURE 4.2 *Entrance at* Immortal Metal Fest, *Finland, 2008. Photo: Marcus Moberg.*

concert experience from the types of spaces more commonly associated with conventional religious practice (Figure 4.2).

As already noted, it is within this alternative temporal space that sensory and bodily practices typical of metal music in general such as headbanging and moshing become consciously intertwined with more conventional Christian practices such as collective prayer and praise poses. It is worth noting that, through such direct and conscious combination of 'Christian' and 'metal' repertoires, Christian metal concerts provide participants with alternative religious sensory and bodily practices that are highly distinctive to Christian metal itself and thus quite different from those commonly encouraged through more conventional worship practices. For example, when compared to the sensory and bodily regimes prevalent in more conventional worship settings (including the more lively regimes of Charismatics and Pentecostals), it would be an understatement to say that Christian metal concerts differ from these contexts by virtue of their high degree of physicality since all-out participation at Christian metal concerts often is directly physically *demanding*.

In close relation to this, we might also want to consider more closely the ways in which Christian metal concerts activate the different human senses in particular ways. Of course, in the multimedia context of the Christian metal concert, the senses are not activated separately but simultaneously. Concerts are at once physically felt in terms of touch and they are seen, heard and even smelled (and perhaps even tasted).

In addition to the concert setting being marked by a high degree of bodily physicality, it also contains a range of *visual* stimuli such as elaborate lighting and special effects of various sorts (e.g. artificial smoke). Moreover, it is not uncommon for musicians to don costumes and elaborate makeup. For example, in order to better convey the idea of being engaged in 'spiritual warfare', some bands wear medieval style armour and wield weapons such as swords and axes on stage. Most participants also tend to be specially dressed for the occasion, wearing various types of costumes, band t-shirts, spike- and stud-armbands, makeup etc. It is therefore worth noting that there is also some degree of *spectacle* involved always.

Concerts are also *heard*. At an archetypical metal concert, the music is played at maximum volume, and Christian metal concerts are no exception in this regard (earplugs are required). Moreover, concerts are physically felt not only when engaged in practices such as headbanging and moshing but also through the loudness of the *music itself*. Concerts thus invoke the feeling of being completely engulfed by the music, both mentally and physically. Lastly, concerts are also experienced in terms of smell (and perhaps even taste) as concert halls become hot and filled with the smell of sweat and artificial smoke.

The Christian metal concert setting is thus one that not only brings together people with a shared religious faith. Within this temporal space, that shared faith becomes intimately intertwined with a shared taste for a particular type of popular music and shared ways of physically appreciating it, a certain style as well as the particular cultural and religious identity that goes with it. Shared aesthetic and stylistic sensibilities contribute to creating a sense of togetherness and fostering a sense of belonging among participants as Christian *metalheads*. Christian metal concerts could therefore be understood as providing participants with an *alternative* set of sensational forms to those most commonly employed in more conventional worship contexts, and this can be viewed as a way of underpinning and strengthening a sense of community, belonging and shared religious-cultural identity.

However, following from its many instrumental aspects, there is clearly also a sense in which Christian metal concerts often limit transcendence through its suppression of the transgressive. Even though Christian metal concert practices may certainly be taken to transgress conventional worship practices, these are nonetheless present at several levels of Christian metal concerts as well. There is thus clearly a sense in which the types of church-like behaviours present at Christian metal concerts as discussed above serve to keep the whole concert experience within 'safe' bounds. Put another way, we might say that there is a sense in which people who attend Christian metal concerts are always, at least partly, attending for purposes *other* than, or at least *in addition to*, the musical experience in itself. These critical observations should, however, be seen as tentative and suggestive. As I have also aimed to highlight, there is also plenty of evidence to suggest that, for its own followers at least, Christian metal's instrumentalism may indeed be one that 'works'.

5

The Contemporary Transnational Scene

This chapter outlines Christian metal's diffusion on a transnational scale. Utilizing the methodological framework of *scene*, the chapter focuses on Christian metal culture as a distinct transnational religious-popular cultural space and maps its diffusion and core regions on a transnational level. The chapter accounts for how Christian metal musicians and followers around the world have formed their own transnationally dispersed independent infrastructure of production and distributions outlets, different print- and online-Christian metal media and different gatherings and festivals. The chapter also discusses how Christian metal has spread to predominantly Catholic countries with significant Protestant minorities such as Brazil and Mexico. The principal aim of the chapter is to provide readers with an account of how the contemporary transnational Christian metal scene, although it consists of a web of national and regional scenes of various sizes which display their own peculiarities, still needs to be viewed as a distinct religious-cultural phenomenon that transcends national and regional borders. The chapter also highlights the impact of the ongoing development of the Internet and digital technologies on the workings of the contemporary transnational scene.

As noted in Chapter 1, the importance of exploring the intersections of religion, media and popular culture has become widely recognized within the broader study of contemporary religion. As argued by an increasing number of scholars,[1] new media and popular culture have come to play an ever more central role in how contemporary religion is experienced, practiced and lived. However, in spite of the long-standing close relationship between music and religion, as Lynch observes, 'the sociological study of the interlocking trends of the decline of traditional religious institutions, the rise of alternative spiritualities and the mediatization of religion have tended to neglect the significance of music in these processes in favor of focusing on other media'.[2] Even so, recent years have seen the emergence of a growing scholarly literature that deals with the intersection of popular music and religion. Calls have, however, been made for future research in this field to be more firmly grounded empirically and ethnographically and focused on what people actually 'do' with music in religiously or spiritually significant ways.[3]

Such an agenda for research raises important issues regarding theory and methodology. In particular, any exploration of what individuals actually might do with particular forms of music in religiously significant ways needs to be based on as solid and clear an understanding of the particular cultural environment in which this occurs as possible. Importantly, researchers also need to be able to communicate this understanding to other researchers within this and related fields. In addition, which is perhaps stating the obvious, the modes of analysis and interpretation employed will no doubt affect how the particular cultural environment under study will be approached and understood.

One way of approaching and making sense of particular musical-cultural environments is through the concept of scene, a methodological framework primarily developed within the field of youth and popular music culture studies. Indeed, this concept has also become frequently employed in research on the intersection of religion and popular music. However, it tends to be mostly used to denote particular popular musical environments more generally. Therefore, what is often lacking is a clearer specification of what a popular music 'scene' actually might be, as opposed to, for example, a popular music 'subculture', 'community' or 'tribe'. Complicating things further, the concept of scene is often used side by side with these other concepts.

In the following, I shall outline the particular version of the concept of scene that is employed here as a way of describing and making sense of the transnational spatial and temporal dimensions and discursive traits of the phenomenon of Christian metal music. My own use and development of scene as a methodological framework owes much to the particular version of the concept developed by Keith Kahn-Harris. In what follows, I will further explicate and elaborate on this version of the concept of scene.

Researchers interested in exploring the place of religion within or in relation to a particular popular musical environment are faced with at least one specific challenge. In one way or another, researchers need to be able to account for how the religious component relates to and connects with the musical-cultural component of the object of their study. By openly acknowledging the strongly interdisciplinary character of the field as a whole, such research needs to use methodological tools suitable for this task in order to be able to sufficiently connect to related types of research within the broader field of popular music culture studies. When re-contextualized for the study of the intersection of religion and popular music, the concept of scene carries much potential in this regard, as it provides researchers interested in exploring the religious significance that particular forms of popular music can have in the everyday lives of individuals with valuable tools for empirically mapping and making sense of the particular cultural environments in which, and in relation to which, this may occur.

Setting the scene: From subcultural theory to post–subcultural theory

As illustrated by the heading of this section, the term 'scene' can hold a range of different meanings. Among many other things, it can denote a space of theater and performance,[4] be used as a way of describing a particular state of affairs connected to a particular geographical location or serve to connote certain attitudes or 'vague notions of lifestyle',[5] for example, when people make statements about themselves by saying 'this is not my scene'. As Kahn-Harris points out, in addition to such uses, scene 'can also mean something much more definite and located that connotes something "subcultural" '.[6] Thus understood, the concept has also developed into a methodological framework aimed at highlighting the interconnectedness of different structural, spatial, temporal and discursive dimensions of particular popular musical environments. Often, together with other so-called 'post-subcultural' theoretical approaches, the concept of scene has also been presented as a way of avoiding and moving beyond the many problematic aspects that have become associated with the concept of 'subculture'.

As subculture has become part of everyday language (and also of many different languages), it has become increasingly ambiguous and difficult to define. As Bennett and Kahn-Harris point out, 'subculture has arguably become little more than a convenient "catch-all" term for any aspect of social life in which young people, style and music intersect'.[7] This also clearly applies to uses of the term within many academic contexts, including the study of religion. Considering the general ambiguity of the concept, vague uses of 'subculture' within the study of religion may be excusable in some cases. However, if employed in studies dealing with the intersection of religion and popular music, it becomes necessary to provide some clarification as to what exactly is meant by the term.

Although the concept of 'subculture' as it is known today was first developed within the so-called 'Chicago School' of urban sociology in the 1950s and 1960s,[8] a differently theorized and subsequently far more enduringly influential understanding of the concept was later developed by scholars associated with the Birmingham Centre for Contemporary Cultural Studies (CCCS) in the mid- and late 1970s,[9] who studied post-war British 'youth cultures', most of which were connected to some form of popular music. Basically, in this perspective, subcultures were viewed as 'sites of counter-hegemonic resistance to dominant ideology', expressed through the creation of spectacular 'styles' and 'counter-hegemonic "rituals"'.[10] However, the CCCS perspective also maintained that, in a society and culture driven by the logic of consumer capitalism, the possibilities for subcultural resistance become limited, thus amounting to little more than resistance of a symbolic kind.[11]

This particular theorization of the concept of subculture has become subjected to continuing criticism since the late 1980s. One particularly significant point concerns the ways in which the focus of CCCS's theory on 'those who were "other" to capitalism' often served to pre-determine its objects of study, thereby also producing 'that otherness through a rigid conceptual framework that read members' activities as implacably resistant'.[12] However, it should be noted that modified and differently theorized versions of subculture have proven continually useful for some types of studies.[13] There have also been successful attempts at redefining subculture as a term and putting it to new uses in combination with other theoretical perspectives.[14] For present purposes, the most important point to note is that debates concerning the analytical value of the concept of subculture and the respective advantages and disadvantages of alternative approaches have proven particularly enduring within the fields of youth and popular music culture studies. It is therefore important to recognize generally the implications of these debates for any exploration of the relationship between religion and popular music.

The development of youth culture towards increasing fragmentation and fluidity in the late 1980s also spurred the development of a range of theoretical frameworks as alternatives to subculture. Usually subsumed under the heading 'post-subcultural theory',[15] these include *neo-tribe*, as originally developed by Maffesoli,[16] *lifestyle*[17] and *scene*.[18] While the concept of neo-tribe aims to highlight the de-individualizing, ever more fluid and temporal character of modes of modern social and cultural engagement, the concept of lifestyle focuses on the material and consumption-related dimensions of personal and cultural identity. As both concepts emphasize the increasing fluidity of contemporary youth culture, they should also be viewed in close relation to macro-level social theoretical ideas which highlight contemporary social and cultural life as marked by increasing rootlessness and the rise of expressive individualism and heightened degrees of self-reflexivity.

While the concepts of neo-tribe and lifestyle are closely connected to a particular perspective on contemporary social and cultural life, the concept of scene is different, as it is most appropriately described as a more practically oriented mapping tool, which focuses on the spatial, place-based and temporal dimensions of particular popular musical environments. Although a range of varyingly theorized versions of the concept have been developed, they all share an emphasis on holism and anti-essentialism. They also share a focus on the intimate interconnectedness that exists between all central dimensions of particular popular musical environments (artists, audiences, media, production, consumption, etc.) without pre-determining their interrelationships or 'imposing predetermined ideas of what scenic involvement consists of'.[19]

Employing scene in the study of religion and popular music

The continuing and accelerating development of new digital media and sound formats, portable media technologies such as smartphones and file-sharing and social networks such as Facebook, has made music more easily accessible, transportable and reproducible than ever before.[20] Considering these developments, the concept of scene allows us to concentrate on the very issues for which the CCCS theory of subculture was poorly equipped through encouraging a holistic approach and form of analysis that does not exclude the combination of different theoretical approaches and perspectives.

A popular music scene can be thought of as a particularly structured, simultaneously musical, discursive and aesthetic temporal space that brings together people who share a passion for, sensibility for or affinity with a given form of popular music. Although a particular form of popular music constitutes the principal locus around which a popular music scene revolves, crucially, the forming of a scene also entails the development of a range of discourses, aesthetics, styles and practices in relation to that particular form of popular music. Indeed, the term 'scene' is often used by members of popular music cultures themselves as a way of conceptualizing their being part of a community which shares musical and stylistic interests and sensibilities. In addition, as they are simultaneously musical, discursive and aesthetic spaces, scenes also become structured along place-based scales and bound to certain geographical or geographically connected locations. As Kahn-Harris explains:

> The term scene is rarely applied to a particular space unless there is a substantial degree of both scenic structure and construction. The term

scene is meaningful to members when it describes a space that is both institutionally distinctive to some degree and has some degree of self consciousness. Scene is most frequently and unanimously used in cases where geographical boundedness (embodied in civic institutions such as cities or in nation states), institutional and aesthetic distinctiveness, and scenic discourses coincide.[21]

As the above points out, scenes display different degrees and forms of scenic *structure* and *construction*. We shall return to what this means exactly. First, however, it is necessary to account for the spatial, geographical, temporal and genre-specific dimensions of scenes.

As noted, scenes are reproduced along place-based scales: locally, nationally, regionally, transnationally and globally. Different local scenes (e.g. the 'London scene') form national scenes (e.g. the 'British scene'). Through the establishment of structural connections and communications with other geographically connected national scenes, regional scenes may develop over time (e.g. the 'Northern European scene'). Sometimes, national and regional scenes come together and form transnational or global scenes. The relationships between the different levels of scenes are, of course, far from simple. The more internationally diffused scenes become the more diverse and difficult they are to conceptualize as particular spaces. The geographical diffusion of scenes is further complicated by scenes being reproduced along *genre-based scales*. For example, a particular local or national metal scene may become closely connected with a sub-genre or style of that form of music, while it may retain close connections with a wider regional or transnational scene.[22] Therefore, the relation between different levels of scenes is characterized by intersection and overlap: 'the quasi-autonomous relation of scenes to each other means that individual scene members are never entirely bound by their location in one particular scene'.[23] Rather, scene members typically interact 'within a complexity of overlapping scenes within scenes, which allows – potentially at least – for movement.... Generic and place-based scenes cross cut and coincide in complex ways'.[24]

For present purposes, it is important to recognize the existence of both similarities and differences in the production, consumption, experience and appreciation of a particular form of popular music across different geographical areas. Indeed, in today's increasingly globalized environment of popular musical production and consumption, very few forms of popular music have remained connected to only one or just some geographical locations or regions. Instead, they float ever more freely in an increasingly globalized popular musical environment that transcends geographical and cultural borders. As Lynch observes in relation to the global spread of popular music scenes with a marked religious component:

In the expansion of genres in mass-produced popular music since the 1960s, there has also been a growing range of popular music scenes that have made explicit use of nature-based, esoteric, and subversive religious ideas and symbolism. Many of these scenes have become globalized.... While these scenes take localized variations, their global reach also creates cultural conditions in which certain alternative religious identities and ideologies can be transmitted across national boundaries to create the possibility of new, alternative religious transnational networks.[25]

Therefore, it is important to note the significance of today's globalized popular musical environment when exploring contemporary linkages and intersections between religion and popular music. In this context, the concept of scene provides a useful mapping tool for identifying and accounting for the various elements that form the building blocks with which popular music cultures (viewed as scenes) are constructed and sustained across different geographical areas at certain points in time. As already noted, the concept aims to highlight how the interconnectedness of the different building blocks results in the formation of a space that constitutes something more than the sum of its individual parts. Further, it is precisely this flexibility that makes it possible to employ the concept of scene in a wide range of different types of research, including the study of religion and popular music. As Kahn-Harris writes: 'the concept of scene allows researchers to produce work that is empirically grounded in specific contexts yet is open to connections with other pieces of research and to everyday language'.[26]

In the following we shall discuss in more detail what is meant by scenic 'structure' and 'construction'. We shall include observations which pertain more directly to Christian metal on the way.

Scenic structure

The development of a scenic structure constitutes an important prerequisite for the reproduction of a popular music scene. Kahn-Harris outlines five main dimensions of scenic structure in his version of the concept: *infrastructure*, *stability*, *relation to other scenes*, *scenic capital* and *production and consumption*.[27]

Infrastructure constitutes the most significant of these dimensions. A scenic infrastructure consists of a web of interconnected institutions through which a scene is sustained and reproduced. The most important of these include (but are not limited to) own means of production (e.g. record labels), promotion and distribution networks, various types of specialized scenic media and the organization of festivals and gatherings. Generally, the degree of institutionalization within scenes correlates with their degree of independence, autonomy and stability over time.[28] For scenes that exist on the margins of mainstream popular music markets, developing independent means of production, distribution and promotion is often crucial for both their establishment as independent scenes as well as their long-term survival.

The creation of independent specialized media channels is also vital for the reproduction of scenes, since they provide members in different geographical locations with forums for sharing information and for interaction. The ongoing rapid development of the Internet and digital technologies has had a particular impact and has also made the infrastructure of some scenes increasingly Internet-based, and the development Christian metal's scenic structure online provides a good illustration of this.[29] Overall, as we shall explore in more detail later on in this chapter, the Christian metal scene has developed its own highly independent scenic infrastructure. When researchers explore the religious elements, dimensions, functions, etc. of a particular popular musical space or environment, the concept of scene provides a framework for making sense of how that environment or space 'works' in practice, by accounting for how it is structured. One needs to keep in mind, however, that scenic infrastructures change and are renewed over time through the establishment of new institutions and the disappearance of existing ones. This is particularly true for small scenes such as the Christian metal scene.

The *stability* of scenes is closely connected to the degree to which they are able to develop independent scenic infrastructures. This is because the development of scenic institutions also increases the number of scenic 'gatekeepers' who support the preservation of scenic distinctiveness. The main point is that long-standing scenes generally gradually develop higher degrees of scenic institutionalization. Therefore, looking at the stability of a scene also involves tracing its history and development over time.[30]

Scenes display different *relations to other scenes*. At various stages in their development, scenes may share institutions with other musically, aesthetically or discursively related scenes. For example, in spite of being strongly institutionalized, the extreme metal scene still shares some institutions with the hardcore punk scene. To take an example more directly related to our main topic in this book, because of their shared general evangelistic ethos, it is not unusual for different Christian music scenes to share institutions. Quite naturally, scenes with similar musical, aesthetic or discursive traits tend to develop closer ties and sometimes 'cross-fertilize considerably', which may, in time, lead to the emergence of new scenes.[31] By contrast, 'weakly institutionalized' scenes risk disappearing or becoming assimilated by other scenes.[32] Such a scenario, however, is highly unlikely for the Christian metal scene since its expressed emphasis on religion makes it unlikely that it would become assimilated into other metal scenes or indeed other non-Christian scenes more generally.

At this point it is necessary to note that, like any concept designed to map the spatial and temporal dimensions of particular social and cultural environments, the concept of scene has limitations. As outlined here, the concept is primarily designed to map more self-consciously delineated popular musical environments in particular geographical or geographically connected areas at certain points in time. Therefore, where a scene and its associated music and style gain sudden international mass popularity and become rapidly globally diffused, the concept can lose much of its descriptive capacity, if it can no longer appropriately describe 'a space that is both institutionally distinctive to some degree and has some degree of self consciousness'.[33]

The reason why the concept of scene as developed here places such a strong emphasis on scenic structure is primarily practical. As noted, in order for scholars to be able to explore the place of religion within a particular popular musical environment, it is crucial to first gain an adequate understanding of the practical workings of that environment. Mapping how that environment becomes manifested in and visible through its particular structure in and across particular geographical locations at particular points in time can make that environment apprehensible, graspable and communicable. It also needs to be openly acknowledged that, similar to using other theoretical or methodological concepts for the purpose of describing the practical workings of a social and cultural environment, researchers themselves inevitably engage, to a degree, in 'scene construction' when they outline and map the structure of a particular scene.

Scenic capital, a notion which builds on Thornton's concept of 'subcultural capital',[34] refers to the different forms of merit, reverence or notoriety that scene members accumulate or acquire in accordance with the logic of a particular scene. For example, individuals involved in the maintenance of the infrastructure or ideological development and reproduction of a scene may achieve a high degree of reverence within that scene.[35] The nature of scenic capital varies according to the general ideological character of scenes.

For example, as discussed briefly in Chapter 1, the black metal scene is generally characterized by its fascination with austere and subversive religious themes, particularly Norse Paganism and Satanism, which sometimes finds expression in a violently adversarial stance towards Christianity, such as in relation to the series of church arsons in Norway in the early 1990s. As has been studied in detail by Kahn-Harris, after having being identified and subsequently convicted for these crimes, some of these individuals gained a considerable amount of scene-specific capital that Kahn-Harris calls 'transgressive subcultural capital' which extended far beyond the Norwegian national scene.[36] By contrast, in the case of the Christian metal scene, a very different form of capital comes into play. As noted above, Christian metal shares the main musical and aesthetic characteristics of metal and its various sub-genres in general, but – in line with the logic of the Christian metal scene – respected members gain what I choose to refer to as 'evangelistic capital' and earn the right to call themselves 'metal missionaries'. This type of capital often also extends beyond the scene in itself into the various immediate church settings of individual Christian metalheads. This form of capital can, of course, no doubt also be viewed as a general characteristic of CCM and indeed of evangelical popular culture more generally. As these examples illustrate, issues of scenic capital provide important insights for a broader understanding of how the place of religion within a scene plays out within everyday scenic activity and practice.

Finally, examining the structure of a scene entails looking at its various modes of *production and consumption*. Especially when we look at larger and more transnationally diffused scenes, it is important to recognize variations in the degree to which local or national scenes contribute to the wider scene. In larger transnational and global scenes, scenic infrastructure tends to be concentrated within core areas or national scenes. However, this does not mean that national scenes which have a great input on a transnational or global level are necessarily the largest markets for the music they produce. Therefore, when researching the place of religion within a particular local or national music scene, it is important to keep in mind that most of the music consumed within that scene may have been produced elsewhere.

Scenic construction

Scenes are constructed in three principal ways: by *internal discursive construction*, *external discursive construction* and *aesthetic construction*. At the risk of over-simplifying, one could say that, if exploring the structure of a scene is mostly about gaining an understanding of how a scene 'works', examining the construction of a scene is mostly about exploring what a scene is 'about'. It is crucial, though, that an exploration of scenic construction is based on, and carried out in relation to, an adequate understanding of its structure. As Kahn-Harris expresses it, *internal discursive construction* 'refers to the extent to which people inside a scene discursively construct that scene as a distinctive space whether or not the term scene is actually used. Through processes of internal discursive construction scenes become "visible" and "recognizable" to members'.[37] Importantly, aided by scenic institutions which are designed to facilitate communication and interaction among members, it is through processes of internal discursive construction that scenes become invested with particular meanings. Examining the internal discursive construction of a scene makes up a vital stage in the study of the place of religion within a particular scene.

Empirically and ethnographically grounded research of the place of religion in a scene has much to gain from examining its internal discursive construction, as this essentially entails looking at the scene from within and exploring what meanings it holds for its members and participants. Indeed, it may be argued that in order to gain an adequate understanding of the scene's significance in its members' lives, such an approach is necessary. However, when exploring the place of religion within a particular scene, researchers need to keep in mind that scenic participation may take many forms and that not all scene members participate in the internal discursive construction of a scene to the same extent. For example, when an individual invests his/her participation in a particular scene with some form of religious significance, this may primarily occur in relation to scenic events, such as concerts, festivals or club nights. However, depending on the character of the scene in question, it may primarily also occur in the privacy of an individual's home – for example, when reading scenic media or interacting with other scene members online.

Therefore, it is vital to examine who is most engaged in the discursive construction within the context of a scene. The reason is that the internal discursive construction of scenes tends to be mostly carried out by people who are directly involved in the maintenance or ideological reproduction of the scene, such as artists, producers of specialized scenic media or administrators of webpages and online discussion forums. When exploring larger regional or transnational scenes, attention also needs to be paid to the locations where such discursive construction primarily takes place.

CCM, characterized as it is by its expressly religious component, provides a particularly good example of this. Transnational Christian music scenes of many kinds can nowadays be found all over the world. However, not only is most of this music still produced in North America, it has also remained intimately connected with the North American strand of evangelicalism, which is itself a highly diverse phenomenon. The internal discursive construction of what a 'Christian scene' is supposedly all 'about' tends to be primarily, although not exclusively, shaped by North American evangelical scene members. The interesting and challenging part is examining how the internal discursive construction of a transnational or global scene, which is more firmly connected to a particular broader social, cultural and religious environment, plays out in another. For example, my earlier research on the Christian metal scene in Finland[38] revealed that the musicians in this national scene commonly tapped into the broader transnational discursive construction of what Christian metal music is supposed to be all 'about'.

However, their discursive representations were simultaneously clearly linked and adapted to the particular social, cultural and religious context of Finland, which is much less marked by evangelicalism than the United States, where the discursive construction of Christian metal primarily originates and still to a large degree is reproduced.

External discursive construction refers to the ways in which scenes become discursively constructed outside the scenic environment itself, for instance, through the way they become represented in mainstream media.[39] For example, the media coverage of the arson attacks of the black metal scene members in Norway in the early 1990s played a considerable part in the construction of the general public's view that black metal was a dangerous, violent and 'satanic' form of music. As already noted in previous chapters, this external discursive construction undoubtedly also influenced the self-understanding of the black metal scene in a number of ways. Typically, extreme forms of metal have received the kind of media attention that has exaggerated their (often supposed) connections to Satanism in particular.[40] The main point is that external discursive construction can affect both public opinion and the self-understanding of a particular scene in various ways.

Lastly, scenes are constructed *aesthetically*. This means that 'scenes are constructed through the development of particular aesthetics, musical and otherwise, that become both internally and externally visible'.[41] Depending on each case, the process through which this occurs is sometimes highly contingent, sometimes highly deliberate and self-conscious.[42] Scholars interested in exploring the religious dimensions of a popular music scene have much to learn from looking more closely at the role that aesthetic and stylistic factors play and how they connect to the ways in which meanings are ascribed to that scene discursively.

In most of its variants, including the one outlined here, the concept of scene is most appropriately described as a practically oriented methodological mapping tool. With specific regard to the study of religion and popular music, the concept of scene offers at least four significant practical methodological advantages. Firstly, the very task of mapping the structure of a scene (which also involves some degree of 'scene construction' by the researcher) considerably aids the initial structuring of a research project. Secondly, the map produced is a great help in making this environment apprehensible and communicable, as it provides a bird's-eye view of the actual general make-up of the scene. A third advantage lies in that scene provides researchers with a framework through which to explore in which ways and through which channels a given scene is discursively constructed and made meaningful by its participants, making them better equipped to account for both the religious- and musical-cultural components of scenes as interrelated parts of the same context. Finally, a fourth and particularly significant advantage of the concept is that it allows researchers to account for both similarities and differences in the ways a particular popular musical environment may become discursively constructed and made meaningful in religiously significant ways across different geographical areas at certain points in time. This enables researchers to account for the way the religious dimensions of a particular scene play out in the everyday lives of participants, who are embedded in different particular religious, social and cultural environments, while simultaneously paying attention to how this relates to a broader regional, transnational or global scenic environment.

However, as the concept of the scene does not require that the interconnectedness of the various elements of which scenes consist or that scenic involvement is interpreted in line with any particular theoretical perspective, it does not have much theoretical weight in itself. It therefore needs to be supplemented with other theoretical frameworks for the purposes of interpretation and analysis. Indeed, the concept of scene does not offer a model for interpreting the reasons *why* individuals ascribe religious significance to their involvement in a scene, but it can provide important insights to *the way* they do this, by helping researchers map and discern the interconnectedness of the structural, spatial, temporal, discursive and aesthetic dimensions of particular popular musical environments.

In the remainder of this chapter we will explore the structure of the contemporary Christian metal scene on a transnational level, while the discursive construction of the scene constitutes the main topic of the next and final main chapter of the book.

Contemporary national and regional scenes

During the late 1980s, Christian metal gradually started gaining a stronger foothold in a number of countries outside of the United States. In the early 1990s, small Christian metal scenes started developing in the Northern European countries of Sweden, Norway, Finland, and to some degree in Germany, The Netherlands and Belgium. A few years later, small scenes also started developing throughout Latin America, particularly in Brazil and Mexico. Australia has produced some of Christian metal's most influential bands and a small scene has also developed there. It is worth noting that these are all countries with long-standing and significant secular metal scenes.

It is also important to note that Christian metal has remained firmly rooted in evangelical Protestantism (broadly defined) and hence also remained more rare, but not nonexistent, in predominantly Catholic countries. Today, predominantly Catholic countries such as Brazil and Mexico have significant Protestant minorities that have partly emerged as a result of the rapid growth of evangelicalism, Charismatic and Pentecostal Christianity throughout Latin America during recent decades. In addition, other traditionally Catholic countries such as Italy and Poland have also produced some known Christian metal bands. So, although there is clearly an affinity between Christian metal and evangelical Protestantism, it is also characterized by an open stance towards other forms of Christianity. Whereas secular metal has gained considerable popularity in many Islamic countries such as Indonesia and Morocco,[43] Christian metal has so far mostly remained confined to North America, (mainly Northern) Europe, Latin American countries such as Brazil and Mexico and, arguably, Australia. Today's transnational scene is mainly confined to these core regions, although there are some known Christian bands coming from outside these regions as well. For example, the Indonesian Christian extreme metal band Kekal is well known at a transnational level. However, more vibrant and significant national scenes have so far only developed in a smaller number of countries. The more significant national scenes mentioned above produce the majority of bands today, and also control and maintain most of today's transnational scenic infrastructure of record labels, distribution channels and specialized media. The Christian scene has so far not diffused on a scale that would warrant using the label 'global'. This is the main reason for referring to it in terms of a transnational scene in this book. What follows is an overview of some of today's most important regional and national scenes.

North America

As mentioned above, today's transnational scene consists of a smaller web of national scenes. The Christian metal scene of the United States – the birthplace of Christian metal – has remained significant to this day. A large part of Christian metal's scenic infrastructure also remains based there. However, because of the geographical size of the country, it has always been fragmented to some degree. A significant portion of US Christian metal bands have come from the so-called 'Sunbelt states' of California (and Southern California in particular), Florida and Texas – all core areas of evangelical youth cultural activity.[44] In the case of the United States, we could therefore also speak of national-regional or local Christian metal scenes, such as for example, the 'Orange County'-, 'Los Angeles'- or 'Florida'-scene. The Canadian scene seems to have become largely integrated with the much larger US scene. From a transnational perspective, these scenes can be said to constitute a wider regional 'North American' scene. Christian metal in North America in many ways continues to be produced under the auspices of the evangelical popular culture industry. Considering the huge market for Christian popular music in North America more generally, this provides North

American Christian metal bands with the opportunity to achieve degrees of commercial success that bands from other countries are ever likely to reach.

The Nordic countries

Another increasingly significant regional scene is formed by the contemporary national scenes of the Nordic countries Sweden, Norway and Finland. Sweden in particular has a long-standing and highly vibrant national scene that continues to produce many successful bands. Some of the most important Christian metal record labels and distribution channels are also based there. Sweden also used to host the *Endtime Festival* that was established to replace the earlier *Bobfest*-festival[45] (1999–2005) named after *Sanctuary International*'s head pastor Bob Beeman. An alternative 'metal parish movement' or 'metal ministry', as they are also called in Christian metal terms, has also been established in Sweden under the name of *Metal Sanctuary*.

The smaller Norwegian scene largely developed in connection with the developments of early- and mid-1990s Norwegian black metal. Indeed, the Norwegian scene has always been particularly associated with unblack metal. Norway also used to host the Christian metal festival *Nordic Fest* (2002–2011). The Swedish and Norwegian scenes have developed close ties. Both of these scenes also have closer ties to the Finnish scene. However, because of the language barrier, overall closer co-operation appears to have remained somewhat limited. The Finnish scene has, however, grown steadily since the beginning of the 1990s and developed into one of the most vibrant national Christian metal scenes of today.

Continental Europe

In the 1990s, small scenes also appear to have developed in Germany, The Netherlands and Belgium. It is, however, difficult to assess their scale. Information regarding the numbers of people involved always has to be derived from scarce, second hand sources such as occasional reports from festivals in various forms of Christian metal media. Of course, membership of music scenes is not something that one generally is able to find statistical data on. A sober and highly tentative estimate would put the number of people involved in these scenes at something around a thousand individuals or less. However, these countries have nevertheless produced a number of bands, some of which have become very successful within the wider transnational scene.

There are many signs of scenic activity though; for example, there is also a metal ministry operating in Germany under the name of *Headbanger's Rest*.

The web forum *Unblack.com* (in German) is also based in Germany and the country also hosts the festival *Blast of Eternity* (2008–). There also used to be a Christian metal record label called *Fear Dark* based in The Netherlands. *Fear Dark* also organized Christian metal events in The Netherlands, Germany and Switzerland under the heading of *Fear Dark Festivals*, but these events appear to have become more un-regular occurrences in recent years. Currently the largest annual Christian metal festival in Europe, *Elements of Rock* (2004–) is held in Switzerland and a formerly widely known Christian metal online discussion forum *JesusMetal*, that now appears to be defunct, used to be based in Belgium. Christian metal has clearly gained a foothold in these countries but it is unclear as to whether they have actually developed distinct national scenes of their own. Instead, they might be seen to form a Northern European continental regional scene. Such scenic structure differs from that of the larger scenes of the United States, Sweden, Norway, Finland, Brazil and Mexico, which have all developed distinctively national scenic structures. In addition, as noted, there are also some contemporary Christian metal bands coming from Italy and Poland. For example, the currently defunct Christian metal webzine *Holy Steel* was based in Italy and the still active webzine *Uzvart Zine* remains based in Poland.

Latin America

In Latin America, the Brazilian scene has grown significantly during recent years with new bands, magazines and webzines constantly emerging. A larger scene has also appeared in Mexico. Both of these scenes are marked by a high degree of commitment and preoccupation with evangelistic outreach. For example, scene members in Brazil and Mexico have also created their own Christian 'metal parish-movements' or 'metal ministries'. Brazil has seen at least two such movements. One based in the city of Recife was known as *Comunidade Zadoque*, but it is unclear as to whether it is still active. Another still very active one is based in Florianópolis and goes by the name of *Crash Church*. As observed above with the US-based *Sanctuary*-movement and the metal ministries in Sweden and Germany, Christian metal musicians and fans in different parts of the world have decided to create their own parish-movements in order to be able to worship in an alternative metal-inspired way and attract people who feel alienated from more traditional church activities. Brazil has also had a number of groups dedicated to supporting and maintaining the country's national scene such as, for example, *Christian Metal Force Brasilia*. The Brazilian scene has also developed its own Portuguese-language webzines and online stores and distribution channels. In Mexico City, members of the successful band Exousia reportedly started a movement known as the *Underground Outreach* at the end of the first decade of the new millennium.[46] There is also some evidence of the existence of Christian metal in other Latin American countries. For example, a metal ministry called *Theocracy Ministry* in Paraguay appears to have been active still a few years prior to the time of writing, and there also used to be a Christian metal Internet-site called *Insacris* based in Colombia. Lastly, there is a festival called *Dikaion Fest* that is held in Ecuador.

Considering the larger populations (and sheer numbers of metal fans) of these countries, one would assume that the number of people involved in these Latin American scenes would be higher than those in Europe. But, again, any assessment of the total number of people more actively involved must remain tentative at best. While it has become somewhat easier to obtain some general information about the larger scenes of Brazil and Mexico, assessing the spread of Christian metal in other Latin American countries on the basis of the scarce information that does exist remains a very difficult task.

It is important to note here that all of these scenes are connected to each other through the complex web of shared infrastructure and channels of communication and interaction that make up the overarching transnational scene. Today's transnational scene is clearly reproduced along place-based scales at regional and national levels. Through the development of a largely Internet-based scenic infrastructure and different forms of scenic media, the transnational scene is now also able to facilitate interaction between different regional and national scenes with increasing speed and ease. This also makes it possible for people living in countries with only small scenes or no scene at all to participate in scenic activity on a transnational level.

Scenic structure

As noted, one of the most important ways in which music scenes are sustained is through their various forms of scenic structure. First, examining the structure of the Christian metal scene involves looking at the development of its own infrastructure of record labels, promotion and distribution channels (so called 'distros'), specialized media and festivals. Significantly, this scenic infrastructure is not shared with any other scene. Examining its structure also involves looking at the ways in which the scene is sustained and kept stable and largely autonomous through its degree of institutionalization. In addition, the Christian metal scene's relation to other scenes, both Christian and secular, also needs to be explored. Its relation to the secular metal scene naturally becomes of particular importance in this regard. Finally, exploring the structure of the contemporary Christian metal scene involves exploring the ways in which it produces its own forms of cultural and evangelistic capital and considering how variations across different social and cultural circumstances between national scenes affect their activities and positions within the wider transnational scene.

The structure of the transnational scene is constantly changing. Small scenic institutions, such as various types of semi-regular festivals and various types of websites, may sometimes disappear quite rapidly without leaving much of a trace at all. The same, in principle, applies for Christian metal's scenic structure as a whole. It needs to be openly acknowledged, therefore, that the information provided in this chapter is likely to be outdated in only a few years time.

Infrastructure and scenic institutions

Today's transnational scene has developed its own highly independent, and largely Internet-based, scenic infrastructure of record labels, promotion and distribution channels, magazines, fanzines, webzines, online communities and discussion forums and festivals. These different forms of scenic infrastructure are referred to as *scenic institutions*. Different national scenes have also developed their own smaller scenic institutions concentrating on bands and events in their own respective countries. It is important to note that some national scenes are more vibrant that others, with more bands, fans and events. All scenic institutions have to start on a local or national level. The Internet has had a decisive impact on the construction and structure of most popular music scenes and, indeed, become of crucial importance to many. By being initially established or by relocating to the Internet, an increasing part of Christian metal's scenic infrastructure has become transnational in scope. The following account does not aim to include every single scenic institution. It is intended to provide a general birds-eye view of the most significant scenic institutions of today's transnational scene as a whole.

Record labels

As mentioned above, the 1980s saw the establishment of small, specialized Christian metal record labels in the United States, such as *Pure Metal Records*, *Intense Records* and *R.E.X. Records*. Subsequently established US labels releasing Christian metal bands include *Armor*

Records, Rugged Records, Open Grave Records/Sullen Records, Facedown Records, Solid State Records, Bombworks Records, Retroactive Records, Bloodbough Records, Tooth & Nail Records, E.E.E. Recordings, *Flicker Records* and *Frontline Records*. As Christian metal has spread to other countries, a number of new labels mostly catering to national or regional scenes have also emerged. Most of these labels release Christian bands only, although there are a few that release bands on the borderline between Christian and secular as well. Record labels thus also serve important gatekeeping functions. There is a strong sense in which Christian metalheads rely on these labels to guarantee that the albums they release more or less conform to the basic 'requirements' of Christian metal outlined above. There are, however, some labels which choose not to call themselves 'Christian' even though, in practice, they only release Christian bands. Such labels could be called 'Christian by association'.[47] There are, however, also many labels that openly express their Christian approach in this regard. For example, the official webpages of Sweden-based label *CM Sweden/Rivel Records*, currently *Liljegren Records*, used to contain the following information:

> CM SWEDEN/RIVEL RECORDS was formed in 1999 by Christian Liljegren. The focus with the recordlabel is to release good hardrock and metal with a good message that lifts up people.[48]

CM Sweden/Rivel Records played an important role in the formation of a Nordic regional scene and released records by a large number of known Nordic bands such as Divinefire, Pantokrator and Crimson Moonlight from Sweden and Immortal Souls, Oratorio and Parakletos from Finland. Another significant Sweden-based label *Endtime Productions* mostly concentrates on extreme metal styles. It has released records by many well-known Norwegian unblack bands such as Antestor, Drottnar and Extol. *Endtime Productions* has also established another label called *Momentum Scandinavia* in cooperation with the Norway-based online Christian metal distro *Nordic Mission*. Another already mentioned significant but now defunct European label *Fear Dark* was based in The Netherlands.

Although most Christian metal labels are based in either North America or Northern Europe, a few have also been established elsewhere. These include the long-established and well-known Australia-based label *Rowe Productions* founded by Mortification's front man Steve Rowe. This label has released many important bands, including by Australian unblack band Horde and Christian thrash metal band Ultimatum from the United States. There is also a larger label called *Extreme Records* based in Brazil.

The establishment of record labels such as these has meant that it has become relatively easy for Christian metal bands to release records at early stages of their musical careers. Indeed, it is not uncommon for bands to release their first record after having played only a few concerts. On the other hand, most Christian labels operate with fairly or very limited resources. A few of the larger ones have distribution deals with larger secular or general Christian labels. Although some of the labels mentioned above primarily cater to the regional scenes in which they are based, following the rapid development and growing accessibility of the Internet, labels of all sizes have become increasingly transnational in scope. Lastly, it should be noted that some bands choose to release their music themselves.

Promotion and distribution channels

Developing means of promotion and distribution becomes of crucial importance for every music scene existing on the fringes of wider mainstream secular markets. Marginal underground scenes have always found innovative ways of promoting and distributing their music to their members. For example, in the 1980s and early 1990s, secular extreme metal culture developed its own institution of tape-trading and letter writing that eventually spread all over the globe. Two or three decades ago, promoting and distributing both old and new music often involved considerable voluntary grassroots organization and networking on a non-profit basis. The development and increasing availability of the Internet throughout the world has brought fundamental changes to such earlier means of promotion and distribution. Today, nearly all Christian metal promotion and distribution channels are Internet-based, that is, promoting and offering their products solely online. The establishment of specialized Christian metal record labels has been of particular importance in this regard. Primarily, they offer Christian bands channels through which to release their music in the first place. But record labels not only produce records, they promote and distribute them as well. For example, many record labels run online distribution services through their webpages. Moreover, many also distribute various forms of band merchandise such as t-shirts, patches, posters and stickers.

A number of Internet-based channels dedicated solely to distribution have also developed. Larger US-based distros include *Girder Music* and *Shaver Audio and Video*, *Rugged Cross Music*, *Divine Metal Distro* and *Roxx Productions*. Christian metal records could also be ordered through previously existing general online Christian music stores such as *Rad Rockers.com*. A number of Christian metal distros have been established in other regions as well. Both active and currently defunct distros include *Soundmass.com*, *unDark Webstore*, *Iron Guardian Industries*, *Metal Mission*, *Forca Eterna Records* and *Lament Distributions*.

Although most of these distros have a transnational scope, some are more concentrated on distributing bands within their own national or regional scenes. For example, the website of Sweden-based *Metal Community* is in Swedish only and the sites of Brazilian *Metal Mission* and *Forca Eterna Records* are both in Portuguese. Much like Christian metal record labels, distros also serve important gatekeeping functions. Their catalogues typically contain only Christian bands. Some distros also openly acknowledge this function. For example, the 'about us' section of Norway-based *Nordic Mission* previously contained the following information:

So what is NORDIC MISSION?

We were established in late 1997 wanting to be the new Christian underground metal distribution and mail order company. At that time, there weren't hardly any stuff to get hold of, at least in Norway, and the bigger labels were not interested in hardly any Christian stuff. At that time we had a lot of demo tapes and underground releases. Things have changed quite a bit, both for us and for the whole scene. We now try to bring you most releases within the Christian metal and hard music scene, everything from hard rock/heavy metal to the more extreme death/black metal and quite a bit of punk and hardcore. But we still think it is important to represent and get hold of band demos and upcoming unknown bands that need to be recognized. So, if you play in a band or run a label, feel free to send you demos or promos for a possible distribution deal.[49]

As illustrated here, *Nordic Mission* previously stated the distribution of Christian metal specifically as being its main objective. The above excerpt also highlights the importance of the establishment of independent Christian metal distros, especially since the larger secular labels tend not to be interested in 'Christian stuff'. However, not all distros include such information about their main aims and objectives on their websites. All of the distros mentioned above are nevertheless widely known as 'Christian' throughout the scene, and they often cooperate with each other in various ways as well. Today's network of distros has made it possible for scene members to get hold of virtually any Christian metal recording, old or new. Distros thus play an important role in aiding bands to reach their core Christian audiences throughout the world. Moreover, they also give new and upcoming bands much needed exposure and visibility. Much like labels, distros thus simultaneously function as both promoters and distributors.

Scenic media

Specialized media constitutes another crucial component of all music scenes. Because of the small scale of the Christian scene and its limited resources, an increasingly large portion of scenic media has become entirely Internet-based. Despite this, Christian metal media can still be roughly divided into two main categories: printed and online.

First, we have printed magazines and fanzines, which offer reports, interviews and reviews. These days, the distinction between magazines and fanzines has become somewhat unclear. Generally speaking, magazines tend to display higher production values, contain more pages, be published regularly, be printed in colour on smooth or glossy paper and sometimes distributed to regular stores selling books and magazines. Only a few magazines exist that are dedicated to Christian metal and hard rock. US-based *HM: The Hard Music Magazine* is probably the most widely known among these. In Sweden, there is also a Swedish-language magazine mainly concentrating on Christian metal and hard rock called *Noizegate Music* (earlier *Noizegate*). Fanzines, on the other hand, are generally characterized by lower production values. Essentially, a fanzine is an amateur-magazine, usually produced entirely by only one person or a few people and published irregularly according to time and resources. Fanzines are usually distributed through their own webpages or Christian metal distros. They tend to be photocopied on rough paper, usually in black and white. They also usually contain fewer pages than magazines. However, some fanzines display much higher production values and sometimes also call themselves magazines. Presently, most Christian metal fanzines are entirely Internet-based and hence referred to as webzines. However, a few printed fanzines still exist, including the well-known *Heaven's Metal* based in the United States and *Extreme Brutal Death* based in Brazil. A fanzine called *Devotion HardMusic Magazine* also used to be produced in Sweden and the Finnish scene also used to produce its own Finnish-language fanzine called *Ristillinen*. Some of these fanzines are transnational in scope, reporting, interviewing and reviewing bands from all over the world. *Heaven's Metal* in particular has enjoyed enduring popularity within the wider transnational scene.

Second, we also have a whole range of various forms of online Christian metal media. Importantly, online media does not require many resources in order to operate. The Internet also enables webzines and other types of sites to store a large amount of reports, reviews and interviews. Christian metal webzines proper – some of which are defunct at the time of writing – include *The Whipping Post*, *Eternal Reign*, *Victory Zine*, *Holy Steel* (partly in Italian),

The Buried Scrolls Webzine, *Screams of Abel*, *Metal Land* (in Portuguese), *Immortal Zine* (in Spanish) and *Usvart Zine* (mostly in Polish).

These magazines, fanzines and webzines essentially all work with the expressed goal of promoting Christian metal and some also express their aims in the form of 'mission statements'. For example, a note from the editor in issue 3 of *Devotion HardMusic Magazine* stated the following:

> Devotion hardmusic magazine started with a purpose to show that there is a living music culture with a positive message ... its exiting to see that more and more christian bands entering the secular market .... Its important that christian bands are in the secular market ... to be a light in the darkness and let jesus be known .... Jesus is the main reason why we do this and try to reach those who is lost ....[50]

In addition to underlining the evangelistic purpose of Christian metal, this statement also emphasizes the importance of Christian bands reaching beyond the confines of both the Christian scene and the world of Christian music more generally. By describing Christian bands in terms of a 'light in the darkness', this statement also aims to highlight Christian metal's active engagement with its secular counterpart. Although the types of mission statements frequently found in various types of Christian metal media tend to be very similar to one another, they sometimes adopt a much stronger tone, as in this example from the editorial to the first English-language issue of the Brazilian fanzine *Extreme Brutal Death*:

> EXTREME has the objective of disclosing the bands of Christian extreme metal, and mainly the Word of God. Our wish is to bear fruits, souls in the presence of God. The Portuguese version of this magazine provoked a huge damage in the satanic black metal scene in South America. We want to enlarge this damage and to increase the revolt of Hell everywhere. Therefore, dear reader, we'll need prayer and support.[51]

These quoted excerpts are both illustrative of the ways in which Christian metal's evangelistic element not only surfaces in the lyrics and activities of bands but in the goals and aims of various scenic institutions as well. The latter excerpt also highlights the transformed sense in which Christian metal has embraced the uncompromising metal attitude and rhetoric. Principally, it clearly expresses the commonly held notion of Christians needing to have the courage to take the Christian message to inhospitable environments in the spirit of spiritual warfare. Christian metal media are thus essentially characterized by a twofold purpose: to support the scene through promoting

Christian bands and, in relation to this, to support the spreading of the Christian message beyond the scene itself (Figures 5.1–5.5).

In addition to printed magazines, fanzines and online webzines, there also exists a large number of general Christian metal information or resource sites on the Internet, many of which also contain album reviews and interviews with bands. Among these, *The Metal for Jesus Page*[52] based in Sweden is one of the oldest and best known. The site contains detailed information on the history and purpose of Christian metal, testimonies from Christian metalheads, monthly sermons, detailed Christian and secular metal comparison charts (comparisons between Christian and secular soundalikes)

FIGURE 5.1 *Cover for* Heaven's Metal, *issue 88, July–August, 2011. Reproduced with the kind permission of* HM: The Hard Music Magazine.

FIGURE 5.2 *Cover for* HM: The Hard Music Magazine, *July, 2013. Reproduced with the kind permission of* HM: The Hard Music Magazine.

and a very substantial collection of links to bands and all kinds of other sites somehow related to Christian metal. Moreover, it also contains a lengthy section dedicated to a detailed defense of Christian metal. This practice is commonly referred to as 'Christian metal apologetics'. Creator and administrator Johannes is a central figure in the vibrant Swedish scene. On the Internet, he also runs the Christian metal prayer chain *Prayer Warriors*, the previously mentioned Christian metal distro *Metal Community* and the Christian metal online radio channel *Metal Countdown*.[53] In addition to this, Johannes functions as head coordinator for the *Metal Bible*-project, the first ever special 'metal-edition' of the New Testament containing testimonies from popular Christian metal musicians from all over the world. We shall

FIGURE 5.3 *Cover for* Extreme Brutal Death, *issue 2, 2013. Reproduced with the kind permission of* Extreme Records.

return to the *Metal Bible* below. In an earlier interview, Johannes stated the main objectives of *The Metal for Jesus Page* in the following way:

1. To lead metalheads to faith in Christ.
2. To help Christians grow in their faith and go on with Christ.
3. Show how much good Christian metal there is out there so that people will not miss all the good music that exists within this genre.
4. Answer all Christian critics of Christian rock.[54]

As seen here, Johannes endeavours to engage with many central issues regarding the main purposes and functions of Christian metal through his site.

FIGURE 5.4 *Front page of* The Metal for Jesus Page. *Reproduced with the kind permission of Johannes Jonsson.*

The now defunct *JesusMetal*-site also used to contain a substantial bank of interviews and reviews. Another fairly recently (2006–) established US-based Christian metal resource site is called *Angelic Warlord.com*.[55] This site offers a particularly substantial collection of interviews, reviews and articles from a wide range of both past and present Christian metal magazines, fanzines and webzines. General Christian metal sites come in a range of different forms. Larger information and resource sites such those mentioned above all operate on a more 'professional-type' basis. For example, they may also contain sound-files and advertisement banners for other Christian metal sites, online stores and distributors. In addition to such sites, however, one also finds various forms of more personal sites mostly dedicated to the particular interests of their administrators such as, for example, the blog *Sanctified Steel*.[56]

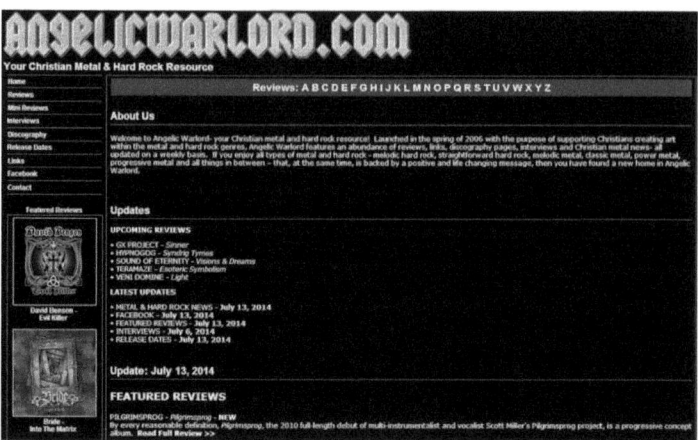

FIGURE 5.5 *Front page of* Angelic Warlord.com. *Reproduced with the kind permission of* Angelic Warlord.com.

Sites designed to aid communication and interaction between scene members constitute a final significant category of online Christian metal media. Such sites are typically designed in the format of the discussion forum or online community. Indeed, such modes of more direct communication and interaction have come to constitute important components of many contemporary music scenes. This is because discussion forums or online communities greatly aid fast interaction between individual scene members in different parts of the world and thus contribute to fostering a sense of being part of a larger transnational community of people with shared interests and concerns. A number of Christian metal forums and communities have developed throughout the years. The largest one of these is US-based *Firestream.net*[57] with members from all over the world. On *Firestream.net* both artists and fans can come together and discuss a wide array of topics ranging from musical styles and lyrics to Satanism and details of Christian theology. In an earlier interview, its creator and administrator explained that the main purpose for the site is to 'be an open, growing community of Christian metal listeners that can come together in discussion and glorify the name of Jesus Christ'.[58] Another larger and long-standing online discussion forum is *The Christian Metal Realm*.[59] Some national scenes have also created their own national-language forums. For example, the Finnish scene has developed its own Finnish-language forum *Kristillinen metalliunioni* (Christian Metal Union).[60]

In addition to these various forms of online media, the official webpages of bands themselves also need to be mentioned, some of which are more elaborate than others. The more simple ones only offer some basic information about the band, its members, releases and concert dates. Others may contain such things as substantial biographies of the band and its individual members, detailed information about its releases and lyrics, large galleries of promotion and live pictures, video sequences from concerts and sample mp3s. Band webpages may also contain smaller mini-forums through which fans can interact directly with the band. It is also not unusual for bands to offer their albums and merchandise for purchase directly through their own webpages. During recent years, Myspace and Facebook have also developed into increasingly important additional online avenues for bands to communicate their music to larger audiences.

Finally, a number of Christian metal online radio channels have also been established. These include *Intense Radio*[61] run by *Sanctuary International*, *Reign Radio*,[62] *Heaven's Metal* (not the fanzine),[63] *Metal Countdown*,[64] *Full Armor of God*,[65] *The Refinery Rock Radio*,[66] *Classic Christian Rock Radio*[67] and *The Cross Stream*.[68] Previously active but now defunct channels include *Almighty Metal Radio* and *91.7FM The Underground Church*. Christian metal online radio channels also typically aim to guarantee that all the music they broadcast is Christian, that is, metal that conforms to the basic 'requirements' of Christian metal discussed above. In addition, they often have an expressed aim of promoting new and upcoming Christian bands. Among these online radio channels, *Intense Radio* and *Reign Radio* have developed into particularly significant transnational scenic institutions.

Although some scenic media mainly concentrate on the respective national scenes of the countries in which they are based, there is also a sense in which transnational scenic media, and Internet-based media in particular, are never, in practice, bound to any particular place or geographical location. It is important to note that, in the absence of such scenic media, Christian metal might not receive much media attention at all. Scenic media can thus be said to play a particularly important role within the overall infrastructure of the scene. This is because they constitute virtually the only channels through which scene members can receive news about Christian metal developments in countries other than their own.

As noted many times above, the Internet has become an indispensable part of scenic communication and infrastructure as well as one of the primary means by which individual scene members themselves take part in scenic activity. On a transnational level, the scene as a whole has become Internet-based to a considerable degree. Today's transnational scene is both largely structured and sustained through the Internet. It is worth noting that the Internet, unlike many other forms of media, enables individuals to choose from and move between many different forms and degrees of involvement and participation. The Internet has played an important role in the formation of what can be viewed as a transnational Christian metal discursive community with a set of common ideals and goals as it also offers a range of opportunities for communication and interaction among its members. However, in doing so it has not only affected the nature of Christian metal discourse by making it more fixed and concentrated but, arguably, also entailed the formation of certain requirements on participation, such as the acquisition and understanding of a specific use of language. Above all, however, the Internet has greatly enhanced the speed of communication between the larger Northern European and American scenes as well as made Christian metal more easily accessible to people outside of these areas. Importantly, the use of the Internet as a primary means of communication has aided the spreading of central discourses on the meaning and function of Christian metal on a transnational level, as local and national scenes have come together. The spreading of these discourses has enabled artists and fans with different religious affiliations, living in countries with different cultural and religious environments, to shape very similar understandings of what Christian metal is supposed to be all 'about'. We shall return to this issue in greater detail when exploring the discursive construction of the scene in the following chapter.

Festivals and events

Different national scenes have established their own festivals dedicated exclusively to Christian metal. At these events, the scene comes 'alive' as members meet in the flesh. Some of these events attract bands and visitors from different countries around the world. However, like most music festivals, they are mostly attended by scene members from the countries in which they are held. In 1999, the first *Bobfest*-festival was held in Stockholm, Sweden. Over the years, the festival has featured a large number of well-known bands and attracted visitors from all over the world. As mentioned above, the festival was named after head pastor Bob Beeman of *Sanctuary International* and also featured him each year as a speaker, until the festival was suspended in 2005. *Bobfest* was the only larger annual Christian metal festival in the Nordic countries for many years. In 2007, a new festival called *Endtime Festival* was established in its place in the town of Halmstad. *Endtime Festival* continued the transnational scope of *Bobfest* and quickly developed into one of the largest festivals of Northern Europe, attracting bands and participants from many different countries. In 2002, the Norwegian distro *Nordic Mission* established *Nordic Fest*, which was held annually in Oslo until 2011. Finland has hosted an unusual number of Christian metal festivals. These include the long-standing and well-known annual *Immortal Metal Fest* (2001–) as well as onetime events such as the *Underground Festival* that was held in Helsinki in the summer of 2005 and the *Metal Fest of the Creator of Night*-festival that was held in the city of Jounsuu later that same year. All of these events have attracted substantial audiences and featured known Christian metal bands from all over the world. Denmark's first ever Christian metal festival *Green Light District Festival* was held in 2007 in cooperation with *Sanctuary International* and held again in 2008. As mentioned above, the now defunct label *Fear Dark* based in The Netherlands also used to organize small festivals under the name of *Fear Dark Festival* in different locations throughout Northern European countries such as The Netherlands, Germany and Switzerland. *Elements of Rock*, held annually in the town of Uster in Switzerland was established in 2003. It is currently the largest Christian metal festival in Europe and always features many transnationally recognized bands. Lastly, in Europe, the *Blast of Eternity*-festival was established in Neckarsulm, Germany, in 2008.

In the United States, the first ever onetime Christian metal festival *The Metal Mardi Gras* was organized by the *Sanctuary*-movement in Los Angeles already in 1987. US Christian metal bands have also played at large US Christian music festivals such as *Creation Festival* and *Cornerstone Festival*. In cooperation with *Sanctuary International*, the United Kingdom has also hosted smaller annual festivals called *Destruction Fest* in London, and the Ukraine has hosted a Christian metal/ hardcore festival called *Total Armageddon Fest*. Lastly, there is much evidence of festivals being organized in Brazil and Mexico as well, but they are rarely advertised in transnational Christian metal media.

It should be pointed out that festivals and smaller events dedicated exclusively to Christian metal tend to operate with very limited resources. In some cases, they may also be partly sponsored by some particular church, parish or congregation. They are usually organized by only a small number of people on a voluntary and non-profit basis. Because of this, festivals sometimes have to be cancelled. On the other hand, as noted above, from time to time onetime festivals are also organized. This makes it difficult to keep track of all Christian metal festivals and larger gatherings on a transnational scale. Finally, it is worth noting that scenes also may be connected to certain places, such as certain venues, although such places may not have any relevance to the scene as a whole beyond a local level.

Institutionalization beyond the scene

Scenes may also institutionalize themselves further through engaging in activities that extend beyond the scene itself. The establishment of alternative 'metal parish movements' in Sweden, Germany, Brazil and Mexico are clear examples of this. In some rare cases, the notion of metal as being particularly suited for expressing and spreading the Christian message has also been adopted by traditional and institutional Christian churches. One contemporary example from Finland can be found in the creation of the so-called *Metal Mass* Lutheran church service concept.[69] Metal Masses are traditional Lutheran church services (the term 'mass' refers to the Eucharist being included) held in almost full accordance with traditional liturgy and service sequence. All featured music accompanying both liturgy and collectively sung hymns is, however, provided by a live metal band. Metal Masses have managed to attract substantially larger crowds than conventional church services and developed into an institution in itself. Today, Metal Masses are regularly organized by Lutheran parishes of all sizes all across the country. It should also be noted that core members of the Christian metal scene in Finland have played an important role in the initial creation and subsequent development of the Metal Mass-concept. For example, the bands playing at the Metal Masses tend to be mainly comprised by Finnish Christian metal musicians. The success of the Metal Mass-concept has undoubtedly also lent the Finnish Christian metal scene some increased public visibility.

Another notable way that the transnational scene has institutionalized itself in a way that extends beyond the scene itself is through the so-called *Metal Bible*-project.[70] The *Metal Bible* is a pocketsize special edition of the New Testament published by Bible for the Nations in Sweden and contains testimonies from Christian metal musicians and fans from all over the world. It also has a metal-inspired layout. The cover displays the contours of an electric guitar against the backdrop of a nighttime church with the title 'Metal Bible' printed in metallic gothic letters. Many concert pictures have also been included of the testimony-writers. At the time of writing, the *Metal Bible* is available in seven languages: Swedish, English, Spanish, German, Polish, Danish and Dutch. Work is underway for further editions in Portuguese, Russian, Italian, Slovak, Finnish and Norwegian.

The *Metal Bible* clearly has evangelistic aims. The main purpose behind the included testimonies is to encourage metalheads to reflect on their life situation and the Christian message. In addition, the coordinators also state broader aims. The *Metal Bible* website contains the following purpose statement:

> The purpose of this special Bible is to break down prejudices and misconceptions that many metalheads have about the Bible and help people to realize that the Bible is not a boring book but an interesting and living book that has a lot to tell us today. My prayer is that many metalheads through the Metal Bible will realize that the Bible is a cool book and that its timeless message is something for them too.[71]

The many testimonies included in the *Metal Bible* are also clearly aimed at highlighting how Christian faith can be expressed in many different forms. Most are written in a typical evangelical testimonial style. Writers contrast their earlier unhappy and sinful lives with their new happy lives as believers. Indeed, conversion is often described in terms of having been 'born again'. They also typically stress the importance of establishing a personal relationship with God. Importantly, nearly all of these writers also explicitly relate their conversion stories to having come into contact with Christian metal. Some testimony writers highlight how finding faith rescued them from earlier self-destructive lives of drug- and alcohol abuse, suicidal thoughts and Satanism. A bit strangely, however, most of the testimonies of this type are written by fans rather than musicians and many of them hardly discuss music at all. One would surely not be entirely mistaken to argue that they have, at least partly, been included in order to associate secular metal with self-destructive behaviour, Satanism and the occult. Another category of testimonies includes testimonies that explicitly focus on Christian metal as a means of evangelism and alternative form of Christian expression. Many of these writers focus on how Christian metal has enabled them to form an alternative Christian identity and point out that Christian faith also can be expressed in a form that 'relates' more to metalheads. For example, many emphasize that people need not change their taste in music and appearance just because they are or become Christians. In this way, the testimonies of the *Metal Bible* also take the form of a collective testimony that serves to express a sense of a shared Christian identity. It is also worth noting that the people behind the *Metal Bible* are actively involved in distributing it at metal festivals all over Europe.

Relation to other scenes

As already noted, the most significant Christian metal scenes of today have all developed in countries with long-standing secular metal scenes. Whether Christian metal can be said to have gained any real foothold within the secular metal communities of these countries is, however, an altogether different matter. Generally speaking, by forming its own separate and independent scene, Christian metal has so far remained confined to the very margins of the wider metal community. Even so, as already noted, because of the highly visible evangelistic efforts of some early bands, it has nevertheless become widely known throughout global metal culture. In some countries, the Christian scene has developed closer ties with the wider secular scene. In others, however, it remains completely segregated. In such environments, Christian metal bands sometimes have difficulties finding secular venues in which to play. For example, grassroots secular metal concert organizers are usually not interested in featuring Christian bands at their events because of the negative effect it might have on ticket sales and the possibility that problems and trouble may ensue during the event itself.

However, there is also clearly a sense in which the Christian scene also deliberately has excluded itself from the wider secular scene. For example, some Christian bands choose not to play secular venues at all. Moreover, even though it is uncommon, secular events may sometimes feature Christian bands. The reverse, however, is extremely rare. Christian metal events are nearly always kept totally 'Christian' in this regard. Its exclusion from the secular scene is thus partly self-imposed. On the other hand, individual scene members may still interact with and participate in the secular scene in various ways. For example, they may regularly follow secular scenic media and attended secular metal concerts.

As noted above, in contrast to the North American and European scenes, the Latin American scenes appear to be particularly concerned with engaging with the secular scene in a more expressly evangelistic and sometimes confrontational way.

In countries with several other larger Christian music scenes, such as the United States and Canada in particular, the Christian metal scene has usually formed closer relationships with other musically related Christian scenes such as Christian hardcore punk, hard rock or goth scenes.

Scenic capital, production and consumption

Most global and transnational music scenes create their own forms of scenic or cultural capital. In the case of the Christian metal scene, the term 'cultural capital' or 'scenic capital' basically refers to the different forms of merit and respect that individual members may accumulate or be ascribed within the context and logic of this particular scene. In the main, scenic capital is gained by people who are seen to represent or embody the scene's main ideals or who are involved in maintaining scenic structures. There are two main forms of scenic capital within the Christian metal scene. The first type has to do with musical creativity. Such capital is gained by musically creative bands and individual band members who pioneer new sounds and thereby further the overall musical development of the scene. For example, Christian bands such as Mortification have been afforded much such capital for pioneering Christian death metal. Because of the musical creativity of the band, Mortification has also gained quite a degree of respect in the secular metal community. Similar examples include Tourniquet, which has developed its own highly technical signature sound of Christian thrash and Australian musician Jayson Sherlock (also a former member of Mortification) who pioneered the unblack metal style through his one man band Horde.

A related form of scenic capital that is more characteristic of the Christian metal scene has to do with furthering the scene's evangelistic aims and goals. Such capital is gained by Christian bands that have over a long period relentlessly aimed to spread the Christian message through their music. The Christian scene has seen many such bands, including Stryper, Deliverance and Mortification. As noted above, members of such bands gain what could be called 'evangelistic capital' and become widely known and respected throughout the scene as 'metal ministers' or 'metal missionaries'. Examples of individual persons invested with particularly high degrees of such capital include Michael Sweet of Stryper, Steve Rowe of Mortification and Bob Beeman of *Sanctuary International*. However, every national scene has a number of particularly respected core members. Indeed, all band members are generally afforded at least some degree of evangelistic capital just for being in a Christian band. People in gatekeeping roles who are known for their long-time involvement with the maintenance of both national and transnational scenic infrastructure and institutions may also gain much such capital. Significantly, this type of evangelistic capital also extends beyond the scene itself into the respective Christian communities of respected scene members themselves.

National scenes differ in the degrees to which they contribute to the wider transnational scene regarding the production and consumption of such things as Christian metal albums and media. As observed above, most transnational infrastructure is maintained by the North American and Nordic scenes in particular. For example, even though the Nordic scenes are much smaller than the US scene, a considerable portion of overall record production is still based there. These countries also produce many successful bands. This means that a substantial portion of all Christian metal is produced in the United States, throughout Northern continental Europe and the Nordic countries Sweden, Norway and Finland. Christian record labels based in these countries also tend to produce a significant number of records by bands from other regions. Although there are no statistics, it is also fair to assume that these more affluent countries also constitute the most important markets for Christian metal. Even though a substantial amount of Christian records are also produced in Latin America, a considerable portion of all records are still imported from the United States and Northern Europe. Generally speaking, one would assume that the resources of the Latin American scenes are slightly more limited because of the relatively lesser economic affluence of countries such as Brazil and Mexico. For example, records may not be as easily affordable for many Latin American scene members as they are for scene members in the Nordic countries. This affects the activities of bands as well. Establishing a band requires instruments and various forms of technical equipment, all of which are quite expensive. However, although it may be more difficult, people involved in music scenes in less affluent countries still tend to find ways of acquiring records and equipment. The point to note is that national and regional scenes are always affected by the general socio-economic conditions of the countries in which they are embedded. However, such differences or inequalities between regional scenes in different parts of the world should not be exaggerated, although they do need to be noted. The same goes for the commercial aspect of Christian metal in a broader sense. Christian metal does indeed offer its musicians and fans an alternative form of religious expression and a form of entertainment that is in line with Christian values. However, this should not make us lose sight of the fact that Christian metal also is a form of Christian expression and entertainment that is promoted and marketed in order to sell, and preferably sell well. Of course, such a commercial aspect constitutes an integral and indispensable part of every music scene. Indeed, it would be difficult to imagine how a Christian metal scene would be possible to sustain without such a commercial aspect. These issues fall beyond the scope of our discussion here, but they do need to be noted nonetheless.

As seen above, the Christian metal scene has developed a highly independent scenic infrastructure. Many of its record labels, promotion and distribution channels, media and festivals have developed into long-standing and important transnational scenic institutions. At this stage, the most important respects in which the scene should be described as being 'highly independent' have been clarified. Although the Christian metal scene retains close connections to evangelical Protestantism in general, it has remained highly independent from particular denominational influence and control. Also, its development of its own scenic infrastructure and institutions has also afforded it a large degree of independence from the wider, and increasingly global, evangelical popular culture industry. Although Christian metal in the United States in particular partly remains more closely connected to the evangelical popular culture industry, the situation throughout other core regions of today's transnational scene, such as Northern Europe and Latin America, is very different. In addition, through the development of its own scenic infrastructure, the Christian metal scene has also been able to achieve a high degree of independence from the infrastructures and institutions of the world of secular metal, many of which have traditionally not been particularly accepting of the very idea of Christian metal in the first place. It is important to note therefore that, in the specific case of the Christian metal scene, the development of such a comprehensive and highly independent scenic infrastructure has been of crucial importance for the establishment and survival of a transnational scene in the first place.

Without its own specialized record labels, promotion and distribution channels and different forms of media, a transnational scene would become nearly impossible to sustain. It would likely dissolve into separate and largely isolated national scenes. The scene's high degree of institutionalization has also ensured its development and stability over time. As has been remarked on earlier, Christian metal's particular religious outlook also makes it highly unlikely for it to be assimilated into other scenes. Lastly, because of its relatively small scale, scene members in different parts of the world tend to be very knowledgeable about transnational scenic infrastructure and institutions. Today's scenic infrastructure is present and implicated at most basic levels of scenic activity. For example, it is often possible to purchase US fanzines such as *Heaven's Metal* or Brazilian fanzines such as *Extreme Brutal Death* at Christian metal festivals in Europe. However, as we have also seen, although Christian metal scenes have developed closer ties to secular metal scenes in certain countries, in most cases, the two remain thoroughly separated.

6

Main Ideological and Discursive Traits

In this final main chapter of the book, we will focus on the central ideological traits of Christian metal through focusing on the ways in which Christian metal musicians and followers themselves *discursively* construct Christian metal as a particular type of phenomenon that serves a certain set of main functions and purposes. Through employing a discourse analytic approach, this chapter thus explores what specific meanings and functions Christian metal is ascribed by its own creators and followers through looking at the ways in which it is talked about and represented in different forms of Christian metal media in particular. We will focus on four key discourses that still dominate the discursive construction of the phenomenon of Christian metal on a transnational level and continue to affect the ways in which Christian metal typically is both represented and understood among its own creators and followers. This chapter thus also highlights the functions that Christian metal culture fills in the everyday religious lives of its followers; how it provides its followers with a rationale for the forming of alternative modes of religious expression, alternative ways of 'doing' religion and important resources for the construction of alternative Christian identities.

In order for our talk of the 'discursive' construction of the scene to make any real sense, we must first consider the concept of 'discourse' in more detail. It is important to note at the outset that the concept of discourse has developed in different directions and come to be understood and utilized in a wide range of different ways.[1] Indeed, it is no exaggeration to say that there has always existed some degree of confusion about what the concept of discourse can or should be taken to mean. Moreover, the fact that scholars have all too frequently employed, and still continue to employ, the concept of discourse in a wide variety of different and often contrasting ways without adequately clarifying what precisely it is that they take the concept to mean (or not to mean) has only served to exacerbate the general ambiguity that has come to surround the concept on the whole. Vague and ambiguous uses of the concept of discourse have not been uncommon among scholars who have argued for the employment of discourse analytic perspectives in the study of religion either. In the following, we shall therefore begin with a discussion of the concept of 'discourse', how it has been understood and employed in the scholarship on religion and how it will be understood and employed in the context of our present discussion.

Theoretical and methodological perspectives: Social constructionism, discourse and the study of religion

In our increasingly media-saturated general social and cultural environment, communication and representation have come to constitute increasingly important, and indeed inescapable, aspects of social and cultural life on the whole.[2] Since the so-called 'linguistic' turn of the humanities and social sciences in the 1960s, and the subsequent 'discursive' turn in the early 1980s,[3] there have emerged a wide range of varyingly related approaches for studying how our language use and modes of representation fundamentally affect and shape our understandings of reality and our constructions of meaningful worlds. Frequently coupled together under the heading of 'discourse analysis', these various approaches have become firmly established and widely employed in many disciplines throughout the humanities and social sciences.

Although there are some notable exceptions, much of the work that has been done on discourse and religion thus far has been almost exclusively meta-theoretical in character and mainly been concerned with pondering the nature of the discipline of religious studies itself, critically assessing scholarly constructions of the category of religion and highlighting the importance of scholarly self-reflexivity.[4] As I have argued elsewhere,[5] the work that has been produced on discourse and religion thus far can roughly be divided into three main intersecting types, situated at different points along a continuum, ranging from purely meta-theoretical work, to work that contextualizes meta-theoretical reflection in relation to theorizing within particular sub-fields in the study of religion, to work that actually implements and performs actual discourse analysis in practice.

Moreover, in close relation to the above, further clarification is also needed with regard to the main theoretical underpinnings of discourse analytic approaches. Indeed, notwithstanding the large variety of different versions, in general, most discourse analytic perspectives nevertheless share the same meta-theoretical underpinning – *social constructionism*. A brief general discussion of this meta-theoretical orientation is therefore also warranted here at the outset.

Social constructionism

The term 'social construction' was first introduced by Berger and Luckmann in their hugely influential treatise *The Social Construction of Reality*,[6] which also played an important role in establishing the issue of social construction as a topic of scholarly inquiry.[7] Important precursors for social-constructionist perspectives can be found across many different disciplines (e.g. philosophy, psychology, the sociology of scientific knowledge). Indeed, it is not uncommon for different commentators to locate the principal roots of social constructionism in slightly different disciplines and broader scholarly debates. One common way of doing this is to trace social constructionism back to 1960s debates on the nature of language and representation within the fields of semiotics and literary theory.[8] These debates, which are often coupled together under headings such as 'post-structuralism' and 'postmodernism/postmodern critique', centred on a radical questioning of modernist meta-narratives and the modernist 'picture metaphor' view of language, that is, the view that words and language correspond to and are able to communicate pictures of the world 'as it is'.[9] In sharp contrast to this view, post-structuralist and postmodern scholars instead emphasized how words and sentences always gain their particular meanings in the particular human interactional and relational contexts in which they appear and are used.[10] Particular focus was directed at how our ways of constructing our conceptions of reality together through language and other modes of representation not only fundamentally shape our own understandings of ourselves and the world but also play a central role in mediating, validating and strengthening power relations and hegemonic views of reality within society and culture on the whole.[11]

Although it is important to recognize 'post-structuralism' and 'postmodernism' as umbrella terms that encompass a wide range of different viewpoints and perspectives,[12] for the purposes of our present discussion, it is enough to note that the post-structuralist and postmodernist questioning of modernist epistemologies and meta-narratives became instrumental in bringing about what is sometimes referred to as a general 'legitimation crisis' and subsequent cultural turn within the humanities and social sciences.[13] As Murphy points out, 'although many theoretical and philosophical questions remained unanswered by this labor, its net effect was to change the way many scholars understood their own research'.[14]

Generally speaking, drawing on the above understanding of the nature of language and representation, in a social constructionist perspective, communication and relationships are viewed as central to human meaning-making as it is primarily through our language use and other modes of representation that we construct and maintain meaningful worlds. From a social constructionist perspective, then, language is not adequately understood as being reflective of reality, but as being thoroughly *constitutive* of reality. In other words, language is not to be approached in terms of a 'neutral information-carrying vehicle' but rather as something that always also 'creates what it refers to'.[15]

It is important to note, however, that theoretical perspectives on the notion of 'social construction' come in many different versions.[16] Hence, rather than constituting a specific theory, social constructionism is more appropriately described in terms of a certain *meta-theoretical orientation* to the general notion of social construction that directs particular focus at how our conceptions of meaningful worlds are constructed through relationships, language and discourse.[17] Although social constructionism has itself been developed in different versions, it is still possible to outline a set of interrelated key assumptions commonly shared by most social constructionists. First and foremost among these comes a *critical stance towards realist, received and taken-for-granted understandings of knowledge and reality*. As Burr points out, social constructionism 'invites us to be critical of the idea that our observations of the world unproblematically yield its nature to us, to challenge the view that conventional knowledge is based upon objective unbiased observation of the world'.[18] Second, as possible constructions of reality and the world are multiple, *all modes of understanding are viewed as being intimately tied to a particular historical, social and cultural context*. Third, social constructionism holds that all forms of *knowledge and understanding are relational and consensual in character* and 'sustained by social processes'.[19] Fourth, 'knowledge and *social action* go together'.[20] Different constructions of the world invite different forms of social action. The concept of *discourse* is central to all of these key assumptions.

Social constructionism thus provides researchers with a sober way of approaching the very nature of scholarly activity and practice on the whole. Indeed, as Engler notes: 'In one sense the study of religion is inherently constructionist. Extreme relativist views notwithstanding, *the contextualization of the sacred* in an ineluctable characteristic of the field'.[21] As noted, in a way that reflects the general ambiguity that has come to surround the concept of discourse on the whole, scholars who have utilized the concept of discourse in the study of religion have seldom clearly explicated what precisely they take the concept of discourse to mean – or not to mean.

It becomes crucial, therefore, to provide some clearer explication of how the concept of discourse is approached and understood within the context of any given study, and it is to this issue that we now turn.

Discourse

As noted above, the concept of discourse has been developed in a range of different directions, and it has been used, and continues to be used, in a wide range of different ways. Even so, when based on a general social constructionist understanding of language as thoroughly constitutive of reality, it is possible to formulate an understanding of the concept of discourse that is sufficiently specific while simultaneously retaining sufficiently broad applicability.

In a social constructionist perspective, discourses are generally understood as constituting more or less coherent ways of constructing and representing reality in particular ways through language and other forms of representation and communication. Burr provides the following general definition:

> A discourse refers to a set of meanings, metaphors, representations, images, stories, statements and so on that in some way together produce a particular version of events. It refers to a particular picture that is painted of an event, person or class of persons, a particular way of representing it in a certain light.[22]

Indeed, this definition is of a very general character. But we need to keep in mind that, as a scholarly analytical construct, the particular way in which the concept of discourse is defined will always be dependent on the particular perspectives and interests of particular researchers and the particular form of discourse analysis that they use.[23] For example, definitions provided and employed by scholars working with a critical-discourse analytic perspective will most likely be more focused on issues related to power relations in society. Moreover, scholars interested in empirically exploring the function of discourse in relation to certain social phenomena (such as religion, for example) may also opt for a definition that better suits that type of research, such as, for example, the following one provided by Hall:

> Discourses are ways of referring to or constructing knowledge about a particular topic of practice: a cluster (or formation) of ideas, images and practices, which provide ways of talking about, forms of knowledge and conduct associated with a particular topic, social activity or institutional site in society.[24]

Although there are many similarities, the differences between this definition and the one provided by Burr above are nevertheless obvious. However, given the huge variety of different definitions of discourse, an 'all-purpose' definition is not only unattainable but even undesirable. For the purposes of our discussion here the most important point to note is that, when the concept of discourse occupies a central role in any given piece of research (such as on religion, for example), it becomes, at the very least, necessary to provide some clearer specification as to how that concept is understood in the context of that particular piece of research.

In spite of their differences, the vast majority of all understandings of discourse nevertheless share some main elements. Central to most is the notion that, like all forms of language and representation, discourses are constitutive; they 'serve to construct the phenomena of our world for us'.[25] The basic point to note is that different discourses construct the world in different ways, each presenting a different account of a given phenomenon or states of affairs, each highlighting certain aspects or elements at the expense of others, and each purporting to articulate and present the 'truth' about that given phenomenon or states of affairs.[26] It is, however, important to recognize that we always base our continuous relational constructions of reality on already existing constructions and ways of understanding the world. Discourses, therefore, are never static. Instead, they constantly mutate and cross-fertilize in various ways.[27] More often than not, particular phenomena or states of affairs tend to be simultaneously surrounded by multiple, related, mutually supporting or competing, discourses.[28] It needs to be noted, therefore, that there exists a 'two-way' mutually affective relationship between discourses and people's utterances and writings. A discourse, therefore, 'can be thought of as a kind of frame of reference, a conceptual backcloth against which our utterances can be interpreted'.[29] Discourses thus constitute more than just ways of representing and conveying particular accounts of certain phenomena or states of affairs. They also constitute resources for meaning-making, that is, ways of making certain phenomena or states of affairs meaningful in particular ways in particular contexts.[30]

Although there exists no 'correct' way of analysing discourse, such analyses nevertheless generally focus on identifying patterns and recurring key elements in a given body of material or collection of material which appear to be central to how particular meanings are produced.[31] Typical types of material include (but are far from limited to) different forms of media texts such as newspaper articles and TV shows, webpages, statements and documents produced within various societal institutions and in-depth interviews. It is worth noting that it is quite possible for different researchers to identify different recurring key elements, different discourses, and different relationships between discourses, in any particular body of material.

It becomes of crucial importance, therefore, that researchers adequately account for exactly how they have gone about identifying recurring patterns and key elements in their material.[32]

For example, when conducting ethnographic research that involves interviewing people affiliated (and who expressly affiliate themselves) with some particular religious group or type of religiosity, a researcher needs to thoroughly acquaint him/herself with the particular types of religious language use, discursive practices and discursive complexes prevalent within that particular religious context. A researcher then also needs to investigate how the discourses that surface in interviews with individuals affiliated with a particular religious group relate to the types of discourses that circulate in various forms of group-related media such as books, magazines and webpages. It is also worth noting the often peculiar character of religious language and discourse on the whole. Although it is not always the case, generally speaking, religious language often aims to refer to, articulate and make meaningful that which, so to speak, 'cannot be expressed in words'.

Moreover, when examining a religious group or phenomenon such as Christian metal that has spread on a transnational scale, a researcher may also want to explore whether differences can be discerned with regard to how people affiliated with that group discursively construct such things as the main purpose of that group or their own personal involvement with it differently across various geographical areas and social and cultural contexts.[33]

Like social constructionist approaches more generally, discourse analysis can be described in terms of an approach that, so to speak, aims to play with 'open cards' and to keep the entire research process as transparent as possible, particularly through forcing researchers to base their interpretations on various texts produced by religionists themselves.

A social constructionist and discourse analytic approach to Christian metal

When based on a social constructionist approach as outlined above, a basic starting point for a discourse analytic approach to religion in general must be to regard the very category of 'religion' as an 'empty signifier' that has no intrinsic meaning in itself.[34] The meaning of the category of 'religion' needs to be viewed as always being constructed and informed by the particular discourses that surround it in particular historical, social and cultural contexts.[35] Importantly, this most certainly applies to academic discourses on religion as well. Approaching religion from a discourse analytic perspective thus essentially entails developing an understanding of the category of religion to which discourse, communication and representation are intrinsic.[36]

Clearly, Christian metal music and culture could, and has been, studied in a number of different ways. The choice of theoretical and methodological approaches not only depends on the nature of the study itself. It will also form, inform and direct that study in fundamental ways. Here, we are interested in directing particular focus on the discursive construction of Christian metal on a transnational level. At its most general, in the approach employed here, particular attention is directed at how the various meanings that Christian metalheads themselves attach to Christian metal as a phenomenon is constructed and maintained though different forms of scenic social interaction. In this approach, in order to gain a fuller understanding of a phenomenon such as Christian metal, one needs to allow academic understandings of the processes whereby religious meanings are constructed to enter into a dialogue with the processes whereby religious meanings are constructed within the Christian metal scene itself. This entails looking at how these meanings and constructions are expressed, communicated and represented through language and discourse.

In order to provide a general illustration of what this approach might entail, let us for a moment consider the circulation of discourses within the more or less globalized realm of popular music more generally. Approaching how particular meanings are attached to particular kinds of popular music by particular groups of people through focusing on how such meanings are constructed discursively can be very revealing of the processes of negotiation that are typically involved in the construction of musical meaning and value. As has been pointed out by Walser with specific reference to metal music and culture, the texts produced within music genres 'are developed, sustained, and reformed by people, who bring a variety of histories and interests to their encounters with generic texts'.[37] Being produced by people in particular historical, social and cultural contexts, these generic texts 'come to reflect the multiplicities of social existence'.[38] From this viewpoint, therefore, music in itself has no intrinsic meaning. Instead, its particular meanings are informed by the particular discourses that surround it, or as Walser puts it: 'Musical meanings are always grounded socially and historically, and they operate on an ideological field of conflicting interests, institutions, and memories.'[39]

A largely similar point is made by Frith when he argues that, in various ways, we often use music to express who we are. We also often assume, or indeed presuppose, that other people's tastes in music will tell us something about who they are and what they are like. This, argues Frith, is most clearly illustrated by the ways in which we tend to talk about popular music through making value judgements about it. However, the value judgements we make in such situations 'are not about likes and dislikes as such, but about ways of listening, about ways of hearing, about ways of being'.[40] In order to understand

and make sense of the cultural value judgements people make, we need to pay closer attention to the wider social, cultural and discursive contexts in which they are embedded. Hence, we need to examine the particular discourses or sets of discourses through which music is invested with certain meanings. Everyday disagreements or disputes about music are rarely about music in itself but, as Frith expresses it, 'about something with music'.[41]

To reiterate, discourses, then, are not only ways of representing and conveying particular accounts of different phenomena and states of affairs but also *resources of meaning-making*, that is resources for constructing different phenomena and states of affairs as meaningful in particular ways, be they musical, religious or, as in the case of Christian metal, a combination between the two.

Thus, to put things in very basic terms, the central discourses pertaining to the meaning and function of Christian metal that we will explore in more detail in following sections are understood broadly as ways of talking about and representing Christian metal music and culture in certain ways and in a certain light, thereby investing it with certain meanings. We are not, therefore, interested in the situated use of these discourses in particular interactions, although that aspect is far from unimportant, but rather, with how the discursive construction of Christian metal relates to broader contemporary developments and transformations of religious life and practice throughout much of the Western world and various strands of evangelical Christianity in particular. To illustrate the discursive construction of the scene, our exploration below will draw on a wide range of different materials and sources.

At its most general, our analysis will proceed as follows: Having accounted for the main musical, verbal, visual, aesthetic and bodily practices of Christian metal in previous chapters, we will now proceed by asking its own producers and followers what Christian metal looks and sounds like to them. In doing this, we approach Christian metal by exploring scenic media such as magazines and fanzines and Christian metal Internet-sites and discussion forums to get an idea of the ways in which it is presented and talked about there. In relation to this, we identify and focus on a set of recurring ways of talking about and representing Christian metal as a whole – that is we identify and focus on a set of key Christian metal discourses. In doing this, we also explore how the key Christian metal discourses identified relate to other similar and connected discourses within wider evangelical contexts. Lastly, we also explore how Christian metal tends to be discursively represented and interpreted within secular metal culture. It is worth reiterating here that, as we will repeatedly talk about the 'discursive construction' of the 'meaning' and 'function' of Christian metal below, what is intended thereby is the basic meaning and function that scene members themselves *discursively* – that is, through text and talk – ascribe and attach to the Christian metal scene and their own personal involvement with it. To put it another way, the discursive dimension explored below should therefore not be viewed as being able to highlight in itself or on its own what other possible types of functions the Christian metal scene may or may not hold for its members.

The discursive construction of the Christian metal scene

As we now move into an analysis of the discursive construction of the Christian metal scene we mainly approach it from *within*. That is, we approach it from the perspective of its musicians, fans and other people involved in maintaining Christian metal scenes at different national levels as well as at a transnational level. What do Christian metal musicians and fans get out of their involvement with the scene culturally, religiously, identity-wise, etc.? What meanings and functions does Christian metal music and culture have for the people who make, play and listen to it, who create and administer Christian metal Internet-sites, produce and distribute magazines and fanzines, organize concerts and festivals and so on?

In the following, we shall thus concentrate on the ways in which today's transnational scene constitutes a particular type of discursive space. As outlined above, scenes are generally marked by three main forms of scenic construction through which they 'are discursively and aesthetically constructed through talk and a range of other practices'.[42] Firstly, looking at the internal discursive construction of the scene involves exploring the degree to which scene members 'discursively construct that scene as a distinctive space', making it 'visible' and 'recognizable' to other members of the scene.[43] Importantly, it is through such discursive construction, communication and interaction among members that scenes become invested with certain meanings. Exploring the internal discursive construction of the Christian metal scene thus involves looking at different ways of representing it that appear to be both stable and recurring as well as central to the ways in which certain meanings are produced.

The first part of this section will be dedicated to exploring these issues. In the second part, we will also briefly discuss the external discursive construction of the Christian metal scene, that is, the ways in which it is discursively constructed and identified as a distinct space from outside of itself within wider Christian settings as well as within the secular metal community. Although our discussion of the external discursive construction of the Christian metal scene will be much less detailed than our exploration of its internal discursive construction, it is important to keep in mind that the external discursive construction of the scene can never be totally separated from its internal discursive construction. This was illustrated in relation to our discussion of the 'double controversy' of Christian metal in Chapter 2. Issues pertaining to the external discursive construction of the scene will therefore always surface in its internal discursive construction as well.

Internal discursive construction

Today's transnational Christian metal scene has developed into a space that greatly aids the forming of some basic shared understandings of what Christian metal is, or is supposed to be, all 'about'. The development of a transnational scene has greatly aided the forming of such shared understandings as it brings together people with different Christian affiliations and shared passions for metal music from different parts of the world. Again, the 'metal part' of this equation is every bit as important as the religious/Christian one. As different national scenes have developed, Christian metal has also become increasingly integrated into the everyday religious lives of scene members.

It is worth reiterating here that the overwhelming majority of Christian metalheads worldwide are Protestant. This is not surprising considering Christian metal's roots in North American evangelicalism. Particular national scenes do need to be understood in their respective social, cultural and religious contexts, but as Christian metal has spread on a transnational level, the transnational scene as a whole has also become increasingly detached from the cultural and religious peculiarities of particular countries or regions. Today's transnational scene is not controlled by any particular Christian group or institution and advocates no particular denominational creed. It can thus be described in terms of a small cross-denominational, both religious and musical, transnational movement. Partly as a consequence of this, Christian metal is, in practice, not reproduced along genre-based scales, that is different Christian metal scenes have in practice not emerged around particular Christian metal styles. Instead, since all Christian metal styles are characterized by largely the same concerns, they all come together within one single scene.

One could, of course, argue that the transnational scene is reproduced along 'ideological' or 'religious' scales (using the term 'ideology' to denote different denominational views on particular religious issues). However, the high degree of uniformity between scenes regarding the ascribed basic meaning and function of Christian metal has ensured that they are largely reproduced along one general and widely shared ideological and religious scale. Debates and disagreements on religious topics constitute an important part of internal scenic discourse but become secondary to the notion of the scene as a particular type of Christian musical space. For example, as one Christian metalhead involved in the maintenance of an online Christian discussion forum pointed out in an earlier interview:

> Since there are so many denominations and that people come from different backgrounds, disagreements are bound to happen. In the Christian metal culture disagreements happen with lyrical interpretation a lot. Disagreements also pop up since there are so many genres of Christian metal. Some people disagree and debate on which metal style a band belongs too, or which metal style sounds best, etc.[44]

According to this scene member, it is not unusual for Christian metalheads to disagree on interpretation of lyrics. This further attests to the importance attached to the content of lyrics in Christian metal more generally. A large portion of disagreements also revolve around musical styles and tastes. This, in turn, again attests to the central part that metal music itself plays in this context.

Indeed, these same types of disagreements may surface just as well within any music scene. However, these types of disagreements and disagreements on the basic meaning of the scene in itself are different things. For example, when asked in an earlier interview whether religious disagreements ever cause problems within the scene, central transnational scenic figure Johannes commented:

> Practically, no. We all share the same basic Christian faith, so there is no problem.... The important thing is the core of the Christian message which all Christian metal bands share.... It is simply not an important subject to raise when it is the core of the Christian message, the gospel, that is the important and central message the bands wish to spread and not specific 'denominational teachings'.[45]

According to Johannes, various teachings and differing views on more specific religious issues become secondary to 'a basic Christian faith' within the scene. Thus, even though discussions on religious topics may constitute an important part of internal scenic discourse, disagreements are not allowed to overshadow the notion of unity and solidarity within the scene.

How does such unity come about? How have such shared notions about the basic meaning and function of Christian metal developed and come to be so widely shared on a transnational level? The discourse analytic approach

MAIN IDEOLOGICAL AND DISCURSIVE TRAITS

employed here searches for answers to these questions through examining the ways in which the scene is constructed discursively, that is the ways in which it is recurrently represented and talked about among scene members themselves.

Obviously, a range of different discourses can be seen to circulate within the scene. At closer inspection, however, scene members tend to represent what they regard to be the basic meaning and function of Christian metal through four main and often overlapping discourses. I have chosen to call them the 'Christian metal is an alternative form of religious expression'-discourse, the 'Christian metal is an alternative means of evangelism'-discourse, the 'Christian metal is a legitimate form of religious expression and evangelism'-discourse and the 'Christian metal is an alternative to secular metal'-discourse. In spite of a range of other discourses circulating within the scene, these four closely related and often overlapping discourses play a central role in expressing and encapsulating the essence of what Christian metal is all 'about' from the perspective of its musicians and fans. They can thus be seen to constitute the basic building blocks for the wider discursive construction of Christian metal on a transnational level.

I have chosen to focus on these four discourses for three main reasons: (1) they are stable and recurring on a transnational level, (2) they surface at every level of scenic activity and (3) they appear to be central to the ways in which particular meanings are produced. This means that these four discourses have featured throughout today's transnational scene for a long time; that they surface in many different contexts, such as in scenic media, in song lyrics or in speeches during concerts; and that they appear to be particularly important for ascribing the Christian metal scene with certain main meanings and functions on a transnational level.

As already mentioned, these four discourses often overlap. They support and uphold each other. This is to say that the ascribed basic meaning and function of Christian metal is never conveyed or expressed through any of these discourses alone. Instead, it is through their convergence and coexistence that such meanings are produced. Much of the wider discursive construction of the scene can hence be viewed in terms of threads spun from the ground- or 'mother-web' formed by these four discourses. Taken together, these discourses thus serve to express the basics of a meaningful whole that becomes something more than the sum of its parts. It is important to note here that variations of these discourses, and particularly the notion of music being an effective medium for spreading the Christian message, also circulate within the wider world of CCM as well as within numerous other distinct evangelical popular music scenes. For example, as discussed in previous chapters, CCM has represented itself as a fully legitimate 'wholesome' or 'sound' alternative to secular popular music ever since its emergence in the late 1960s. The long-standing discourses that underpin the idea of CCM thus constitute a wider discursive context in relation to which the discursive construction of Christian metal also needs to be understood.

In the following, these four discourses are explored in direct relation to the particular ways in which they are formulated and the particular meanings they produce within the particular context of the Christian metal scene. It is important to keep in mind, though, that although these discourses are both stable and recurring this does not mean that they are static. Instead, within certain bounds, they are constantly contested, debated and modified depending on the particular contexts in which they appear. As we are primarily interested in exploring how these discourses appear on a transnational level, most examples will be taken from various forms of transnational Christian metal media. Examples that illustrate variations in the ways in which these discourses may appear will also be included.[46]

'Christian metal is an alternative form of religious expression'

This discourse essentially represents Christian metal as a non-traditional and non-conventional but equally sincere way of expressing Christian faith. However, compared to the other three main discourses, this general and broad discourse rarely appears in 'purer' form. That is to say, when examining the Christian metal scene, one rarely comes across statements which explicitly state that 'Christian metal is an alternative form of religious expression'. In many ways, this broad discourse serves to underpin the other three key internal discourses of the scene. For instance, it clearly surfaces in the following excerpt from the 'Frequently asked questions' section of *The Metal for Jesus Page*:

Why the need of Christian metal?

First of all because many Christians love metal music, and since we are Christians it's only natural to combine it with our faith. Just because you are Christian that doesn't mean that you have to listen to gospel or pop music! God is much bigger than the regular church music. Great music also deserves a great message, so why not combine them and take the best from both worlds. The reason that we want to spread the message of Jesus is because we care for people and don't want anyone to burn in hell, but instead find a living relationship with God (cause that's what the real Christian life is all about, it's a living relationship with God and not a boring religion!). Christian metal is also needed to encourage and help believers that love metal to grow in faith and come closer to Christ through the lyrics.[47]

This excerpt highlights an entire range of issues pertaining to how the basic meaning and function of Christian metal is represented by Christian metalheads, and particularly by core scene members such as musicians and people involved in maintaining important scenic institutions. Indeed, this excerpt is primarily intended as information for outsiders on what Christian metal is all about. That is the broader discursive context in which this excerpt needs to be understood. It represents Christian metal as an alternative form of religious expression through stating that it is 'only natural' for Christians to combine their taste in music with their faith. It is also stated that 'God is much bigger than the regular church music' and, moreover, that 'Christian metal is ... needed to encourage and help believers that love metal to grow in faith and come closer to Christ.' This statement thus suggests that Christian metal plays an important role in the personal religious lives of individual Christian metalheads. This excerpt is also illustrative of how the four main discourses of Christian metal often overlap. For example, it clearly draws on and articulates the 'Christian metal is an alternative means of evangelism'-discourse as well.

Another example of this discourse at play can be found in an article in *Heaven's Metal* from 2006 by Steve Rowe of Mortification:

There is a sick and dying world out there on its way to hell. I am so happy to be part of an extreme Christian music culture that still holds fast to the truth of salvation through Jesus, when the majority of 'Christian' rock acts have sold out to little or no Jesus message. Let all who play Christian Metal stand strong together as people who present powerful music with the most powerful message of salvation.[48]

This excerpt is taken from a short article in which Rowe discusses the combination of evangelism with the extreme musical form of death metal. As in the previous excerpt cited above, Rowe also highlights Christian metal's evangelistic aims. We should note here that spreading the Christian message through metal is also represented as constituting an alternative form of religious expression. For musicians, however, Christian metal is not merely about using metal to express their own religiosity to themselves and their fans, although it does serve that function too. As an alternative form of Christian expression, Christian metal is also directed outward as a means of evangelistic outreach. In addition, Rowe also argues that it is the duty of Christian musicians to convey a clear Christian message through their music. He expresses joy in being 'part of an extreme Christian music culture' that still holds true to that ideal.

Discussing the main objectives of today's transnational scene, Johannes further elaborated on these issues:

> Christian metal is a complement to other ways of spreading the Christian message. Through this music it is possible to reach out to many who would never take the message to themselves if they got it served in a more traditional way.... There is quite much contact with like-minded people in other countries and more and more all the time. We are like a big team working together since we have the same faith and like the same music. It is important and it means a lot to meet like-minded people and exchange experiences and have fun together.[49]

Here, Johannes clearly emphasizes contact between different scenes, describing the transnational scene as a 'big team' of 'like-minded people' working towards a shared goal. Moreover, as is also pointed out, scene members not only 'have the same faith', they also 'like the same music'. The common notion of the music functioning as a tool for 'reaching out' with the Christian message in an alternative form is likewise stressed.

Let us consider a final example of this discourse from the official webpages of *Sanctuary International*, where one finds the following introductory statement:

> Sanctuary International continues to promote Christian Music 'On The Edge' as we celebrate our faith in Jesus Christ. Pastor Bob travels around the globe teaching the basics of the Christian Faith without the legalism of traditional religion. Our message remains powerful and life-changing.[50]

Here, the promotion of 'Christian Music "On The Edge"' (i.e. metal) is related to a 'powerful and life-changing' message that avoids the 'legalism of traditional religion'. For one thing, this statement appears to express the general cross-denominational aims of *Sanctuary International*. In addition, though, the promotion of music 'On The Edge' is also contrasted with the practices of 'legalist' and 'traditional religion'.

These examples all illustrate how the 'Christian metal is an alternative form of religious expression'-discourse can be seen to underlie the other three main discourses. Again, the alternativeness of Christian metal is not directed against traditional modes of religious expression in a confrontational spirit. Rather, it is represented as being characterized by non-legalistic cross-denominational concerns. All of the examples cited above also draw attention to Christian metal as a means of evangelistic outreach, which brings us to the 'Christian metal is an alternative means of evangelism'-discourse.

'Christian metal is an alternative means of evangelism'

The pervasiveness of the evangelistic element in Christian metal culture has already been pointed out several times. We saw it surfacing in lyrics as well as in the main objectives of many scenic institutions such as record labels, distros and media. As already noted, although Christian metalheads nowadays rarely view the music purely as an evangelistic tool, the general notion of a 'metal ministry', of representing a Christian voice in the world of metal, has remained important. This discourse thus continues to be drawn upon by bands as well as other core members of the scene. Indeed, Christian metal sometimes comes close to being represented as the *only* means to reach certain people, especially secular metalheads. In this way the scene as a whole is also invested with a clear and important evangelistic mandate. Although this discourse may appear in many guises, it is often also expressed quite explicitly. The 'Christian metal is a powerful tool!'-section of *The Metal for Jesus Page* provides a particularly illustrative example of this and is thus worth quoting at length:

> Christian metal is a very powerful tool to spread the Gospel. The best with this tool is that thru this wonderful tool we can reach people that never will be reached otherways. Thru Christian Metal we can talk the metalheads language and have their attention. When we have got their attention they will also be open to the great message of salvation in a way that they relate and understands. So Heavenly Metal is a great way to communicate the gospel to people that wouldn't be reached in other ways.
>
> Christian Metal is a powerful tool and now is time that we start to use it!
>
> **DON'T BE SELFISH!**
> Don't just listen to your Christian Metal Cds by yourself but let non-Christians around you borrow them. Don't be so selfish! Buy Christian Metal Cds for your non-Christian friends. Let them know that there is a good and positive alternative to all the crap that many of the secular bands are offering!
>
> ...

USE YOUR CHRISTIAN METAL MAGS!

Also use your Christian metal mag's. Lend them to your friends. And why don't you give a subscription to them so they can check out the bands and the message for themselves.

WE WILL BE ACCOUNTABLE TO GOD

Christian Metal is a very powerful tool. So let's use it to bring metalheads to Christ. Jesus will soon return and we will be accountable for how we have used these great tools He has given us.

Thru this powerful music you can help your non-Christian friends to come to know the wonderful love of Jesus, and escape Hell too. Don't just hold your records for yourself but use them to let more people know about Jesus. That's what it's all about.

Of course God has also created Christian Metal for our enjoyment and to help us to grow in faith. But the main reason Christian Metal exist is because God wants people to get to know Christ so they can have a living relationship with Him and in the end go to Heaven instead of Hell.[51]

In this excerpt, Christian metal's role as an effective evangelistic tool is emphasized repeatedly. Indeed, all activities related to Christian metal are represented as being guided by evangelistic purposes. This also includes the entire scene in itself, which is represented as a God-given evangelistic tool. The 'effectiveness' of Christian metal as an evangelistic tool is represented as essentially lying in its ability to reach people who 'never will be reached otherways' through approaching them in their own language and thereby getting their attention. Christian metal media are also represented as offering non-Christians opportunities to 'get to know Christ'. Spreading the Christian message, it is stated, is 'what it's all about'. Although Christian metal serves additional religious functions for Christian metalheads as well, evangelistic outreach is presented as 'the main reason' for its very existence in the first place.

However, as noted, this discourse comes in many different forms; the 'effectiveness' of Christian metal as an evangelistic tool can be emphasized to varying degrees. In its many forms, this discourse also appears on the official webpages of many bands. Let us consider a few examples. The following excerpt is taken from the webpages of the Swedish band Majestic Vanguard and was posted already in 2005:

The day of tomorrow and what it will bring to us, will we never know. However for those who have chosen to live there life with Jesus Christ, there will always be a great future. Majestic Vanguards future lies in the hand of our bringer of the day. Nothing can ever chance that fact. The only thing we can do is to serve the one who once served us. The purpose with Majestic Vanguard is to present Jesus Christ to a fallen mankind. Too many voices in our time speak the fall prophet's words. It will all end up in misery. Jesus is the only way to God and through him we can all go free. Majestic Vanguard accepts that fact, and we are Gods respectfully servants![52]

In this excerpt, the band focuses on representing themselves as servants of God whose main purpose is 'to present Jesus Christ to a fallen mankind'. Their evangelistic aims are explicitly connected to their musical activity. It is important to note, as is also hinted at in this excerpt, that spreading the word may also take the form of musicians themselves stating examples and functioning as living proof of the advantages and 'great futures' of people (who are also metalheads) who have embraced the Christian faith.

Bands are also frequently asked about these issues in interviews for scenic media. For example, when asked about the main purpose and goals of the band in an interview for *Devotion Hard Music Magazine* back in 2003, the Finnish unblack band Bleakwail simply stated: '1. To preach the gospel for metal people. 2. To play good music to the same people.'[53] However, not all bands represent their understandings of themselves and their activities in such unambiguous terms. Some bands rather choose to pursue a form of evangelism more geared towards encouraging discussion and debate. Let us consider one final example of such an approach that appears in the form of a purpose-statement on the webpages of the German band Ancient Prophecy. Originally written in German, it also attests to how the main internal discourses of the transnational scene have spread to different countries and transcended language barriers:

We make music in praise of God. He should stand center stage, not us. Our lyrics are not about great feats, dragons, superficial love, or direct social critique…We want to be present as Christians in the metal scene and testify to the possibility of having a real relationship to the God described in the Bible. The band was founded with the purpose of passing on the 'good news' described in the New Testament.[54]

This excerpt offers an example of musicians representing themselves as servants or tools of God. As the band states, God occupies 'center stage' in their activity as a band and, moreover, that spreading the 'good news' of the Bible is their principal aim. It is important to note that, although it can be formulated in different ways, this way of representing one of the principal aims and purposes of Christian metal has proven enduring. This particular discourse has thus remained relatively stable over time. When appearing in written form in Christian metal media or in the mission statements of bands, this discourse tends to appear in largely similar and often quite explicit forms. Moreover, this discourse typically also represents metal music in itself in terms of a God-given tool that is in turn neutral in itself. Musicians also repeatedly represent themselves as servants of a higher evangelistic cause, and their musical activities, on the whole, are also typically represented as being primarily directed towards this cause rather than personal gain or fame. Moreover, Christian metal is also often represented as an alternative, and frequently also as an *effective*, means of evangelism that is particularly suited for reaching certain groups of people such as secular metalheads. This is essentially what makes it 'alternative' in this context. Even so, in various ways, all of the examples cited above express the notion of a 'metal ministry' that is able to reach places that more traditional modes of evangelism cannot. Many of these examples also simultaneously highlight Christian metal's edifying and inspirational functions for Christian metalheads themselves. As such, this discourse also connects with the broader 'Christian metal is an alternative form of religious expression'- discourse discussed above.

'Christian metal is a legitimate form of religious expression and evangelism'

As has been noted many times, the seemingly radical ideas, aesthetics and imagery used within Christian metal have not always been accepted within more conservative Christian circles. Indeed, some Christian metalheads may even feel rejected within more traditional church settings. This was one of the main reasons behind the establishment of the *Sanctuary*-movement in 1984 as well as the forming of alternative 'metal parish-movements' in countries such as Sweden, Germany, Brazil and Mexico. Although attitudes have become increasingly accepting, Christian metal is still repeatedly defended against detractors and represented as a fully legitimate means of religious expression and evangelism. This discourse also underlies the already mentioned practice of writing so-called 'Christian metal apologetics', that is, detailed defenses of Christian metal that are primarily directed towards Christian critics of Christian metal. Essentially, this discourse represents Christian metal as a fully viable contemporary means of religious expression and evangelism that does not shun the new and innovative. Christian metalheads' choice of music and look is defended in a number of ways, one of the most common being the already mentioned argument that a musical style as such cannot be regarded as either good or bad/evil, the lyrics and how one uses the music being the all-important question. All this, however, depends much on the general religious mood and milieu of the social and cultural contexts in which Christian metalheads find themselves. In spite of the increasingly accepting attitudes of most churches towards Christian metal, the 'Christian metal is a legitimate form of religious expression and evangelism'-discourse continues to constitute a central element of the internal discursive construction of today's transnational scene. This discourse has also lurked in the background in many of the examples discussed above. Importantly, there is also a sense in which it functions as a way for the scene as a whole to legitimize itself for itself. The well-known *The Metal for Jesus Page*, which has been quoted several times above, contains a particularly detailed defense of Christian metal. The section 'Christian rock – friend or foe?' outlines '7 Reasons Why It's OK To ROCK FOR JESUS!' The section starts out thus:

> **You can't limit God to only work thru worship and gospel music.** GOD IS much BIGGER THAN YOUR MUSICTASTE and He can use anyone and anything to spread his Word. The Bible tells us that God even spoke thru a Donkey!! <Numeri 22> And if He can speak thru a donkey He can surely speak thru Christian Metal!
>
> Cause there is no limitations to God. He works thru any musicstyle and anyone that are submitted to Him.<Luke 1:37, Jer 32:27> And who are you that try to take God's place and say that He doesn't like this or that music style just because you don't?? Do you really know??[55]

A bit further down, it continues:

> **God wants EVERYONE to be saved** not just the ones who wear three-piece-suits! <1 Tim 2:3-4, 2 Peter 3:9> Therefore He speaks and works in different ways to spread His kingdom. We are all different therefore God use us in different ways. And you can't win these Heavy Metal dudes with gospelmusic! They would just laugh at you and walk away. Therefore there need to be Christian bands that play Heavy Metal so these dudes can have something to relate to and then be able to get the message in a way and language they understand.
>
> ...
>
> <1 Cor 9:19-23> said that we should **be all to all men to at least win some for Jesus!** There we got it. God wants us to go the extra mile for these people so they can get the message and go to heaven instead of hell. Therefore the Christian Metal bands dress like the audience so they can get their ear so they can relate to them and then understand that Jesus is something for them too![56]

Here, Christian metal is defended on the basis of constituting an effective means of reaching out to people who would never be interested in receiving the Christian message served in a more traditional way. In addition, it is also suggested that Christian 'metal missionaries' consciously choose to evangelize to groups that tend to fall outside the grasp of the evangelistic outreach of most other Christian churches and groups. Christian metal is distinguished from these other forms of evangelism through consciously approaching possible converts in a language they can relate to. This is the primary argument most commonly employed to establish Christian metal's legitimacy as an alternative, fully viable, and indeed effective, means of evangelism. As seen here, this discourse may also become intimately connected with the other two main discourses outlined above. As the text quoted above also includes biblical references the argument for Christian metal's legitimacy is also made on biblical grounds.[57] At one point in the defense, drawing on Psalms 150, worshipping the Lord through metal is represented as an updated version of a style of worship that is encouraged by the Bible in the first place. This makes it possible for the author to also proclaim that the Bible actually 'supports heavy music' and that 'God supports heavy metal',[58] the louder the better. At other points in this defense, the author also goes on to express astonishment and frustration over the fact that Christian criticism of Christian metal ever existed in the first place and still to some degree continues to exist today. It is argued that if all Christians realized that Christian metal is 'a friend to the church'[59] the door could be closed on such debates once and for all. However, since the author also seems to suggest that it is unlikely for that to happen any time soon, a continued aggressive defense of Christian metal's legitimacy is necessary.

However, this discourse is not always expressed in such detailed ways. For example, when musicians touch upon these issues in interviews for scenic media, they usually only use some of the arguments outlined in the above excerpt or just allude to some of them in passing. Nevertheless, scenic media dealing with these issues do provide scene members with clearly articulated and detailed versions of this discourse. Let us now consider parts of a different type of Christian metal defense called 'Christian metal: A Defence' that used to be posted on a now defunct New Zealand-based site dedicated to extreme Christian metal styles called *Unblack Noise*:

> It has been said that metal stands for power and rebellion against the prevailing culture, values and structures in which it finds itself. This is considered incompatible with the assumed 'submission' that Christians uphold.... A Christian is the most rebellious type, as they will rebel against a society that allows permissive or zero morality to run rampant. As for being 'counter-cultural', metal and Christians share something in common, though maybe only in part and not in the way expected. While census' here show that about 70% of people are 'Christian', let's cut the crap. If that were true, then Sunday would be a hell busy day for most

churches.... Being a Bible-believing Christian, (and I am not referring to the so-called Liberal Christian crap), is about as counter-cultural as one can get while remaining within the law. Metal has nothing uncommon with Christians on that score.... The bottom line is that it is just music, connected absolutely to no particular lifestyle or value system and, like any other art form, open to reinterpretation. Christians will always be in it.[60]

This defense provides a rather different approach to the issue of Christian metal's legitimacy than the previous excerpts quoted above. For one thing, the author chooses to approach widespread notions about the meaning of secular metal in a much more straightforward way. However, exactly *who* the author wishes to address with these arguments remains less clear. When Christians are talked about as 'the most rebellious type', this could be interpreted as being directed against detractors within the secular metal community who accuse Christian metal of not being sufficiently 'rebellious'. However, it may just as well be directed at Christian detractors who accuse Christian metalheads of having accommodated metal music and style to such a degree as to having lost their identity as Christians. In addition, it also clearly alludes to the notion of the 'true believer's' rebellion and resistance against a fallen society and culture. Significantly, towards the end, the author also expresses the commonly held notion of all musical forms being neutral in themselves and 'open to reinterpretation'. Christian metal is thus legitimated in a somewhat reversed manner. It is not represented as something that is supported by biblical texts or as a particularly effective way for reaching certain groups of people. Instead, it is legitimated on the grounds that 'it is just music'; hence, Christians may well 'be in it'.

These above examples serve to illustrate the many forms in which the 'Christian metal is a legitimate form of religious expression and evangelism'-discourse may appear, sometimes more explicitly, sometimes more vaguely. The important point to note, though, is that this discourse continues to appear in spite of Christian metal having achieved wider acceptance in Christian circles during the past decade. As noted above, representing Christian metal as a legitimate form of religious expression and evangelism also functions as a way for the scene as a whole to legitimate its own existence and evangelistic mandate.

'Christian metal is an alternative to secular metal'

This discourse principally deals with distinguishing Christian metal's 'positive' message from the perceived potentially destructive messages presented by many secular metal bands. As in the case of CCM more generally, this discourse thus also underlies the rationale for the very existence of a separate Christian metal scene, that is, a scene that is at least partly separated from other secular metal scenes by the virtue of being comprised by Christian people and having an expressed aim of making metal that strives to convey and spread a 'basic' Christian message. As noted in the previous chapter, some Christian metal general resource websites contain detailed comparison charts designed to aid Christians in finding 'positive' Christian sound-a-likes of popular secular bands. In this way, although the most obvious difference between Christian and secular metal lies in the content of the lyrics, this discourse is also directed at distinguishing Christian metal *culture* from secular metal culture more generally through representing it as providing a more 'positive' and 'meaningful' alternative.

As with the other key discourses discussed above, this discourse also appears in many shapes and forms. For example, it surfaced in many of the mission statements of scenic institutions quoted in the previous chapter. A more typical example of this discourse at play can be found in the following statement that used to be posted on the front page of the Christian metal Internet site *JesusMetal*:

> Here at JesusMetal we will introduce you to the Extreme Side of Christianity, or the safe side of Metal, it's both really. Here you'll find all about positive metal, with sometimes christian lyrics, sometimes a band just has a Christian background. We try to keep the site 100% christian, but it might happen that accidentally a secular band is added, because it was promoted by a Christian company. If you find any band on here that is not christian, please e-mail. We will dig deeper into a band and decide whether or not we'll delete the band from our archives.[61]

As mentioned above, scenic institutions are often seen as serving important gatekeeping functions and this excerpt clearly illustrates how the administrators of *JesusMetal* have assumed this role. They can be said to draw on the 'Christian metal is an alternative to secular metal'-discourse through stating that *JesusMetal* 'will introduce you to the Extreme Side of Christianity, or the 'safe side of Metal'. In this way, Christian metal is primarily distinguished from secular metal by the virtue of being 'safe'. However, by also stating that *JesusMetal* 'will introduce you to the Extreme Side of Christianity', the administrators also draw on the 'Christian metal is an alternative form of religious expression'-and 'Christian metal is a legitimate form of religious expression and evangelism'-discourses. The above excerpt, in any case, clearly aims to convey the idea that Christian metal should not only be clearly distinguished from secular metal but be thoroughly separated from it as well. As already noted, this is a much-contested approach within the wider transnational scene.

Indeed, bands who seek acceptance within the wider metal community may regard separation as hampering their opportunities to represent a Christian voice in the wider metal-world. Most Christian metalheads seem to favour a delicate balance between separation and integration. However, such a balance may be extremely difficult to uphold since notions about absolute separation on the one hand and full integration on the other seem ultimately incompatible. Bands who favour integration typically choose to downplay the directness of their Christian message. Because of this, they are sometimes seen as yielding to the demands of both the secular metal community as well as commercial pressures of the wider secular popular cultural mainstream. The question of lyrical content thus lies at the very core of these debates. This, however, has not changed the general notion of Christian metal as constituting a positive alternative to secular metal. Christian metal bands who make compromises with their message in exchange for the possibility of wider success in the secular market may still continue to emphasize that they make 'positive' metal. As already noted, in such cases what kind of a message a band actually conveys through its lyrics usually becomes secondary to what kinds of messages it consciously leaves out. But bands are rarely judged solely on the basis of how clearly or explicitly they convey a Christian message anyway. Purely musical merits also play an important role. In other words, a band that conveys an explicitly Christian message also needs to be musically creative in order to achieve wider success even within just the Christian scene.

The 'Christian metal is an alternative to secular metal'-discourse may therefore also simply be used to represent Christian metal as lacking the perceived potentially destructive messages of much secular metal. On the other hand, it may also be used to emphasize the 'meaningfulness' of Christian metal *culture* on the whole as opposed to the 'meaninglessness' of much of secular metal culture, associated as it often tends to be with destructive lifestyles involving such things as alcohol and substance abuse. This discourse thus also has important bearings for internal scenic understandings of the Christian scene as an alternative metal scene more broadly. However, even though Christian metal is commonly distinguished from and sometimes directly juxtaposed to secular metal in various ways, not all Christian metalheads are as concerned with actually replacing their favourite secular bands with Christian alternatives. Many Christian metalheads are avid fans of secular metal as well, which is not to say that they always approve of the messages they encounter through it. While some Christian metalheads consciously and deliberately eschew all secular metal, many others opt for a less unconditional stance and only avoid listening to bands with the most overt satanic and anti-Christian lyrics. Others just simply ignore the whole issue altogether.

External discursive construction

The Christian scene is also discursively constructed from 'outside' of itself in various ways. When approaching the external discursive construction of the scene, we might begin by looking more closely at Christian metal's position within broader Protestant denominational contexts. As we have seen above, in addition to the extreme music, Christian metal has also fully embraced the metal rhetoric and aesthetic and no other contemporary form of popular music has been as consistently criticized and condemned by conservative Christian groups as metal has.

Indeed, there are still some conservative Christian groups (for example US-based *Dial the Truth Ministries*[62]) who vehemently oppose all forms of rock music and everything related to it, including Christian rock. Such groups tend to represent metal as an utterly unredeemable 'satanic' style of music. In such a view, the very notion of 'Christian' metal is therefore viewed as oxymoronic. Other strictly conservative Christian groups who accept some forms of popular music being used for religious purposes often nevertheless tend to be particularly suspicious towards metal. In such cases, metal is simply not regarded as a suitable form of music through which to express the Christian faith.

As noted above, there is also the additional question of the metal style and look. Long hair for men, black clothes, leather jackets, spikes and chains may still not be deemed as suitable ways for Christians to appear within certain more strictly conservative Christian circles. It is also worth noting that, if approached separately from the overall internal discursive construction of the scene, the 'Christian metal is a legitimate form of religious expression and evangelism'-discourse examined above might lead us to think that Christian metal continues to encounter much resistance within wider Christian circles. However, as pointed out above, viewing it separately from the other three key internal scenic discourses would be highly misleading. As noted, this is because this discourse has also come to function as a principal way for the Christian metal scene to legitimate itself for itself.

It has become difficult to find sufficient grounds for arguing that Christian metal would remain commonly criticized by Christian groups nowadays. As Christian metal has become more visible through the development of a lively transnational scene, and following the increasingly accepting attitudes of most churches, the earlier wave of initial Christian resistance to Christian metal as explored above seems to have largely ebbed away. This is not to say that such resistance may not still exist; only that it is no longer commonplace. I wish to point out, however, that these are general conclusions that I have arrived at based on my own reading of Christian metal media and my many interviews and discussions with people involved in the maintenance of transnational scenic media as well as core members of the Christian metal scene in Finland.[63] The situation in much more religiously diverse countries such as the United States, however, is impossible to assess. Considering the exceptionally wide range of different types of Christian churches in the United States, it is fair to assume that attitudes towards Christian metal range across the whole spectrum from total acceptance to fierce opposition, even though outright opposition does indeed appear to have become much less common than it once used to be. This may, at least partly, be one reason for the continuing need to legitimate and defend Christian metal in transnational scenic discourse.

However, by and large, Christian metalheads and musicians appear to have good relationships to their own churches. The activities of Christian metal bands may not be interpreted in terms of extensions of the activities of their respective churches, but it appears that the evangelistic efforts of bands tend to be appreciated by their own churches. It should be noted, however, that individual members of the same band may well be affiliated with different churches. For example, in a Nordic context, it is not unusual for bands to have both Lutheran and Pentecostal members. It should also be noted here that discourses pertaining to Christian metal within different Christian churches are never all that far removed from similar discourses within the scene itself. There is thus a sense in which such discourse is only partly 'external'. To varying degrees, depending from case to case, the key internal discourses of the scene outlined above are all affected by the external discursive construction of the scene. A more thorough examination might of course bring some particular forms of external Christian discursive construction to light, but such an inquiry would extend beyond the purview of our discussion here.

As has been noted several times already, another significant form of external discursive construction that more directly also influences the internal discursive construction of the scene is that of the wider secular metal community. This particular form of discursive construction has so far presented a rather different picture of what Christian metal is all 'about'. As noted, although they may not approve of it (and many certainly do not), the existence of Christian metal is still widely known among secular metal audiences. Because of its religious outlook and more or less pronounced evangelistic agenda, Christian metal has, however, never gained wider acceptance within the wider secular metal community. To the contrary, it has often been ridiculed, discriminated against and at times been vehemently opposed within certain sections of secular metal culture. As noted above, metal has often been interpreted as constituting a form of rebellion against the stifling confines of post-industrial late modern society and culture – an understanding that also undoubtedly has become at least partly internalized by metal culture itself. Because of this, Christian metal is often viewed as completely antithetical to what metal is 'supposed' to be about. The above mentioned notorious example of the secular black metal fan who became so provoked by the very existence of the Swedish unblack band Admonish that he set up his own anti-Admonish website in the mid-1990s may serve as one example of this. To take another example, the major secular label *Nuclear Blast Records* reportedly received a series of threats after having released unblack band Horde's controversial release *Hellig Usvart*.[64]

From the vantage point of many secular metalheads, then, Christian metal is typically viewed as oxymoronic, a complete contradiction in terms. The lyrics of Christian metal have also frequently been the subject of ridicule within secular metal culture. For example, it is not unusual for secular metal commentators, such as album-reviewers, who happen to like the music of a Christian band to dismiss its lyrics, and thereby often also the band as such. Christian metal is thus typically represented as an appropriation of metal music and style for purely evangelistic purposes and, therefore, as constituting a 'treason' against metal.

In addition, Christian metal bands are also often accused of being musically poor. As seen above, earlier bands emphasized evangelistic outreach over musical creativity and technical ability; a way of approaching music-making that has become increasingly widely contested within the Christian scene itself. However, although they are likely to disapprove of the lyrics, secular audiences tend to be more accepting of Christian bands that are particularly musically creative. For example, bands such as Mortification, Extol, Crimson Moonlight and Immortal Souls have managed to gain some degree of wider respect in the secular metal community in spite of being widely known as Christian bands. The main criterion seems to be that, if the music is truly creative and innovative, then it is possible to simply ignore the content of the lyrics. But, unless it is simply dismissed as a laughing matter, direct evangelistic activity is rarely accepted by secular audiences. This also has to do with the pervasive and deeply engrained individualistic ethos of secular metal culture, which is perhaps where the problem that secular audiences tend to have with Christian metal is essentially rooted.

As we have seen, such external discursive construction also affects the internal discursive construction of the Christian scene to some degree. However, as already noted and further illustrated by the key internal discourses discussed above, today's Christian metal scene seems primarily concerned with constructing an understanding of itself as an alternative way of 'doing' religion, and this includes evangelism as well. As such, it could be argued that the Christian metal scene's engagement with the broader secular metal community so far has largely remained outweighed by its engagement with itself.

7

Concluding Remarks: Christian Metal, Alternative Religious Expression and Identity

Throughout the chapters of this book, we have explored the phenomenon of Christian metal from a range of different angles. It is now time to briefly summarize and discuss some of the most important insights about the phenomenon of Christian metal that previous chapters have aimed to convey.

In full accordance with metal's uncompromising attitude and general lyrical and aesthetic conventions, we have seen that Christian metal song lyrics often deal with strong and sometimes radical themes supported by equally strong imagery and aesthetics. We might now pose the tentative question of whether Christian metal's use of such uncompromising themes, imagery and aesthetics perhaps could be seen to reflect more uncompromising religious views among its musicians and fans. Indeed, as we discussed in Chapter 3, Christian metal musicians often point out the 'radical' character of the Christian message itself. On closer inspection, however, the rhetoric and imagery used in Christian metal should perhaps not be interpreted as being all that 'radical' after all. It all depends on how that concept is understood. It is important to note that, most of the time, the ideas that Christian metal bands express through their lyrics and imagery do not deviate, to any significant degree, from the teachings of most Protestant traditions. The *way* and *style* in which they are expressed and used, however, frequently does. Calls to spiritual warfare and rebellion against sin do not constitute a particularly visible part of the rhetoric of mainline Protestant traditions such as Lutheranism or Anglicanism, but they do appear all the more frequently in evangelical, Charismatic and Pentecostal contexts. This also needs to be understood in relation to these latter traditions being more concerned with cultivating the experiential and subjective side of faith.[1] Their respective worship styles also emphasize active bodily participation, feeling and emotion rather than simply listening, receiving and interpreting. Even so, none of the worship practices found within any of these traditions can be directly compared with the intensity and aggressiveness of the metal experience. Because of this, Christian metal scenes also provide their members with a space in which they can express their Christian faith in strong and radical terms in close connection to the intense musical experience that metal provides. Importantly, Christian metalheads may not find many, if any, opportunities for such forms of religious expression within the more traditional worship settings of their own churches.

As discussed in Chapter 4, Western popular music always carries with it an 'echo' of its transgressive potential, sometimes actualized and sometimes not. It is a potential that tends to become actualized when popular music scenes are less concerned about maintaining communal structures and institutions and go through periods of aesthetic innovation. It is the drive to innovate that carries with it the threat of transgression, aesthetic and otherwise. While popular music scenes are more often sites of stability than sites of change, the potential for radical aesthetic innovation and the transgression it can produce is nevertheless ever-present. In the long run, a lack of a drive to aesthetically innovate, or at the very least the desire to keep innovation and transcendence within 'safe' bounds, risks limiting Christian metal's transgressive potentials. The 'transgression-free transcendence' typically favoured by Christian popular music in general may indeed bring about experiences of rapturous encounter with the divine among its audiences, but it remains a type of transcendence that is firmly rooted in worldly, bounded being that does not challenge the arbitrary nature of institutions and structures. Whether Christian metal will meet these challenges remains to be seen.

When it comes to its general ideological character, the Christian metal scene can be described as being rather conservative regarding doctrine and beliefs but progressive and innovative regarding expression and practice. Such attitudes regarding issues of religious expression and practice could also clearly be viewed in direct relation to the changing face and increasing diversity of contemporary evangelicalism more generally, as discussed in Chapter 1. This is perhaps particularly so in the case of the larger North and Latin American scenes, which are all embedded in broader social and cultural climates of which evangelicalism, including its Charismatic and Pentecostal variant, constitutes a major religious current. In line with these more general developments, Christian metal is typically represented as a complement and alternative to other more traditional modes of religious expression. This, however, should clearly not be taken to mean that Christian metalheads reject more traditional modes of Christian expression and worship. Generally speaking, the relationships between Christian metalheads and their own churches are overwhelmingly positive. For example, although Christian metalheads may be critical and feel alienated from the worship practices of their own churches, such critical stances rarely translate into an expressed disapproval or dismissal of these churches as such. Besides, larger Protestant traditions tend to be internally diverse and encompass various more liberal, progressive, revivalist, conservative and other types of 'affinity groups'.[2] Christian metalheads can no doubt be viewed as forming precisely such an affinity group. But, importantly, this is an affinity group that is intimately connected to the particular popular cultural form of metal as well as the particular scenic structure through which it is reproduced and sustained on an everyday basis.

As explored in Chapter 6, Christian metal scene members from around the world do indeed appear to hold some shared understandings regarding what they view as constituting the 'basics' of Christian faith and life. However, as just noted, some of the countries in which Christian metal has thrived differ considerably in religious mood and milieu. But even though these differences do surface in scenic discourse, they are usually represented as being secondary to a wider and more encompassing notion of Christian metal as an alternative community of believers. Again, its 'alternativeness' is rarely directed against scene member's own churches in a confrontational sense. Rather, this alternativeness mostly has to do with innovation and renewal, not rejection and open criticism. Even so, Christian metalheads from around the world nevertheless still appear to share an experience of being part of a particular form of affinity group that extends beyond their own respective churches. More importantly, through the development of a transnational Christian metal scene, they are also aware of the fact that similar affinity groups that share their concerns exist across a range of different churches and denominations in a number of other countries as well. They thus also share a notion of being part of what could be described as a wider transnational religious-musical movement, that is, a wider transnational Christian metal scene.

This sense of fellowship is further reinforced through the sense of being part of a larger community of Christian metalheads who not only share some basic aims and concerns but also a common aesthetic and style. As we have seen, the contemporary transnational scene is socially constructed as an open Christian space in which people with different denominational affiliations can meet, exchange ideas and, equally importantly, share and express their appreciation for metal with likeminded people. The scene should thus primarily be understood to function as a space in which Christians who are into metal can express their faith in an alternative and complementary way that is fully in line with their cultural sensibilities. It might thus also be possible to describe it in terms of a cross-denominational religious community with a set of shared aims and concerns. Indeed, this is also how the scene is frequently represented in transnational internal scenic discourse.

Finally, what can be said about the Christian metal scene providing its members with resources for the forming of an alternative Christian identity? Although scene members may be critical of certain aspects of traditional church practice, particularly regarding musical issues, the scene can nevertheless be described as a space that is characterized by a 'conscious counter-identification against institutionally and socially assigned identities, and the meanings and values that they are seen to represent' (Weedon, 2004). While it is clear that scene members do not hold directly dismissive attitudes towards traditional and conventional modes of religious expression and practice in general they do, however, actively choose to express their religiosity in an alternative and complementary way. The manner and style in which scene members choose to express their faith and thereby their understanding of themselves in relation to their own churches is also fundamentally influenced by the particular popular musical form of metal and thus very different from more institutionally bound and traditional understandings of religious identity, expression and practice. Christian metal can therefore be described as an expressly different way of 'doing' religion. A more multifaceted picture of Christian metal's ability to function as an alternative way of 'doing' religion also emerges when issues of style and the experiential, sensory and bodily dimensions of Christian metal also are taken into account.

In a broader perspective, all present-day cases of groups of Christians embracing new media and popular cultural forms need to be understood in relation to wider processes of religious change, and particularly in connection to accelerating processes of de-traditionalization and a corresponding increasingly general widespread individualization and privatization of religious life and practice on the whole. De-traditionalization, however, also occurs *within* religious communities, as witnessed by modern-time transformations of evangelicalism. Generally speaking, it seems clear that popular cultural forms and new media have come to play an ever more central role in relocating religious expression and practice beyond the borders of traditional religious communities into the much more unpredictable and essentially non-regulated wider popular cultural realm. Depending on the broader context, however, it might be useful to distinguish between thoroughgoing de-traditionalization on the one hand and particular de-traditionalizing *tendencies* on the other. It seems reasonable to presume that the 'locations' of religion may have changed, diversified and multiplied more in some particular broader social, cultural and religious contexts than they have in others. This, I would argue, applies more generally to Christian/evangelical popular cultural groups in different parts of the world as they are embedded in different religious climates. Christian metal is no exception in this regard. Any exploration of the meanings and functions that Christian metal is ascribed by its musicians and fans needs to take account of the particular social, cultural and religious environments in which these musicians and fans find themselves. Although this book has focused on Christian metal on a transnational level, the core areas of today's transnational scene do not only differ considerably with regard to general religious mood and milieu but also with regard to the degrees and scale on which religious de-traditionalization can be said to have occurred.

Considering the general evangelical orientation of the Christian metal scene, all of the above observations could also be viewed in relation to the changing face and increasing diversity of modern evangelicalism in the main, which has increasingly moved away from traditional institutional organizational structures and hierarchical forms of oversight, become ever more occupied with the self and subjective experiences and embraced a wide range of new media and cultural practices in the creation of new forms of religious expression and styles of worship. As with many other Christian popular music scenes, the transnational Christian metal scene should clearly be viewed in relation to such more widespread trends.

Notes

Chapter 1

1 E.g. Robert Walser, *Running with the Devil. Power, Gender and Madness in Heavy Metal Music* (Hanover, CT: Wesleyan University Press, 1993), p. 28.
2 Jeremy Wallach, Harris M. Berger and Paul D. Greene, eds, *Metal Rules the Globe: Heavy Metal Music Around the World* (Durham, NC: Duke University Press, 2011).
3 E.g. Deena Weinstein, *Heavy Metal: The Music and Its Culture* (New York, NY: Da Capo Press, 2000).
4 E.g. Weinstein, *Heavy Metal*; Walser, *Running*; Keith Kahn-Harris, *Extreme Metal: Music and Culture on the Edge* (Oxford: Berg, 2007).
5 Andy A. Brown, 'Heavy Metal and Subcultural Theory: A Paradigmatic Case of Neglect?', in *The Post-subcultures Reader*, eds, David Muggleton and Rupert Weinzierl (New York, NY. Berg, 2003).
6 Kahn-Harris, *Extreme Metal*, p. 17.
7 Jeffrey Arnett, *Metalheads: Heavy Metal Music and Adolescent Alienation* (New York, NY: Westview Press, 1996).
8 Harris M. Berger, *Metal, Rock and Jazz: Perception and the Phenomenology of Musical Experience* (Hanover, NH: University Press of New England, 1999).
9 Kahn-Harris, *Extreme Metal*.
10 Kahn-Harris, *Extreme Metal*, p. 10.
11 Kahn-Harris, *Extreme Metal*, p. 10.
12 E.g. Walser, *Running*, p. xvii.
13 A different version of such an argument is also presented in Thomas Bossius, *Med framtiden i backspegeln. Black metal och transkulturen. Ungdomar, musik och religion i en senmodern värld* [With the Future in the Rear-view Mirror: Black Metal and Trance Culture: Youth, Music, and Religion in a Late Modern World]. Diss. (Göteborg: Diadalos, 2003).
14 Kahn-Harris, *Extreme Metal*, p. 11.
15 E.g. Stan Denski and David Sholle, 'Metal Men and Glamour Boys: Gender Performance in Heavy Metal', in *Men, Masculinity and the Media*, ed. Steve Craig (Newbury Park, CA: Sage, 1992).
16 E.g. Niall R. W. Scott, 'Heavy Metal and the Deafening Threat of the Apolitical', in *Heavy Metal: Controversies and Countercultures*, eds, Titus Hjelm, Keith Kahn-Harris and Mark LeVine (London: Equinox Publishing, 2013).

NOTES

17 Robert Wright, '"I'd Sell You Suicide": Pop Music and Moral Panic in the Age of Marilyn Manson', *Popular Music* 19/3 (2000), pp. 365–385.
18 See the contributions to Wallach, Berger and Greene, *Metal Rules the Globe*.
19 Gerd Bayer, ed., *Heavy Metal Music in Britain* (Hampshire: Ashgate, 2009).
20 Wallach, Berger and Greene, *Metal Rules the Globe*.
21 Titus Hjelm, Keith Kahn-Harris and Mark LeVine, eds, *Heavy Metal: Controversies and Countercultures* (London: Equinox Publishing, 2013).
22 These include Philip Bashe, *Heavy Metal Thunder* (London: Omnibus Press, 1986); Gavin Baddeley, *Lucifer Rising: A Book of Sin, Devil Worship and Rock'n' Roll* (London: Plexus Publishing Limited, 1999); Natalie Purcell, *Death Metal Music: The Passion and Politics of a Subculture* (Jefferson, NC: McFarland & Company, Inc. Publishers, 2003); Michael Moynihan and Didrik Söderlind, *Lords of Chaos: The Bloody Rise of the Satanic Metal Underground* (Venice, CA: Feral House, 2003[1998]); Ian Christe, *Sound of the Beast: The Complete Headbanging History of Heavy Metal* (New York, NY: HarperCollins Publishers, 2004); Albert Mudrian, *Choosing Death: The Improbable History of Death Metal & Grindcore* (Los Angeles, CA: Feral House, 2004).
23 Kahn-Harris, *Extreme Metal*, p. 9.
24 Matt Hills, *Fan Cultures* (London: Routledge, 2002).
25 Ronald Byrnside, 'The Formation of a Musical Style: Early Rock', in *Contemporary Music and Music Cultures*, eds, Charles Hamm, Bruno Nettl and Ronald Byrnside (Englewood Cliffs, NJ: Prentice Hall, 1975).
26 Weinstein, *Heavy Metal*, pp. 6–8.
27 Weinstein, *Heavy Metal*, pp. 6–8.
28 Weinstein, *Heavy Metal*, pp. 6–8.
29 Weinstein, *Heavy Metal: A Cultural Sociology* (New York, NY: Lexington Books, 1991), pp. 11–21.
30 Weinstein, *Heavy Metal: A Cultural*, p. 14.
31 Weinstein, *Heavy Metal: A Cultural*, p. 22.
32 Weinstein, *Heavy Metal: A Cultural*, p. 12.
33 Weinstein, *Heavy Metal: A Cultural*, pp. 93–98.
34 Walser, *Running*, pp. 63–107.
35 Weinstein, *Heavy Metal: A Cultural*, p. 23, pp. 21–30.
36 Walser, *Running*, p. 2.
37 Walser, *Running*, pp. 41–51; Weinstein, *Heavy Metal: A Cultural*, pp. 21–28.
38 Kahn-Harris, *Extreme Metal*, p. 2.
39 Weinstein, *Heavy Metal: A Cultural*, pp. 28–34, 121–129.
40 Weinstein, *Heavy Metal*, p. 35.
41 Walser, *Running*, p. 151.
42 Weinstein, *Heavy Metal: A Cultural*, p. 39.
43 Weinstein, *Heavy Metal: A Cultural*, pp. 38–39.

44 Kahn-Harris, *Extreme Metal*, p. 3.
45 Weinstein, *Heavy Meta*, pp. 50–52.
46 Kahn-Harris, *Extreme Metal*, p. 5.
47 Kahn-Harris, *Extreme Metal*, p. 35; Cf. Mudrian, *Choosing Death*.
48 Kahn-Harris, *Extreme Metal*, pp. 34–37; see also Andy Bennett, *Cultures of Popular Music* (Maidenhead: Open University Press, 2001), pp. 42–56.
49 Bennett, *Cultures of Popular Music*, p. 5.
50 Cf. Marcus Moberg, 'Popular Culture and the 'Darker Side' of Alternative Spirituality: The Case of Metal Music', in *Postmodern Spirituality*, ed., Tore Ahlbäck Scripta Instituti Donneriani Aboensis XXI (Åbo: The Donner Institute for Research in Religious and Cultural History, 2009), p. 139.
51 Kahn-Harris, *Extreme Metal*, p. 30.
52 Kahn-Harris, *Extreme Metal*, pp. 34–43.
53 Kahn-Harris, *Extreme Metal*, p. 43.
54 Kahn-Harris, *Extreme Metal*, pp. 3–5.
55 Weinstein, *Heavy Metal*, p. 39.
56 Weinstein, *Heavy Metal*, p. 39.
57 Weinstein, *Heavy Metal*, pp. 245–262.
58 E.g. Weinstein, *Heavy Metal*, p. 254; Walser, *Running*, p. 139; for a detailed account of metal-related controversies in the 1980s and 1990s, see Titus Hjelm, Keith Kahn-Harris and Mark LeVine, 'Introduction: Heavy Metal as Controversy and Counterculture', in *Heavy Metal: Controversies and Countercultures*, eds, Titus Hjelm, Keith Kahn-Harris and Mark LeVine (London: Equinox Publishing, 2013); Wright, 'I'd Sell You Suicide'.
59 E.g. Walser, *Running*, p. 138; Lynn Schofield Clark, *From Angels to Aliens: Teenagers, the Media, and the Supernatural* (New York, NY: Oxford University Press US, 2005), p. 47.
60 Weinstein, *Heavy Metal*, pp. 258–262; Walser, *Running*, pp. 139–143; Eileen Luhr, *Witnessing Suburbia: Conservatives and Christian Youth Culture* (Berkeley: University of California Press, 2009), pp. 46–47.
61 E.g. Carl A Raschke, *Painted Black: From Drug Killings to Heavy Metal: The Alarming True Story of How Satanism Is Terrorizing Our Communities* (San Francisco, CA: Harper & Row, 1990).
62 E.g. Wright, 'I'd Sell You Suicide', p. 370.
63 Kahn-Harris, *Extreme Metal*, pp. 141–156; Weinstein, *Heavy Metal: A Cultural*, pp. 42–43, 53–57.
64 These extraordinary events have been documented by Moynihan and Söderlind in *Lords of Chaos* which also contains rich interview material with many scene members who were implicated in these events.
65 E.g. Moybihan and Söderlind, *Lords of Chaos*; *Metal: A Headbanger's Journey* (2005).
66 Cf. Christopher Partridge, *The Re-enchantment of the West (vol. 2): Alternative Spiritualities, Sacralization, Popular Culture and Occulture* (London: Continuum, 2005), p. 235.

67 Arnett *Heavy Metal*, pp. 121–129.
68 Kahn-Harris, *Extreme Metal*, p. 145.
69 E.g. Bossius, *Med framtiden*; Helen Farley, 'Demons, Devils and Witches: The Occult in Heavy Metal Music', in *Heavy Metal Music in Britain*, ed., Gerd Bayer (Aldershot: Ashgate, 2009); Jonathan Cordero, 'Unveiling Satan's Wrath: Aesthetics and Ideology in Anti-Christian Heavy Metal', *Journal of Religion and Popular Culture* 21/1 (2009); Gry Mørk, '"With my Art I am the Fist in the Face of God": On Old-School Black Metal', *Contemporary Religious Satanism: A Critical Anthology*, ed., Jesper A. Petersen (Aldershot: Ashgate, 2009); Kennet Granholm, '"Sons of Northern Darkness": Heathen Influences in Black Metal and Neofolk Music', *Numen: International Review for the History of Religions* 58/4 (2011), pp. 514–544; Kennet Granholm 'Ritual Black Metal: Popular Music as Occult Mediation and Practice'. *Correspondences* 1/1 (2013). http://correspondencesjournal.files.wordpress.com/2013/09/11302_20537158_granholm.pdf, accessed 10 July 2014.
70 Granholm, '"Sons of Northern Darkness"'.
71 Cf. Kahn-Harris, *Extreme*, pp. 10–11.
72 Gordon Lynch, 'What is this "Religion" in the Study of Religion and Popular Culture?', in *Between Sacred and Profane: Researching Religion and Popular Culture*, ed., Gordon Lynch (London: I.B. Tauris, 2007), p. 129.
73 E.g. David Chidester, *Authentic Fakes: Religion and American Popular Culture* (Berkeley: University of California Press, 2005), p. 16.
74 Lynch, 'What is this "Religion"', pp. 127–129.
75 Sean McCloud, 'Popular Culture Fandoms, the Boundaries of Religious Studies, and the Project of the Self', *Culture and Religion* 4/2 (2003), p. 193.
76 Lynch, 'What is this' Religion', p. 128.
77 Weinstein, *Heavy Metal: A Cultural*, p. 214.
78 Weinstein, *Heavy Metal: A Cultural*, pp. 231–232.
79 Weinstein, *Heavy Metal: A Cultural*, p. 194.
80 Weinstein, *Heavy Metal: A Cultural*, p. 232.
81 E.g. Nick Couldry, *Media Rituals: A Critical Approach* (London: Routledge, 2003).
82 Robin Sylvan, *Traces of the Spirit: The Religious Dimensions of Popular Music* (New York: New York University Press, 2002).
83 Sylvan, *Traces of the Spirit*, p. 6.
84 Sylvan, *Traces of the Spirit*, p. 5.
85 Sylvan, *Traces of the Spirit*, p. 163.
86 Sylvan, *Traces of the Spirit*, p. 163.
87 Sylvan, *Traces of the Spirit*, p. 164.
88 Sylvan, *Traces of the Spirit*, p. 164.
89 Sylvan, *Traces of the Spirit*, pp. 166–168.
90 Cf. McCloud, 'Popular Culture Fandoms', pp. 191–192.
91 The same criticism also applies to the arguments on the religious dimensions of metal presented in Rupert Till, *Pop Cult: Religion and Popular Music* (London: Continuum, 2010).

NOTES

92 E.g. Stewart M. Hoover, *Religion in the Media Age* (New York, NY: Routledge, 2006); Christopher Partridge, *The Re-enchantment of the West (vol. 1): Alternative Spiritualities, Sacralization, Popular Culture and Occulture* (London: Continuum, 2004); *The Re-enchantment (vol. 2)*.

93 Jeremy Stolow, 'Religion, Media, and Globalization', in *The New Blackwell Companion to the Sociology of Religion*, ed., Bryan S. Turner (Chichester: Blackwell, 2010), p. 544.

94 E.g. Don Slater, *Consumer Culture and Modernity* (London: Wiley, 1997), pp. 24–25.

95 Tuomas Martikainen and François Gauthier, 'Introduction: Religion in Market Society', in *Religion in the Neoliberal Age: Political Economy and Modes of Governance* (Farnham: Ashgate, 2013), p. 2.

96 E.g. Anthony Giddens, *Modernity and Self-Identity: Self and Society in the Late Modern Age* (Stanford: Stanford University Press, 1991); Zygmunt Bauman, *The Individualized Society* (Cambridge: Polity Press, 2001); Ulrich Beck and Elisabeth Beck-Gernsheim, *Individualization: Institutionalized Individualism and Its Social and Political Consequences* (London: Sage, 2002).

97 Cf. Marcus Moberg, Sofia Sjö and Kennet Granholm, 'Introduction', in *Religion, Media, and Social Change*, eds, Kennet Granholm, Marcus Moberg and Sofia Sjö (London: Routledge, 2015).

98 For a good general overview of the development of the field of religion, media and culture, see, for example, Gordon Lynch, 'Media and Cultures of Everyday Life', in *The Routledge Companion to the Study of Religion*, Second edition, ed., John R. Hinnells (Oxon: Routledge, 2010).

99 E.g. Bruce D. Forbes and Jeffrey H. Mahan, eds, *Religion and Popular Culture in America* (Berkeley, University of California Press, 2000); Daniel A. Stout and Judith M. Buddenbaum, eds, *Religion and Popular Culture: Studies on the Interaction of Worldviews* (Ames: Iowa State University Press, 2001), Gordon Lynch, ed., *Between Sacred and Profane: Researching Religion and Popular Culture* (London: I.B. Tauris, 2007); Lynn Schofield Clark, *From Angels to Aliens*; Partridge, *The Re-enchantment (vol. 1); The Re-enchantment (vol. 2)*; Adam Possamai, *Religion and Popular Culture: A Hyper-Real Testament* (Brussels: P. I. E. Peter Lang, 2005).

100 Gordon Lynch, *Understanding Theology and Popular Culture* (Oxford: Blackwell Publishing, 2005), p. 2.

101 Lynch, *Understanding Theology*, p. 14.

102 Lynch, *Understanding Theology*, p. 15.

103 Lynch, *Understanding Theology*, pp. 15–16.

104 Lynch, *Understanding Theology*, p. 19.

105 Partridge, *The Re-enhantment vol. 1*, p. 123.

106 Cf. Marcus Moberg and Sofia Sjö, 'Mass-Mediated popular Culture and Religious Socialisation', in *Religion, Media, and Social Change*, eds, Kennet Granholm, Marcus Moberg and Sofia Sjö (London: Routledge, 2015).

107 Stewart M. Hoover, *Religion*, p. 284.

108 Stewart M. Hoover, *Religion*, p. 290.
109 Lynch, 'Media and Cultures', p. 552.
110 Bruce D. Forbes, 'Introduction' in *Religion and Popular Culture in America*, eds, Bruce D. Forbes and Jeffrey H. Mahan (Berkeley. University of California Press, 2000), pp. 10–17.
111 E.g. Manuel A. Vasquez, 'Tracking Global Evangelical Christianity', *Journal of the American Academy of Religion* 71/1 (2003).
112 Heather Hendershot, *Shaking the World for Jesus. Media and Conservative Evangelical Culture* (Chicago: University of Chicago Press, 2004), p. 2.
113 David W. Bebbington, *Evangelicalism in Modern Britain: A History from the 1730s to the 1980s* (London: Routledge, 1989), pp. 2–3; James Davison Hunter, *Evangelicalism: The Coming Generation* (Chicago: The University of Chicago Press, 1993).
114 Clark, *From Angels to Aliens*, p. 30.
115 Hendershot, *Shaking*, p. 97, 112, 124.
116 Hendershot, *Shaking*, p. 124.
117 Hendershot, *Shaking*, p. 97, 124.
118 Hendershot, *Shaking*, p. 178.
119 Hendershot, *Shaking*, pp. 179–180.
120 Hendershot, *Shaking*, p. 101.
121 Clark, *From Angels to Aliens*, p. 34.
122 Hendershot, *Shaking*, p. 179.
123 Crawford Gribben, *Writing the Rapture: Prophecy Fiction in Evangelical America* (Oxford: Oxford University Press, 2009).
124 Clark, *From Angels to Aliens*, p. 37.
125 Hendershot, *Shaking*, pp. 177–180.
126 E.g. Clark, *From Angels to Aliens*, p. 41.
127 Clark, *From Angels to Aliens*, p. 32; Luhr, *Witnessing*, pp. 5–8.
128 E.g. Hendershot, *Shaking*; William D. Romanowski, 'Evangelicals and Popular Music: The Contemporary Christian Music Industry', in *Religion and Popular Culture in America*, eds, Bruce D. Forbes and Jeffrey H. Mahan (Berkeley. University of California Press, 2005).
129 E.g. Hoover, *Religion*, p. 78, 150.
130 Hunter, *Evangelicalism*, p. 71.
131 Donald E. Miller, *Reinventing American Protestantism: Christianity in the New Millennium* (Berkeley: University of California Press, 1997).
132 Luhr, *Witnessing*.
133 Hendershot, *Shaking*, p. 6.
134 Hendershot, *Shaking*, p. 7.
135 Hendershot, *Shaking*, p. 13.
136 E.g. Romanowski, 'Evangelicals and Popular Music', p. 105.
137 Hendershot, *Shaking*, p. 28.

138 Hendershot, *Shaking*, p. 7.
139 Jay R. Howard and John M. Streck, *Apostles of Rock: The Splintered World of Contemporary Christian Music* (Lexington, NC: Kentucky University Press, 1999).
140 Howard and Streck, *Apostles of Rock*, pp. 8–13.
141 Howard and Streck, *Apostles of Rock*, pp. 8–13.
142 Howard and Streck, *Apostles of Rock*, p. 14.
143 Cf. Romanowski, 'Evangelicals and Popular Music', p. 108.

Chapter 2

1 Weinstein, *Heavy Metal*. See also Bossius, *Med framtiden*.
2 See, for example, Marcus Moberg, *Faster for the Master! Exploring Issues of Religious Expression and Alternative Christian Identity within the Finnish Christian Metal Music Scene*. Diss (Åbo: Åbo Akademi University Press, 2009); Marcus Moberg 'Portrayals of the End Times, the Apocalypse and the Last Judgment in Christian Metal Music', in *Anthems of Apocalypse: Popular Music and Apocalyptic Thought*, ed., Christopher Partridge (Sheffield: Sheffield Phoenix Press, 2012); Marcus Moberg 'Turn or Burn? Approaching the Peculiar Case of Christian Metal', in *Reflections in the Metal Void*, ed., Niall W. R. Scott (Oxford: Inter-Disciplinary Press, 2012); Marcus Moberg 'The "Double Controversy" of Christian Metal', in *Heavy Metal: Controversies and Countercultures*, eds, Titus Hjelm, Keith Kahn-Harris and Mark LeVine (London: Equinox Publishing, 2013).
3 E.g. Perry L. Glanzer, 'Christ and the Heavy Metal Subculture'. Applying Qualitative Analysis to the Contemporary Debate about H. Richard Niebuhr's Christ and Culture', *Journal of Religion and Society* 5 (2003), http://moses.creighton.edu/jrs/2003/2003-7.pdf, accessed 9 July, 2014; Charles M. Brown, 'Apocalyptic Unbound. An Interpretation of Christian Speed/Thrash Metal Music', in *Religious Innovation in a Global Age. Essays on the Construction of Spirituality*, ed., George N. Lundskow (Jefferson, NC: McFarland & Company, Inc., Publishers, 2005); Eileen Luhr, *Witnessing*; Eric S. Strother, *Unlocking the Paradox of Christian Metal Music*, Diss. (University of Kentucky, 2013); Henna Jousmäki, 'Translocal Religious Identification in Christian Metal Music Videos and Discussion on YouTube', in *Cosmopolitanism and Transnationalism: Visions, Ethics, Practices*, ed. Leena Kaunonen (Helsinki: Helsinki Collegium for Advanced Studies, 2014); 'Spiritual Quest and dialogicality in Christian metal lyrics'. *Journal of Religion and Popular Culture* 25/2 (2013), pp. 273–286; 'Bridging into the Metal Community and the Church. Entextualization of the Bible in Christian Metal Discourse'. *Discourse, Context and Media* 1 (2012), pp. 217–226. Christopher Partridge, *The Lyre of Orpheus: Popular Music, the Sacred, and the Profane* (Oxford: Oxford University Press, 2014).
4 E.g. Howard and Streck, *Apostles of Rock*; Hendershot, *Shaking*; Forbes, 'Introduction'.

5   Luhr's *Witnessing* is an exception to this.
6   E.g. Bruce Moore, *Metal Missionaries: The Assimilation of Extreme Christian Music into Mainstream Consciousness*, E-book (Australia: Undark.net, 2010).
7   John J. Thompson, *Raised by Wolves: The Story of Christian Rock & Roll* (Toronto: ECW Press, 2000).
8   Mark Allan Powell, *Encyclopedia of Contemporary Christian Music* (Peabody, MA: Hendrickson Publishers, 2002).
9   http://fi.wikipedia.org/wiki/Kristillinen_metallimusiikki, accessed 11 July 2014. The English-language Wikipedia article is nearly as comprehensive.
10 Stryper, *To Hell with the Devil* (Enigma Records, 1986).
11 Stryper, *To Hell with the Devil*, p. 153.
12 Stryper, *To Hell with the Devil*, pp. 152–162; see also Weinstein, *Heavy Metal*, pp. 53–54.
13 Luhr, *Witnessing*, p. 115.
14 Glanzer. 'Christ and the Heavy Metal Sunculture', p. 15.
15 Glanzer, 'Christ and the Heavy Metal Subculture', pp. 32–34.
16 Glanzer, 'Christ and the Heavy Metal Subculture', p. 24.
17 Brown, 'Apocalyptic Unbound', p. 125.
18 Glanzer, 'Christ and the Heavy Metal Subculture', pp. 42–44; see also interview with Bob Beeman in the Finnish Christian metal fanzine *Ristillinen* 3 (2002), pp. 22–29.
19 Luhr, *Witnessing*, p. 84.
20 Thompson, *Raised by Wolves*, p. 161, 164; http://en.wikipedia.org/wiki/Christian_metal, accessed 11 July 2014.
21 E.g. Brown, 'Apocalyptic Unbound', p. 124.
22 Thompson, *Raised by Wolves*, p. 162; Weinstein, *Heavy Metal*, p. 54.
23 Glanzer, 'Christ and the Heavy Metal Subculture', p. 21.
24 Cf. Luhr, *Witnessing*, pp. 114–115.
25 http://www.metalforjesus.org/faq.html, accessed 11 July 2014.
26 IF mgt 2007/69. Author's translation from the Finnish original.
27 Steve Rowe, *Heaven's Metal* 62 (2006), p. 10.
28 E.g. Weinstein, *Heavy Metal*, p. 249.
29 E.g. Luhr, *Witnessing*; Hunter, *Evangelicalism*.
30 E.g. Wright, 'I'd Sell You Suicide', p. 370.
31 Moberg, 'The "Double Controversy" of Christian Metal'.
32 Weinstein, *Heavy Metal*, p. 245.
33 Luhr, *Witnessing*, p. 124.
34 Luhr, *Witnessing*, p. 112.
35 Rhys H. Williams, 'Religious Social Movements in the Public Sphere: Organization, Ideology, and Activism', in *Handbook of the Sociology of Religion*, ed., Michele Dillon (Cambridge: Cambridge University Press, 2003), p. 322.

36 Williams, *Handbook of the Sociology of Religion*, p. 322, emphasis added.
37 Williams, *Handbook of the Sociology of Religion*, pp. 322–327.
38 Weinstein, *Heavy Metal*, p. 270.
39 Williams, 'Religious Social Movements', p. 370.
40 Weinstein, *Heavy Metal*, p. 261; cf. Wright, 'I'd Sell You Suicide', p. 370.
41 Cf. Luhr, *Witnessing*, p. 52.
42 Cf. Jeff Manza and Nathan Wright, 'Religion and Political Behavior', in *Handbook of the Sociology of Religion*, ed., Michele Dillon (Cambridge: Cambridge University Press, 2003), p. 306.
43 Cf. Luhr, *Witnessing*, p. 143.
44 Luhr, *Witnessing*, p. 155
45 Luhr, *Witnessing*, p. 199.
46 Luhr, *Witnessing*, p. 118; cf. Manza and Wright, 'Religion and Political Behavior', p. 306.
47 Luhr, *Witnessing*, p. 118.
48 Luhr, *Witnessing*, p. 123.
49 Luhr, *Witnessing*, pp. 146–148.
50 Luhr, *Witnessing*, p. 62.
51 Jimmy Swaggart, *Religious Rock 'n' Roll: A Wolf in Sheep's Clothing* (Baton Rouge, LA: Swaggart Ministries, 1987).
52 Jeff Godwin, *Dancing with Demons: The Music's Real Master* (Chino, CA: Chick Publications, 1988).
53 E.g. Godwin, *Dancing with Demons*.
54 Luhr, *Witnessing*, pp. 49–50.
55 Weinstein, *Heavy Metal*, pp. 84–85.
56 Luhr, *Witnessing*, p. 115.
57 E.g. Miller, *Re-Inventing*, p. 173.
58 Moberg, *Faster for the Master!*, p. 228.

Chapter 3

1 For a less detailed but somewhat similar categorization, see Brown, 'Apocaplyptic Unbound', pp. 130–133.
2 Saint, *The Mark* (Armor Records, 2006).
3 Cf. Brown, 'Apocalyptic Unbound'. p. 125.
4 Saint, 'Primed and Ready', *Time's End* (Pure Metal, 1986). Reproduced with the kind permission of Retroactive Records and Saint.
5 Deliverance, 'No Time', *Deliverance* (Intense Records, 1989). Reproduced with the kind permission of Retroactive Records.
6 Hendershot, *Shaking*, p. 179.

7   Hendershot, *Shaking*, p. 97, 124.
8   David Morgan, *The Lure of Images: A History of Religion and Visual Media in America* (London: Routledge, 2007), p. 199.
9   Saint, 'Crime Scene Earth', *Crime Scene Earth* (Armor Records, 2008). Reproduced with the kind permission of Armor Records and Saint.
10 Luhr, *Wintessing*, p. 117.
11 Ephesians 6: 11–17, *Bible*, New International Version.
12 Stryper, *Soldiers Under Command* (Enigma, 1985).
13 Deliverance, *Weapons Of Our Warfare* (Intense Records, 1990).
14 Recon, *Behind Enemy Lines* (Intense Records, 1990).
15 Recon, 'Behind Enemy Lines', *Behind Enemy Lines* (Intense Records, 1990).
16 Deliverance, 'Flesh and Blood', *Weapons Of Our Warfare* (Intense Records, 1990).
17 Impending Doom, 'There Will be Violence', *There Will Be Violence* (Facedown Records, 2010). Reproduced with the kind permission of Facedown Records.
18 Ultimatum, 'Violence and Bloodshed', *The Mechanics of Perilous Times* (Gutter Records/Massacre Records, 2000).
19 War of Ages, 'Salvation', *Arise And Conquer* (Facedown Records, 2008). Reproduced with the kind permission of Facedown Records.
20 https://www.blessedresistance.com/index.php, accessed 12 July, 2014.
21 http://www.ultimatum.net/mainframe.html, accessed 12 July, 2014.
22 Luhr, *Witnessing*, p. 136.
23 Luhr, *Witnessing*, p. 135.
24 Andras Häger, 'Visual Representations of Christianity in Christian Music Videos', *Temenos: Nordic Journal of Comparative Religion* 41/2 (2005), pp. 258–260.
25 For examples of this, see the album covers for Mortification's *The Evil Addiction Destroying Machine* (Rowe Productions, 2009) or War of Age's *Arise and Conquer* (2008).
26 Saint, *Time's End* (Pure Metal Records, 1986).
27 Bride, *Show No Mercy* (Pure Metal Records, 1986).
28 Impending Doom, *There Will Be Violence*.
29 Stryper, *The Yellow and Black Attack* (Enigma Records, 1984).
30 Mortification, *Post Momentary Affliction* (Intense Records, 1993).

Chapter 4

1   See, for example, Graham St. John, ed., *Rave Culture and Religion* (London: Routledge, 2004).
2   Timothy Fitzgerald, 'Experience', in *Guide to the Study of Religion*, ed., Willi Braun and Russell T. McCutcheon (London: Cassell, 2000), p. 134.

3. Rudolph Otto, *The Idea of the Holy: An Inquiry into the Non-Rational Factor in the Idea of the Divine and Its Relation to the Rational* (Oxford: Oxford University Press, 1958).
4. Birgit Meyer, 'Media and the Senses in the Making of Religious Experience: An Introduction', *Material Religion* 4/2 (2008), p. 129.
5. Ann Taves, *Religious Experience Reconsidered: A Building-Block Approach to the Study of Religion and Other Special Things* (New Jersey: Princeton University Press, 2009).
6. Birgit Meyer, 'Religious Sensations: Why Media, Aesthetics, and Power Matter in the Study of Contemporary Religion', in *Religion: Beyond a Concept*, ed., Hent de Vries (New York, NY: Fordham University Press, 2008), p. 707.
7. Cf. Charles Hartshorne, 'Transcendence and Immanence', in *Encyclopaedia of Religion*, Vol. 13. Second edition, ed., Lindsey Jones (Detroit, MI: Macmillan Reference USA, 2005).
8. Cf. Taves, *Religious Experience*, p. 66.
9. Georges Bataille, *Literature and Evil* (London: Marion Boyars, 1985); Georges Bataillee, *The Accursed Share: An Essay on General Economy* (New York, NY: Zone Books, 1993).
10. Victor Turner, *Dramas, Fields and Metaphors: Symbolic Action in Human Society* (London: Cornell University Press, 1974).
11. Mary Douglas, *Purity and Danger: An Analysis of the Concepts of Pollution and Taboo* (London: Ark Paperbacks, 1984).
12. E.g. Petru Calianu and Craig A. Burgdoff, 'Sacrilege', in *Encyclopaedia of Religion*, Vol. 12. Second edition, ed., Lindsey Jones (Detroit, MI: Macmillan Reference USA, 2005), p. 8011.
13. Max Weber, 'The Nature of Social Action', in *Weber: Selections in Translation*, ed., Walter Garrison Runciman (Cambridge: Cambridge University Press, 1991).
14. Jürgen Habermas, *The Theory of Communicative Action, Vol. 1: Reason and the Rationalization of Society* (Boston, MA: Beacon Press, 1984).
15. Lawrence Grossberg, 'Another Boring Day in Paradise: Rock and Roll and the Empowerment of Everyday Life', *Popular Music* 4 (1984), pp. 225–258.
16. Simon Reynolds, *Blissed Out: The Raptures of Rock* (London: Serpents Tail, 1990).
17. Michael Chanan, *Musica Practica: The Social Practice of Western Music from Gregorian Chant to Postmodernism* (London: Verso, 1994).
18. Cf. Gordon Lynch, 'Religion, Media, and Cultures of Everyday Life', in *The Routledge Companion to the Study of Religion*, Second edition, ed., J. R. Hinnells (Oxon: Routledge, 2010), p. 552.
19. E.g. Romanowski, 'Evangelicals and Popular Music', p. 112.
20. Kahn-Harris, *Extreme Metal*, p. 30.
21. Kahn-Harris, *Extreme Metal*.
22. A similar argument is presented in Partridge, *The Lyre of Orpheus*, pp. 212–216.
23. Fitzgerald, 'Experience', p. 134.
24. Fitzgerald, 'Experience', p. 134.

25 The results of this work is presented in detail in Moberg, *Faster for the Master!*.
26 E.g. Weinstein, *Heavy Metal*, pp. 27–31; Kahn-Harris, *Extreme Metal*, pp. 73–74.
27 Andreas Häger, 'Christian Rock Concerts as a Meeting Between Religion and Popular Culture', in *Ritualistics*, ed., Tore Ahlbäck, Scripta Instituti Donneriani Aboensis XVIII. (Åbo: The Donner Institute for Research in Religious and Cultural History, 2003), pp. 49–51.
28 Häger, 'Christian Rock Concerts as a Meeting between Religion and Popular Culture', pp. 49–51; Andeas Häger, 'Visual Representations of Christianity in Christian Music Videos', *Temenos: Nordic Journal of Comparative Religion* 41/2 (2005), p. 259.
29 Luhr, *Witnessing*, p. 80.
30 E.g., Häger, 'Visual Representations', p. 259.
31 Häger, 'Christian Rock Concerts'.
32 Häger, 'Christian Rock Concerts', p. 42.
33 Birgit Meyer, *Religious Sensations: Why Media, Aesthetics, and Power Matter in the Study of Contemporary Religion* (Professorial Inaugural Address, Amsterdam: Faculty of Social Sciences, Free University, 2006), p. 18. http://www.fsw.vu.nl/nl/Images/Oratietekst%20Birgit%20Meyer_tcm30-44560.pdf18
34 Meyer, 'Religious Sensations', p. 707.
35 Meyer, 'Media and the Senses', p. 129, emphasis added.
36 Meyer, 'Religious Sensations', p. 707.
37 Birgit Meyer and Jojada Verrips, 'Aesthetics', in *Key Words in Religion, Media and Culture*, ed., David Morgan (New York, NY: Routledge, 2008), p. 27.
38 Meyer and Verrips, 'Aesthetics', p. 28.
39 Meyer and Verrips, 'Aesthetics', p. 28.

Chapter 5

1 E.g. Partridge, *Re-enchantment (vol. 1)*; Lynch, 'Media and Cultures'.
2 Gordon Lynch, 'The Role of Popular Music in the Construction of Alternative Spiritual Identities and Ideologies', *Journal for the Scientific Study of Religion* 45/4 (2006), p. 482.
3 E.g. Lynch, 'The Role of Popular Music'; Graham St John, 'Electronic Dance Music Culture and Religion: An Overview', *Culture and Religion* 7/1 (2006); Giles Beck and Gordon Lynch, '"We Are All One, We Are All Gods": Negotiating Spirituality in the Conscious Partying Movement', *Journal of Contemporary Religion* 24/3 (2009).
4 Kahn-Harris, *Extreme Metal*, p. 91.
5 Kahn-Harris, *Extreme Metal*, p. 15.
6 Kahn-Harris, *Extreme Metal*, p. 15.
7 Andy Bennett and Keith Kahn-Harris, 'Introduction', in *After Subculture: Critical Studies in Contemporary Youth Culture*, eds Andy Bennett and Keith Kahn-Harris (London: Palgrave McMillan, 2004), p. 8.

8 Kahn-Harris, *Extreme Metal*, p. 15.
9 E.g. Stuart Hall and Tony Jefferson, eds, *Resistance Through Rituals: Youth Subcultures in Post-War Britain* (London: Hutchinson, 1976); Paul Willis, *Profane Culture* (London: Routledge, 1978); Dick Hebdige, *Subculture: The Meaning of Style* (London: Routledge).
10 Kahn-Harris, *Extreme Metal*, p. 16.
11 Bennett and Kahn-Harris, 'Introduction', pp. 4–6.
12 Kahn-Harris, *Extreme Metal*, p. 17.
13 E.g. Paul Hodkinson, *Goth: Identity, Style, and Subculture* (Oxford: Berg, 2002).
14 E.g. Sarah Thornton, *Club Cultures: Music, Media and Subcultural Capital* (Cambridge: Polity Press, 1995).
15 David Muggleton and Rupert Weinzierl, eds, *The Post-subcultures Reader* (New York, NY: Berg, 2003).
16 Michel Maffesoli, *The Time of the Tribes: The Decline of Individualism in Mass Society* (London: Sage, 1996) For more on the application of the concept of neo-tribe in the study of popular music, see, for example, Andy Bennett, 'Subcultures or Neo-Tribes? Rethinking the Relationship between Youth, Style and Musical Taste', *Sociology* 33/3 (1999).
17 E.g. Steven Miles, *Youth Lifestyles in a Changing World* (Buckingham: Open University Press, 2000).
18 E.g. Will Straw, 'Systems of Articulation, Logics of Change: Communities and Scenes in Popular Music', *Cultural Studies* 5/3 (1991); Will Straw, 'Scenes and Sensibilities', *Public* 22–23 (2001); Kahn-Harris, *Extreme Metal*; Peter Webb, *Exploring the Networked Worlds of Popular Music: Milieu Cultures* (New York, NY: Routledge, 2007).
19 Kahn-Harris, *Exteme Metal*, p. 21.
20 Cf. Lynn Schofield Clark, 'Introduction to a Forum on Religion, Popular Music, and Globalization', *Journal for the Scientific Study of Religion* 45/4 (2006).
21 Kahn-Harris, *Exteme Metal*, p. 101.
22 Kahn-Harris, *Exteme Metal*, pp. 99–100.
23 Kahn-Harris, *Exteme Metal*, p. 99.
24 Kahn-Harris, *Exteme Metal*, p. 99.
25 Lynch, 'The Role of Popular Music', pp. 482–483.
26 Kahn-Harris, *Exteme Metal*, p. 21.
27 Kahn-Harris, *Exteme Metal*, pp. 100–102.
28 Kahn-Harris, *Exteme Metal*, p. 100.
29 Marcus Moberg, 'The Internet and the Construction of a Transnational Christian Metal Music Scene', *Culture and Religion* 9/1 (2008).
30 Kahn-Harris, *Extreme Metal*, pp. 100–101.
31 Kahn-Harris, *Extreme Metal*, p. 101.
32 Kahn-Harris, *Extreme Metal*, p. 101.
33 Kahn-Harris, *Extreme Metal*, p. 101.

NOTES

34 Thornton, *Club Cultures*.
35 Kahn-Harris, *Extreme Metal*, p. 101.
36 Kahn-Harris, *Extreme Metal*, p. 127.
37 Kahn-Harris, *Extreme Metal*, p. 100.
38 Moberg, *Faster for the Master!*
39 Kahn-Harris, *Extreme Metal*, p. 100.
40 E.g. Wright, 'I'd Sell You Suicide'.
41 Kahn-Harris, *Extreme Metal*, p. 100.
42 Kahn-Harris, *Extreme Metal*, p. 100.
43 Kahn-Harris, *Extreme Metal*, p. 118.
44 Luhr, *Witnessing*, p. 84.
45 http://www.bobfest.org/, accessed 13 July 2014.
46 *Extreme Brutal Death* 1 (2005), p. 16.
47 This term was suggested to me by Justin Davisson.
48 http://www.rivelrecords.com/main.php, accessed 8 July 2014.
49 http://www.nordicmission.net/, accessed 26 November 2008.
50 *Devotion HardMusic Magazine* 3 (2001), p. 27.
51 *Extreme Brutal Death* 1 (2005), p. 4.
52 http://www.metalforjesus.org/, accessed 13 July 2014.
53 http://www.metalforjesus.org/MC.html, accessed 13 July 2014.
54 IF 2005/5: 1–7. Author's translation from the Swedish original.
55 http://www.angelicwarlord.com/, accessed 13 July 2014.
56 http://sanctifiedsteel.blogspot.fi/, accessed 13 July 2014.
57 http://firestream.freeforums.org/index.php?sid=089eba790eeb8936bbee1c89c7a08c70, accessed 13 July 2014.
58 IF 2006/9.
59 http://thecmr.forumotion.com/, accessed 13 July 2014.
60 http://www.metalliunioni.com/forum/, accessed 13 July 2014.
61 http://www.intenseradio.com/, accessed 13 July 2014.
62 http://www.reignradio.com/index.html, accessed 13 July 2014.
63 http://www.angelfire.com/wv/heavensmetal/, accessed 13 July 2014.
64 http://www.metalforjesus.org/MC.html, accessed 13 July 2014.
65 http://www.fullarmorradio.com/, accessed 13 July 2014.
66 http://www.therefineryrock.com/, accessed 13 July 2014.
67 http://www.classicchristianrock.net/, accessed 13 July 2014.
68 http://www.thecrossstream.com/, accessed 13 July 2014.
69 http://metallimessu.com/, accessed 14 July 2014.
70 http://www.themetalbible.com/, accessed 14 July 2014.
71 http://www.themetalbible.com/background.html, accessed 14 July 2014.

Chapter 6

1. E.g. Vivien Burr, *Social Constructionism* (London: Routledge, 2003); Steven Engler, 'Constructionism versus What?', *Religion* 34/4 (2004), pp. 291–313; Steven Engler 'Discourse', in *The Brill Dictionary of Religion*, ed., Kocku von Stuckrad (Leiden: Brill, 2006).
2. Cf. Margaret Wetherell, 'Themes in Discourse Research: The Case of Diana', in *Discourse Theory and Practice*, ed., Margaret Wetherell, Stephanie Taylor and Simeon J. Yates (London: Sage, 2001), p. 22.
3. Titus Hjelm, 'Disocurse Analysis', in *The Routledge Handbook of Research Methods in the Study of Religion*, eds, Michael Stausberg and Steven Engler (London: Routledge, 2011), p. 136.
4. E.g. Murphy, 'Discourse'; Kocku von Stuckrad, 'Discursive Study of Religion: From States of the Mind to Communication and Action', *Method and Theory in the Study of Religion* 15/3 (2003), pp. 251–271; Russell T. McCutcheon, *Manufacturing Religion: The Discourse on Sui Generis Religion and the Politics of Nostalgia* (Oxford: Oxford University Press).
5. Marcus Moberg, 'First-, Second-, and Third-Level Discourse Analytic Approaches in the Study of Religion: Moving from Meta-Theoretical Reflection to Implementation in Practice', *Religion* 43/1 (2013), pp. 4–25.
6. Peter L. Berger and Thomas Luckmann, *The Social Construction of Reality: A Treatise in the Sociology of Knowledge* (Harmondsworth: Penguin, 1987 [1966]).
7. E.g. Engler, 'Constructionism', p. 292.
8. E.g. Burr, *Social Constructionism*, pp. 11–15.
9. Kennet J. Gergen, *An Invitation to Social Construction* (London: Sage, 1999), pp. 33–35.
10. Gergen, *An Invitation*, pp. 33–38.
11. Burr, *Social Constructionism*, p. 18.
12. Jonathan Potter, *Representing Reality: Discourse, Rhetoric and Social Construction* (London: Sage, 1996), p. 69, 88.
13. E.g. Burr, *Social Constructionism*, pp. 11–15.
14. Murphy, 'Discourse', in *Guide to the Study of Religion*, ed., Willi Braun and Russell T. McCutcheon (London: Cassell, 2000), p. 329.
15. Stephanie Taylor, 'Locating and Conducting Discourse Analytic Research', in *Discourse as Data: A Guide for Analysis*, eds, Margaret Wetherell, Stephanie Taylor and Simeon T. Yates (London: Sage, 2001), p. 8.
16. Gergen, *An Invitation*, pp. 48–49.
17. Gergen, *An Invitation*, pp. 48–49.
18. Burr, *Social Constructionism*, p. 3.
19. Burr, *Social Constructionism*, p. 4.
20. Burr, *Social Constructionism*, p. 5, emphasis added.
21. Engler, 'Constructionism', p. 298.

22 Burr, *Social Constructionism*, p. 64.
23 E.g. Martin Reisigl and Ruth Wodak, 'The Discourse-Historical Approach', in *Methods of Critical Discourse Analysis*, Second edition, eds, Ruth Wodak and Michael Meyer (London: Sage, 2008), p. 89.
24 Stuart Hall, 'Introduction', in *Representation: Cultural Representations and Signifying Practices*, ed., Stuart Hall (London: Sage, 1997), p. 4.
25 Burr, *Social Constructionism*, p. 65.
26 Burr, *Social Constructionism*, p. 65.
27 Gergen, *An Invitation*, pp. 48–49.
28 E.g. Burr, *Social Constructionism*, p. 65.
29 Burr, *Social Constructionism*, p. 66.
30 Burr, *Social Constructionism*, pp. 63–65.
31 Taylor, 'Locating and Conducting', p. 6.
32 Taylor, 'Locating and Conducting', pp. 16–19.
33 Cf. Robert J. Wuthnow, 'Taking Talk Seriously: Religious Discourse as Social Practice', *Journal for the Scientific Study of Religion* 50/1 (2011), p. 11.
34 Cf. Beckford, *Social Theory*, p. 166.
35 E.g. Kocku von Stuckrad, 'Reflections on the Limits of Reflection: An Invitation to the Discursive Study of Religion', *Method and Theory in the Study of Religion* 22/2 (2010), p. 166.
36 Cf. von Stuckrad, 'Discursive Study of Religion', p. 263.
37 Walser, *Running*, p. 27.
38 Walser, *Running*, p. 27.
39 Walser, *Running*, p. 29.
40 Simon Frith, *Performing Rites. On the Value of Popular Music* (Oxford: Oxford University Press, 1996), p. 8, emphasis added.
41 Frith, *Performing Rites*, p. 26.
42 Kahn-Harris, *Extreme Metal*, p. 100.
43 Kahn-Harris, *Extreme Metal*, p. 100.
44 IF 2006/9.
45 IF 2005/5: 1–7. Author's translation from the Swedish original.
46 The grammar has been left unchanged in all quoted excerpts.
47 http://www.metalforjesus.org/faq.html, accessed 7 July 2014.
48 Rowe, *Heaven's Metal*, p. 21.
49 IF 2005/5: 1–7. Author's translation from the Swedish original.
50 http://www.sanctuaryinternational.com/, accessed 7 July 2014.
51 http://www.metalforjesus.org/greatool.html, accessed 7 July 2014.
52 http://www.majesticvanguard.net/site.php?page=biography.php, accessed 7 July 2014.
53 *Devotion Hard Music Magazine*, issue 5, 2003.

54 http://www.ancientprophecy.de/home.htm, accessed 7 July 2014. German original: Wir machen Musik, Gott zur Ehre. Er soll im Mittelpunkt stehen, nicht wir. Unsere Texte handeln nicht von großartigen Heldentaten, Drachen, oberflächlicher Liebe oder direkter sozialer Kritik…Wir möchten als Christen in der Metalszene zeigen und bezeugen, dass es möglich und real ist, eine echte Beziehung zu dem zu haben, den die Bibel als Gott beschreibt. Die Band wurde zu dem Zweck gegründet, das weiterzugeben was im neuen Testament als die "Gute Nachricht" oder die "Frohe Botschaft" bezeichnet wird.

55 http://www.metalforjesus.org/friorfoe.html, accessed 13 July 2015.

56 http://www.metalforjesus.org/friorfoe.html, accessed 13 July 2014.

57 Cf. Luhr, *Witnessing*, p. 145.

58 http://www.metalforjesus.org/friorfoe.html, accessed 13 July 2015.

59 http://www.metalforjesus.org/friorfoe.html, accessed 13 July 2014.

60 http://unblacknoise.wordpress.com/2008/10/08/christian-metal-a-defence/, accessed 26 November 2008. Link currently defunct.

61 http://home.wanadoo.nl/kemman/homer.htm, accessed 28 November 2008. Link currently defunct.

62 http://www.av1611.org/, accessed 13 July 2014.

63 See Moberg, *Faster for the Master!*

64 http://en.wikipedia.org/wiki/Unblack_metal, accessed 13 July 2014.

Chapter 7

1 E.g. Paul Heelas and Linda Woodhead, et al., *The Spiritual Revolution: Why Religion is Giving Way to Spirituality* (Oxford: Blackwell, 2005), pp. 17–23.

2 Cf. Helen Cameron, 'The Decline of the Church in England as a Local Membership Organization: Predicting the Nature of Civil Society in 2050', in *Predicting Religion: Christian, Secular and Alternative Futures*, eds, Grace Davie, Paul Heelas and Linda Woodhead (Hamphire: Ashgate, 2003).

Bibliography

Arnett, J., *Metalheads: Heavy Metal Music and Adolescent Alienation*, New York, NY: Westview Press, 1996.
Baddeley, G., *Lucifer Rising: A Book of Sin, Devil Worship and Rock'n' Roll*, London: Plexus Publishing Limited, 1999.
Bashe, P., *Heavy Metal Thunder*, London: Omnibus Press, 1986.
Bataille, G., *Literature and Evil*, London: Marion Boyars, 1985.
———, *The Accursed Share: An Essay on General Economy*, New York, NY: Zone Books, 1993.
Bauman, Z., *The Individualized Society*, Cambridge: Polity Press, 2001.
Bayer, G. (ed.), *Heavy Metal Music in Britain*, Hampshire: Ashgate, 2009.
Bebbington, D. W., *Evangelicalism in Modern Britain: A History from the 1730s to the 1980s*, London: Routledge, 1989.
Beck, U. and Beck-Gernsheim, E., *Individualization: Institutionalized Individualism and its Social and Political Consequences*, London: Sage, 2002.
Beck, G. and Lynch, G. ' "We Are All One, We Are All Gods": Negotiating Spirituality in the Conscious Partying Movement', *Journal of Contemporary Religion* 24 (2009), pp. 339–355.
Begbie, J., 'Unexplored Eloquencies: Music, Media, Religion and Culture', in J. Mitchell and S. Marriage (eds), *Mediating Religion: Conversations in Media, Religion and Culture*, London: T&T Clark Ltd, 2003.
Bennett, A., 'Subcultures or Neo-Tribes? Rethinking the Relationship between Youth, Style and Musical Taste', *Sociology* 33 (1999), pp. 599–617.
———, *Cultures of Popular Music*, Maidenhead: Open University Press, 2001.
Bennett, A. and Kahn-Harris, K., 'Introduction', in A. Bennet and K. Kahn-Harris (eds), *After Subculture: Critical Studies in Contemporary Youth Culture*, London: Palgrave McMillan, 2004.
Berger, P. L. and Luckmann, T., *The Social Construction of Reality: A Treatise in the Sociology of Knowledge*, Harmondsworth: Penguin, 1987 [1966].
Bossius, T. *Med Framtiden i Backspegeln. Black Metal och Transkulturen. Ungdomar, Musik och Religion i en Senmodern Värld*, Göteborg: Diadalos, 2003.
Brown, A. A., 'Heavy Metal and Subcultural Theory: A Paradigmatic Case of Neglect?', in D. Muggleton and R. Weinzierl (eds), *The Post-subcultures Reader*, New York, NY: Berg, 2003.
Brown, C. M., 'Apocalyptic Unbound. An Interpretation of Christian Speed/Thrash Metal Music', in G. N. Lundskow (ed.), *Religious Innovation in a Global Age. Essays on the Construction of Spirituality*, Jefferson, NC: McFarland & Company, Inc., Publishers, 2005.
Burr, V., *Social Constructionism*, London: Routledge, 2003.

Byrnside, R., 'The Formation of a Musical Style: Early Rock', in C. Hamm, B. Nettl and R. Byrnside (eds), *Contemporary Music and Music Cultures*, Englewood Cliffs, NJ: Prentice Hall, 1975.

Calianu, P. and Burgdoff, C. A., 'Sacrilege', in L. Jones (ed.), *Encyclopaedia of Religion*, Vol. 12. Second edition, Detroit, MI: Macmillan Reference USA, 2005.

Cameron, H., 'The Decline of the Church in England as a Local Membership Organization: Predicting the Nature of Civil Society in 2050', in G. Davie, P. Heelas and L. Woodhead (eds), *Predicting Religion: Christian, Secular and Alternative Futures*, Hamphire: Ashgate, 2003.

Chanan, M., *Musica Practica: The Social Practice of Western Music from Gregorian Chant to Postmodernism*, London: Verso, 1994.

Chidester, D., *Authentic Fakes: Religion and American Popular Culture*, Berkeley, CA: University of California Press, 2005.

Christe, I., *Sound of the Beast: The Complete Headbanging History of Heavy Metal*, New York, NY: HarperCollins Publishers, 2004.

Clark, L. S. *From Angels to Aliens: Teenagers, the Media, and the Supernatural*, New York, NY: Oxford University Press, 2005.

———, 'Introduction to a Forum on Religion, Popular Music, and Globalization', *Journal for the Scientific Study of Religion* 45 (2006), pp. 475–479.

Cordero, J., 'Unveiling Satan's Wrath: Aesthetics and Ideology in Anti-Christian Heavy Metal', *Journal of Religion and Popular Culture* 21 (2009).

Couldry, N., *Media Rituals: A Critical Approach*, London: Routledge, 2003.

Denski, S. and Sholle, D., 'Metal Men and Glamour Boys: Gender Performance in Heavy Metal', in S. Craig (ed.), *Men, Masculinity and the Media*, Newbury Park, CA: Sage, 1992.

Douglas, M., *Purity and Danger: An Analysis of the Concepts of Pollution and Taboo*, London: Ark Paperbacks, 1984.

Engler, S., 'Constructionism versus What?', *Religion* 34 (2004), pp. 291–313.

———, 'Discourse', in K. von Stuckrad (ed.), *The Brill Dictionary of Religion*, Leiden: Brill, 2006.

Farley, H., 'Demons, Devils and Witches: The Occult in Heavy Metal Music', in G. Bayer (ed.), *Heavy Metal Music in Britain*, Aldershot: Ashgate, 2009.

Fitzgerald, T., 'Experience', in W. Braun and R. T. McCutcheon (eds), *Guide to the Study of Religion*, London: Cassell, 2000.

Forbes, B. D. and Mahan, J. H. (eds), *Religion and Popular Culture in America*, Berkeley, CA: University of California Press, 2000.

Frith, S., *Performing Rites. On the Value of Popular Music*, Oxford: Oxford University Press, 1996.

Giddens, A., *Modernity and Self-Identity: Self and Society in the Late Modern Age*, Stanford, CA: Stanford University Press, 1991.

Glanzer, P. L., 'Christ and the Heavy Metal Subculture: Applying Qualitative Analysis to the Contemporary Debate about H. Richard Niebuhr's Christ and Culture', *Journal of Religion & Society* 5 (2003), 1–16. http://moses.creighton.edu/jrs/2003/2003-7.pdf [accessed 9 July 2014].

Godwin, J., *Dancing with Demons: The Music's Real Master*, Chino, CA: Chick Publications, 1988.

Granholm, K., '"Sons of Northern Darkness": Heathen Influences in Black Metal and Neofolk Music', *Numen: International Review for the History of Religions* 58 (2011), pp. 514–544.
———, 'Ritual Black Metal: Popular Music as Occult Mediation and Practice'. *Correspondences* 1 (2013), pp. 5–33. http://correspondencesjournal.files.wordpress.com/2013/09/11302_20537158_granholm.pdf [accessed 10 July 2014].
Gribben, C., *Writing the Rapture: Prophecy Fiction in Evangelical America*, Oxford: Oxford University Press, 2009.
Grossberg, L., 'Another Boring Day in Paradise: Rock and Roll and the Empowerment of Everyday Life', *Popular Music* 4 (1984), pp. 225–258.
Habermas, J., *The Theory of Communicative Action, Vol. 1: Reason and the Rationalization of Society*, Boston, MA: Beacon Press, 1984.
Häger, A., 'Christian Rock Concerts as a Meeting between Religion and Popular Culture', in T. Albäck (ed.), *Ritualistics, Scripta Instituti Donneriani Aboensis XVIII*, Åbo: The Donner Institute for Research in Religious and Cultural History, 2003.
———, 'Visual Representations of Christianity in Christian Music Videos', *Temenos: Nordic Journal of Comparative Religion* 41 (2005), pp. 241–274.
Hall, S., 'Introduction', in S. Hall (ed.), *Representation: Cultural Representations and Signifying Practices*, London: Sage, 1997.
Hall, S. and Jefferson, T. (eds), *Resistance Through Rituals: Youth Subcultures in Post-War Britain*, London: Hutchinson, 1976.
Hartshorne, C., 'Transcendence and Immanence', in L. Jones (ed.), *Encyclopaedia of Religion*, Vol. 13. Second edition, Detroit, MI: Macmillan Reference USA, 2005.
Hebdige, D., *Subculture: The Meaning of Style*, London: Routledge, 1979.
Hendershot, H., *Shaking the World for Jesus. Media and Conservative Evangelical Culture*, Chicago, IL: University of Chicago Press, 2004.
Hills, M., *Fan Cultures*, London: Routledge, 2002.
Hirschkind, C., 'Media, Mediation, Religion', *Social Anthropology* 9 (2011), pp. 90–97.
Hjelm, T., 'Disocurse Analysis', in S. Stausberg and S. Engler (eds), *The Routledge Handbook of Research Methods in the Study of Religion*, London: Routledge, 2011.
Hjelm, T., Kahn-Harris, K. and LeVine, M., 'Introduction: Heavy Metal as Controversy and Counterculture', in T. Hjelm, K. Kahn-Harris and M. LeVine (eds), *Heavy Metal: Controversies and Countercultures*, London: Equinox Publishing, 2013.
——— (eds), *Heavy Metal: Controversies and Countercultures*, London: Equinox Publishing, 2013.
Hodkinson, P., *Goth: Identity, Style, and Subculture*, Oxford: Berg, 2002.
Hoover, S. M., *Religion in the Media Age*, New York, NY: Routledge, 2006.
Howard, J. R. and Streck, J. M., *Apostles of Rock: The Splintered World of Contemporary Christian Music*, Lexington: Kentucky University Press, 1999.
Hunter, J. D., *Evangelicalism: The Coming Generation*, Chicago, IL: The University of Chicago Press, 1993.
Jousmäki, H., 'Translocal Religious Identification in Christian Metal Music Videos and Discussion on YouTube', in L. Kaunonen (ed.), *Cosmopolitanism and*

Transnationalism: Visions, Ethics, Practices, Studies across Disciplines in the Humanities and Social Sciences 15, Helsinki: Helsinki Collegium for Advanced Studies, 2014.

———, 'Spiritual Quest and Dialogicality in Christian Metal Lyrics', *Journal of Religion and Popular Culture* 25 (2013), pp. 273–286.

———, 'Bridging into the Metal Community and the Church. Entextualization of the Bible in Christian Metal Discourse', *Discourse, Context and Media* 1 (2012), pp. 217–226.

Kahn-Harris, K., *Extreme Metal: Music and Culture on the Edge*, Oxford: Berg, 2007.

Luhr, E., *Witnessing Suburbia: Conservatives and Christian Youth Culture*, Berkeley, CA: University of California Press, 2009.

Lynch, G., *Understanding Theology and Popular Culture*, Oxford: Blackwell Publishing, 2005.

———, 'The Role of Popular Music in the Construction of Alternative Spiritual Identities and Ideologies', *Journal for the Scientific Study of Religion* 45 (2006), pp. 481–488.

——— (ed.), *Between Sacred and Profane: Researching Religion and Popular Culture*, London: I.B. Tauris, 2007.

———, 'What is This "Religion" in the Study of Religion and Popular Culture?', in G. Lynch (ed.), *Between Sacred and Profane: Researching Religion and Popular Culture*, London: I.B. Tauris, 2007.

———, 'Media and Cultures of Everyday Life', in J. R. Hinnells (ed.), *The Routledge Companion to the Study of Religion*, Second edition, Oxon: Routledge, 2010.

———, 'Living with Two Cultural Turns: The Case of the Study of Religion', in S. Roseneil and S. Frosh (eds), *Social Research after the Cultural Turn*, New York, NY: Palgrave Macmillan, 2012.

Maffesoli, M., *The Time of the Tribes: The Decline of Individualism in Mass Society*, London: Sage, 1996.

Manza, J. and Wright, N., 'Religion and Political Behavior', in M. Dillon (ed.), *Handbook of the Sociology of Religion*, Cambridge: Cambridge University Press, 2003.

Martikainen, T. and Gauthier, F., 'Introduction: Religion in Market Society', in T. Martikainen and F. Gauthier (eds), *Religion in the Neoliberal Age: Political Economy and Modes of Governance*, Farnham: Ashgate, 2013.

McCloud, S. 'Popular Culture Fandoms, the Boundaries of Religious Studies, and the Project of the Self', *Culture and Religion* 4 (2003), pp. 187–2016.

McCutcheon, R. T., *Manufacturing Religion: The Discourse on Sui Generis Religion and the Politics of Nostalgia*, Oxford: Oxford University Press, 1997.

Metal: A Headbanger's Journey, J. J. Wise, S. Dunn and S. McFadyen (dir), Warner Home Video, 2005.

Meyer, B., *Religious Sensations: Why Media, Aesthetics, and Power Matter in the Study of Contemporary Religion*, Professorial Inaugural Address, Amsterdam: Faculty of Social Sciences, Free University, 2006 https://www.vu.nl/nl/Images/Oratietekst%20Birgit%20Meyer_tcm9-44560.pdf [accessed 15 July 2014].

———, 'Media and the Senses in the Making of Religious Experience: An Introduction', *Material Religion* 4 (2008), pp. 124–134.

———, 'Religious Sensations: Why Media, Aesthetics, and Power Matter in the Study of Contemporary Religion', in H. de Vries (ed.), *Religion: Beyond a Concept*, New York, NY: Fordham University Press, 2008.

Meyer, B. and Verrips, J., 'Aesthetics', in D. Morgan (ed.), *Key Words in Religion, Media and Culture*, New York, NY: Routledge, 2008.

Miles, S., *Youth Lifestyles in a Changing World*, Buckingham: Open University Press, 2000.

Miller, D. E., *Reinventing American Protestantism: Christianity in the New Millennium*, Berkeley, CA: University of California Press, 1997.

Moberg, M. 'The Internet and the Construction of a Transnational Christian Metal Music Scene', *Culture and Religion* 9 (2008), pp. 67–82.

———, 'Popular Culture and the 'Darker Side' of Alternative Spirituality: The Case of Metal Music', in T. Ahlbäck (ed.), *Postmodern Spirituality, Scripta Instituti Donneriani Aboensis XXI*, Åbo: The Donner Institute for Research in Religious and Cultural History, 2009.

———, *Faster for the Master! Exploring Issues of Religious Expression and Alternative Christian Identity within the Finnish Christian Metal Music Scene*, Diss, Åbo: Åbo Akademi University Press, 2009.

———, 'Turn or Burn? Approaching the Peculiar Case of Christian Metal', in N. R. W. Scott (ed.), *Reflections in the Metal Void*, Oxford: Inter-Disciplinary Press, 2012.

———, 'Portrayals of the End Times, the Apocalypse and the Last Judgment in Christian Metal Music', in C. Partridge (ed.), *Anthems of Apocalypse: Popular Music and Apocalyptic Thought*, Sheffield: Sheffield Phoenix Press, 2012.

———, 'First-, Second-, and Third-Level Discourse Analytic Approaches in the Study of Religion: Moving from Meta-Theoretical Reflection to Implementation in Practice', *Religion* 43 (2013), pp. 4–25.

———, 'The "Double Controversy" of Christian Metal', in T. Hjelm, K. Kahn-Harris and M. LeVine (eds), *Heavy Metal: Controversies and Countercultures*, London: Equinox Publishing, 2013.

Moberg, M. and Sjö, S., 'Mass-Mediated Popular Culture and Religious Socialisation', in K. Granholm, M. Moberg and S. Sjö (eds), *Religion, Media and Social Change*, London: Routledge, 2015.

Moberg, M., Sjö, S. and Granholm, K., 'Introduction', in K. Granholm, M. Moberg and S. Sjö (eds), *Religion, Media and Social Change*, London: Routledge, 2015.

Moore, B., *Metal Missionaries: The Assimilation of Extreme Christian Music into Mainstream Consciousness, E-book*, Australia: Undark.net, 2010.

Morgan, D., *The Lure of Images: A History of Religion and Visual Media in America*, London: Routledge, 2007.

Mørk, G., ' "With My Art I am the Fist in the Face of God": On Old-School Black Metal', in J. A. Petersen (ed.), *Contemporary Religious Satanism: A Critical Anthology*, Aldershot: Ashgate, 2009.

Moynihan, M. and Söderlind, D., *Lords of Chaos: The Bloody Rise of the Satanic Metal Underground*, Venice, CA: Feral House, 2003[1998].

Mudrian, A., *Choosing Death: The Improbable History of Death Metal & Grindcore*, Los Angeles, CA: Feral House, 2004.

Muggleton, D. and Weinzierl, R. (eds), *The Post-subcultures Reader*, New York, NY: Berg, 2003.

Otto, R., *The Idea of the Holy: An Inquiry into the Non-Rational Factor in the Idea of the Divine and Its Relation to the Rational*, Oxford: Oxford University Press, 1958.

Partridge, C., *The Re-enchantment of the West, Vol. 1: Alternative Spiritualities, Sacralization, Popular Culture and Occulture*, London: Continuum, 2004.

———, *The Re-enchantment of the West, Vol. 2: Alternative Spiritualities, Sacralization, Popular Culture and Occulture*, London: Continuum, 2005.

———, *The Lyre of Orpheus: Popular Music, the Sacred, and the Profane*, Oxford: Oxford University Press, 2014.

Possamai, A., *Religion and Popular Culture: A Hyper-Real Testament*, Brussels: P. I. E. Peter Lang, 2005.

Potter, J., *Representing Reality: Discourse, Rhetoric and Social Construction*, London: Sage, 1996.

Powell, M. A., *Encyclopedia of Contemporary Christian Music*, Peabody, MA: Hendrickson Publishers, 2002.

Purcell, N., *Death Metal Music: The Passion and Politics of a Subculture*, Jefferson, NC: McFarland & Company, Inc. Publishers, 2003.

Raschke, C. A., *Painted Black: From Drug Killings to Heavy Metal: The Alarming True Story of How Satanism Is Terrorizing Our Communities*, San Francisco, CA: Harper & Row, 1990.

Reisigl, M. and Wodak, R., 'The Discourse-Historical Approach', in R. Wodak and M. Meyer (eds), *Methods of Critical Discourse Analysis*, Second edition, London: Sage, 2008.

Reynolds, S., *Blissed Out: The Raptures of Rock*, London: Serpents Tail, 1990.

Romanowski, W. D., 'Evangelicals and Popular Music: The Contemporary Christian Music Industry', in B. D. Forbes and J. H. Mahan (eds), *Religion and Popular Culture in America*, Berkeley, CA: University of California Press, 2005.

Rowe, S., Heaven's Metal, 62 (2006), p. 21.

Scott, N. R. W., 'Heavy Metal and the Deafening Threat of the Apolitical', in T. Hjelm, K. Kahn-Harris and M. LeVine (eds), *Heavy Metal: Controversies and Countercultures*, London: Equinox Publishing, 2013.

Slater, D., *Consumer Culture and Modernity*, London: Wiley, 1997.

St. John, G. (ed.), *Rave Culture and Religion*, London: Routledge, 2004.

———, 'Electronic Dance Music Culture and Religion: An Overview', *Culture and Religion* 7 (2006), pp. 1–25.

Stolow, J., 'Religion, Media, and Globalization', in B. S. Turner (ed.), *The New Blackwell Companion to the Sociology of Religion*, Chichester: Blackwell, 2010.

Stout, D. A. and Buddenbaum, J. M. (eds), *Religion and Popular Culture: Studies on the Interaction of Worldviews*, Ames: Iowa State University Press, 2001

Straw, W., 'Systems of Articulation, Logics of Change: Communities and Scenes in Popular Music', *Cultural Studies* 5 (1991), pp. 368–388.

———, 'Scenes and Sensibilities', *Public* 22–23 (2001), pp. 245–257.

Strother, E. S., *Unlocking the Paradox of Christian Metal Music*, Diss., University of Kentucky, 2013.

Swaggart, J., *Religious Rock 'n' Roll: A Wolf in Sheep's Clothing*, Baton Rouge, LA: Swaggart Ministries, 1987.

Sylvan, R., *Traces of the Spirit: The Religious Dimensions of Popular Music*, New York: New York University Press, 2002.
Taves, A., *Religious Experience Reconsidered: A Building-Block Approach to the Study of Religion and Other Special Things*, Princeton, NJ: Princeton University Press, 2009.
Taylor, S., 'Locating and Conducting Discourse Analytic Research', in M. Wetherell, S. Taylor and S. T. Yates (eds), *Discourse as Data: A Guide for Analysis*, London: Sage, 2001.
Thompson, J. J., *Raised by Wolves: The Story of Christian Rock & Roll*, Toronto: ECW Press, 2000.
Thornton, S., *Club Cultures: Music, Media and Subcultural Capital*, Cambridge: Polity Press, 1995.
Till, R., *Pop Cult: Religion and Popular Music*, London: Continuum, 2010.
Turner, V., *Dramas, Fields and Metaphors: Symbolic Action in Human Society*, London: Cornell University Press, 1974.
Vasquez, M. A., 'Tracking Global Evangelical Christianity', *Journal of the American Academy of Religion* 71 (2003), pp. 157–173.
von Stuckrad, K. 'Discursive Study of Religion: From States of the Mind to Communication and Action', *Method and Theory in the Study of Religion* 15 (2003), pp. 255–271.
———, 'Reflections on the Limits of Reflection: An Invitation to the Discursive Study of Religion' *Method and Theory in the Study of Religion* 22 (2010), pp. 156–169.
Wallach, J., Berger, H. M. and Greene, P. D. (eds), *Metal Rules the Globe: Heavy Metal Music Around the World*, Durham, NC: Duke University Press, 2011.
Walser, R., *Running with the Devil. Power, Gender and Madness in Heavy Metal Music*, Hanover, CT: Wesleyan University Press, 1993.
Webb, P., *Exploring the Networked Worlds of Popular Music: Milieu Cultures*, New York, NY: Routledge, 2007.
Weber, M., 'The Nature of Social Action', in W. G. Runciman (ed.), *Weber: Selections in Translation*, Cambridge: Cambridge University Press, 1991.
Weedon, C., *Identity and Culture: Narratives of Difference and Belonging*, New York, NY: Open University Press, (2004), p. 4.
Weinstein, D., *Heavy Metal: A Cultural Sociology*, New York, NY: Lexington Books, 1991.
———, *Heavy Metal: The Music and Its Culture*, New York, NY: Da Capo Press, 2000.
Wetherell, M., 'Themes in Discourse Research: The Case of Diana', in M. Wetherell, S. Taylor and S. J. Yates (eds), *Discourse Theory and Practice*, London: Sage, 2001.
Williams, R. H., 'Religious Social Movements in the Public Sphere: Organization, Ideology, and Activism', in M. Dillon (ed.), *Handbook of the Sociology of Religion*, Cambridge: Cambridge University Press, 2003.
Willis, P., *Profane Culture*, London: Routledge, 1978.
Wright, R., '"I'd Sell You Suicide": Pop Music and Moral Panic in the Age of Marilyn Manson', *Popular Music* 19 (2000), pp. 365–385.
Wuthnow, R. J., 'Taking Talk Seriously: Religious Discourse as Social Practice', *Journal for the Scientific Study of Religion* 50 (2011), pp. 1–21.

Websites

Ancient Prophesy http://www.ancientprophecy.de/home.htm [accessed 7 July 2014].
Angelic Warlord.com http://www.angelicwarlord.com/ [accessed 13 July 2014].
Bobfest http://www.bobfest.org/ [accessed 13 July 2014].
Blessed Resistance https://www.blessedresistance.com/index.php [accessed 12 July 2014].
Classic Christian Rock http://www.classicchristianrock.net/ [accessed 13 July 2014].
Christian Metal http://en.wikipedia.org/wiki/Christian_metal [accessed 11 July 2014].
Christian Metal Realm http://thecmr.forumotion.com/ [accessed 13 July 2014].
Cross Stream http://www.thecrossstream.com/ [accessed 13 July 2014].
Dial the Truth Ministries http://www.av1611.org/ [accessed 13 July 2014].
Firestream.net http://firestream.freeforums.org/index.php?sid=089eba790eeb89 36bbee1c89c7a08c70 [accessed 13 July 2014].
Full Armor of God http://www.fullarmorradio.com/ [accessed 13 July 2014].
Heaven's Metal http://www.angelfire.com/wv/heavensmetal/ [accessed 13 July 2014].
Intense Radio http://www.intenseradio.com/ [accessed 13 July 2014].
JesusMetal http://home.wanadoo.nl/kemman/homer.htm [accessed 28 November 2008].
Kristillinen Metallimusiikki http://fi.wikipedia.org/wiki/Kristillinen_metallimusiikki [accessed 11 July 2014].
Kristillinen Metalliunioni http://www.metalliunioni.com/forum/ [accessed 13 July 2014].
Majestic Vanguard http://www.majesticvanguard.net/site.php?page=biography.php [accessed 7 July 2014].
Metal Bible http://www.themetalbible.com/ [accessed 14 July 2014].
Metal for Jesus Page http://www.metalforjesus.org [accessed 11 July 2014].
Metallimessu http://metallimessu.com/ [accessed 14 July 2014].
Nordic Mission http://www.nordicmission.net/ [accessed 26 November 2008].
Refinery Rock http://www.therefineryrock.com/ [accessed 13 July 2014].
Reign Radio http://www.reignradio.com/index.html [accessed 13 July 2014].
Rivel Records http://www.rivelrecords.com/main.php [accessed 8 July 2014].
Rowe Productions http://www.roweproductions.com/ [accessed 13 July 2014].
Sanctified Steel http://sanctifiedsteel.blogspot.fi/ [accessed 13 July 2014].
Sanctuary International http://www.sanctuaryinternational.com/ [accessed 7 July 2014].
Ultimatum http://www.ultimatum.net/mainframe.html [accessed 12 July 2014].
Unblack Noise http://unblacknoise.wordpress.com/2008/10/08/christian-metal-a-defence/ [accessed 26 November 2008].
Unblack Metal http://en.wikipedia.org/wiki/Unblack_metal [accessed 13 July 2014].

Magazines and Fanzines

Devotion HardMusic Magazine 3, 2001.
Extreme Brutal Death 2005/1.

Heaven's Metal 62, 2006.
Ristillinen 3, 2002.

Discography

Admonish, *Den yttersta tiden*, Admonish, 2005.
Bride, *Show No Mercy*, Pure Metal Records, 1986.
Deliverance, *Deliverance*, Intense Records, 1989.
Deliverance, *Weapons of Our Warfare*, Intense Records, 1990.
Impending Doom, *There Will Be Violence*, Facedown Records, 2010.
Mortification, *Post Momentary Affliction*, Intense Records, 1993.
Mortification, *The Evil Addiction Destroying Machine*, Rowe Productions, 2009.
Recon, *Behind Enemy Lines*, Intense Records, 1990.
Saint, *Time's End*, Pure Metal, 1986.
Saint, *The Mark*, Armor Records, 2006.
Saint, *Crime Scene Earth*, Armor Records, 2008.
Stryper, *The Yellow and Black Attack*, Enigma Records, 1984.
Stryper, *Soldiers Under Command*, Enigma, 1985.
Stryper, *To Hell with the Devil*, Enigma Records, 1986.
Ultimatum, *The Mechanics of Perilous Times*, Gutter Records/Massacre Records, 2000.
Vengeance Rising, *Human Sacrifice*, Intense Records, 1989.
War of Ages, *Arise and Conquer*, Facedown Records, 2008.

Interviews

IF 2005/5: 1–7. Interview with Johannes. The Folkloristic Archive at Åbo Akademi University. The Folkloristic Archive at Åbo Akademi University.
IF 2006/9. Interview with Christian metal scene member. The Folkloristic Archive at Åbo Akademi University.
IF mgt 2007/69. Interview with Finnish Christian metal musician. The Folkloristic Archive at Åbo Akademi University.

Index

AC/DC (band) 11
Admonish (band) 38, 51, 54, 148
Agape (band) 34
Aletheian (band) 38
Almighty Metal Radio 111
Ancient Prophecy (band) 139
Angelic Warlond.com 34, 109–110
Antestor (band) 38, 101
Antichrist 28, 54
anti-Admonish website 51, 148
anti-Christian 15–18, 62, 146
apocalypticism 14, 16, 42
Arch of Thorns (band) 38
Arise and Conquer (album) 63–64
Armor Records 100–101
Arnett, Jeffrey 6–7, 18, 23
As I Lay Dying (band) 39
Ashen Mortality (band) 38
Australia 38–39, 44, 95–96, 101, 116
Austria 8

Balance of Power (band) 38
Barren Cross (band) 2, 35, 48, 54
Bathory (band) 15
Beeman, Bob 35, 97, 112, 117
Behind Enemy Lines (album) 59
'Behind Enemy Lines' (song) 59
Belgium 95, 97–98
Believer (band) 37
Bible 14, 27, 35, 50, 55, 58, 63, 76–77, 107–108, 114–115, 139, 141–143
biblical 14, 16, 35, 50, 55, 58, 63, 76–77, 107–108, 114–115, 139, 141–143
  themes 16, 54, 55, 56
black metal 15, 18–19, 37–39, 50–51, 62, 91, 94, 97, 103, 105, 148
  and church arsons 15, 18, 91, 94
  Norwegian scene 15, 18, 51, 92, 97

  and Satanism 15, 19, 37–38, 91, 94, 105
  in South America 105
Black Sabbath (band) 10–11
Blast of Eternity 98, 113
Bleakwail (band) 139
Blessed Resistance 60
Bloodbought Records 101
Bloodgood (band) 2, 35, 48
Bobfest 97, 112
Bombwork Records 101
Books of Moses 54
Brazil 4, 37–38, 83, 95–96, 98–99, 101, 103–105, 113, 117, 119, 140
Bride (band) 35, 63
Britain 7, 11, 27, 38
Buried Scrolls Webzine 105

Canada 35–36, 38, 116
Centre for Contemporary Cultural Studies (CCCS) 86–87
Children of Bodom (band) 16
Christ 27–28, 41, 45, 48, 54, 56–58, 63, 108, 110, 135–136, 138–139
Christcore 39
Christianity
  Catholic 4, 83, 95–96
  Charismatic 50, 58, 71, 76, 96, 152
  conservative 3, 17, 28, 35, 41, 46–52, 61, 140, 146
  evangelical 1–3, 17, 25–29, 35, 46–48, 51, 58, 72, 74, 76, 78, 95–96, 115, 118, 129, 152, 155
  Orthodox 78
  Pentecostal 58, 76, 96, 147, 152
Christian metal
  aesthetics 62–63, 74–75, 140, 151
  apologetics 107, 140

INDEX

and bodily practices 3–4, 31, 67, 73–81, 129, 154
concerts 72–82, 133
in continental Europe 97–98, 117
controversy 46–52, 131
criticism of 47–52, 146–148
definition of 41–46
development of 34–39
distros 99, 101–103
festivals 112–113
in Latin America 98–99
lyrical themes 53–61
media 104–112
in the Nordic countries 97
in North America 96–97
record labels 100–102
sub-genres 37–39
visual dimension 61-65
Christian Metal Force Brasilia 98
Christian Metal Realm 110
Classic Christian Rock Radio 111
CM Sweden/Rivel Records 101
Colombia 99
Comunidade Zadoque 98
congregation 35–36, 50, 79, 113
Contemporary Christian Music (CCM) 30–31, 41, 45, 62, 92–93, 133–134, 144
definition of 30
Cornerstone Festival 113
corpse-paint 51
counter-culture 9–10, 14, 29, 142–143
Crash Church 98
Creation Festival 113
'Crime Scene Earth' (song) 57
Crimson Moonlight (band) 38, 101, 148
Crimson Thorn (band) 38
Cradle of Filth (band) 15
Cross Stream 111
culture wars 46–47

Daniel Band (band) 34–35
Darkthrone (band) 15
de-traditionalization 154–155
Death (band) 15
death metal 14, 38, 44, 116, 135
Deep Purple (band) 10

Def Leppard (band) 12
Deliverance (band) 37, 56, 59, 117
Demon Hunter (band) 39, 54, 60
Den yttersta tiden (album) 54
Denmark 113
denomination 1, 118, 131–132, 136–137, 146, 153–154
Destruction Fest 113
Deuteronomium (band) 38, 54
Devil, the 6, 14, 17, 35, 39, 58
The Devil Wears Prada (band) 39
Devotion HardMusic Magazine 104–105
Dial the Truth Ministries 146
Dikaion Fest 99
Dimmu Borgir (band) 15
discourse
  analysis 126–127
  definition of 125–127
discursive construction
  external 94, 146–149
  internal 92–93, 130–146
Divinefire (band) 38, 101
Divine Metal Distro 102
Drottnar (band) 38, 101
Durkheim, Emile 21

Ecuador 99
E.E.E. Recordings 101
Elements of Rock 98, 113
Eliade, Mircea 21
Emperor (band) 15
end times 57
Endtime Festival 97, 112
Endtime Productions 101
Enigma Records/Capitol 37
Ephesians (Epistle) 58
eschatology 14, 27, 37, 42, 53–55, 59, 63
Eternal Reign 104
Europe
  continental 37, 97, 99, 101, 115–116, 119
  Northern 88, 95, 112–113, 117–118
evangelical popular culture industry 26–31, 37, 40, 48, 96, 118
Evangelicalism
  evangelicals 26–29
  main characteristics 26–28

INDEX

in North America 28–30, 35, 46–48, 50, 55, 93–94, 96, 131, 152
evangelistic capital 92, 100, 117
Extol (band) 38, 54, 101, 148
Extreme Brutal Death 104–105, 108, 119
extreme metal 6–7, 15–18, 37, 50, 70, 73, 90, 96, 101–102, 105
Extreme Records 101, 108

Facebook 87, 111
Facedown Records 64–65, 101
'Faster for the Master!' 39
Fear Dark 98, 101, 113
Fear Dark Festivals 98, 113
Finland 5, 38, 77, 80, 93–95, 97–98, 101, 112, 114, 117, 147
Fire Throne (band) 38
Firestream.net 110
'Flesh and Blood' (song) 59
Flicker Records 101
Forca Eterna Records 103
Frontline Records 101
Frosthardr (band) 38
Full Armor of God 111

gender roles 24, 41, 49, 56
genre
    code 9–11
    definition of 9
Germany 38, 95, 97–98, 113, 140
Girder Music 102
glam metal 4, 35, 46, 49–50
Godwin, Jeff 49
Goreship 39
Gospel Metal 37
Grateful Dead (band) 11
Green Light District Festival 113

hard rock 9–11, 34, 103–104, 116
hardcore/hardcore punk 13, 16, 39, 90, 103, 113, 116
Harmony (band) 38
Headbanger's Rest 97
headbanging 13, 75–77, 80–81
Heartcry (band) 38
Heaven's Metal (fanzine) 34, 37, 44, 104, 106, 119, 135
Heaven's Metal (online radio) 111

heavy metal
    aesthetics 16, 51, 62–63, 75
    concerts 13, 21–22, 49, 75, 77, 79, 81, 115–116
    development of 9–16
    musical dimension 11–12
    style 12–13
    verbal dimension 13–14
    visual dimension 12–13
Hellig Usvart (album) 38, 148
Hendrix, Jimi 11
HM: The Hard Music Magazine 34, 37, 104, 106, 107
Holy Blood (band) 54
Holy Soldier (band) 35
Holy Spirit 78
Holy Steel 38, 104
Horde (band) 38, 101, 116, 148
Human Sacrifice (album) 37, 63

identity
    Christian 4, 36, 115, 121, 143, 151, 154
    cultural 20, 81, 86
    religious 1, 18, 23, 74, 79, 81, 89, 130, 154
Immortal Metal Fest 77, 80, 112
Immortal Souls (band) 38, 101, 148
Immortal Zine 105
Impending Doom (band) 39, 59, 64–65
Incubus 38
Indonesia 6
infiltration 28, 45
Infiltration Squad 60
Insacris 99
instrumentalism 31, 70–73, 77, 81–82
Intense Radio 111
Intense Records 100
internet
    significance of 83, 90, 99, 100, 102, 104, 111–112
Iron Guardian Industries 103
Iron Maiden (band) 12
Italy 96, 98

Jacobs Dream (band) 38
Jefferson Airplane (band) 11
Jerusalem (band) 34

INDEX

Jesus Movement 30, 76
JesusMetal 98, 109, 144
Jonsson, Johannes 107–109, 132, 136
Judas Priest (band) 11

Kahn-Harris, Keith 6–7, 15–16, 18, 70, 73, 84–85, 87, 89, 91–92
Kekal (band) 96
Kerrang! 35
KISS (band) 11, 49
Kohllapse (band) 39
Korn (band) 16
Kristillinen metalliunioni 111

Lament Distributions 103
Last Judgment 54, 56–57
Latin America 5, 37, 95–96, 98–99, 116–118, 152
Led Zeppelin (band) 10
Leviticus (band) 35
lifestyle (theoretical concept) 86–87
Light Shall Prevail (band) 38
Liljegren Records 101
Limp Bizkit (band) 16
Lion of Judah 63
Living Sacrifice (band) 38
Lutheran 114, 147, 152

machismo 40, 56, 75
Majestic Vanguard (band) 138–139
The Mark (album) 54
Mastodon (band) 16
Mayhem (band) 15
mediation 78
mega-church 50
Megadeth (band) 14
Mercyful Fate (band) 37
Messiah Prophet (band) 35
metalheads 6, 11, 22, 23, 39–40, 61–62, 74, 76, 81, 92, 101, 106, 108, 114–115, 128, 131–132, 135, 137–140, 143, 145, 147–148, 152–153
Metallica (band) 14
Metal Bible 107–108, 114–115
Metal Blade Records 37
Metal Community 103, 107
Metal Countdown 107, 111
Metal Fest of the Creator of Night 113

Metal for Jesus Page 34, 42, 106, 108–109, 134, 137, 141
Metal Land 105
Metal Mardi Gras 113
Metal Mass 114
metal ministry 97–99, 137, 140
Metal Mission 103
metal missionaries 92, 117, 142
metal music
　　controversy 2, 5–6, 17, 23, 41, 46–48, 51
　　and religion 17–23
　　sub-genres 7–8, 11, 13–18, 39
Mexico 4, 37, 83, 95–96, 98–99, 113, 117, 140
Momentum Scandinavia 101
Morbid Angel (band) 15
Mortification (band) 2, 38, 44, 60, 64, 101, 116–117, 135, 148
moshing 13, 73, 75–77, 80–81
Mötley Crüe (band) 49
movement culture 47
MTV 35
musical authenticity 10, 44, 46, 51–53
Myspace 111

Narnia (band) 38
neo-tribe 86–87
Netherlands, The 38, 95, 97–98, 101, 113
New Wave of British Heavy Metal (NWOBHM) 12
97.7 FM The Underground Church 111
'No Time' (song) 56
Noizegate Music 104
Nordic Fest 97, 112
Nordic Mission 101, 103, 112
Norway 5, 38, 51, 91, 94–95, 97–98, 101, 103, 117
Nuclear Blast Records 38, 148
numinous (theoretical term) 21–22, 68

occultism/the occult 14–15, 17, 81, 115
One Way 76–77
Open Grave Records/Sullen Records 101
Oratorio (band) 101

INDEX

Paganism 14–15, 91
Pantokrator (band) 38, 54, 101
Paraguay 99
Parakletos (band) 101
Paramaecium (band) 38
Parent-Teacher Association (PTA) 17
Parents Music Resource Center (PMRC) 17, 47, 50
Petra (band) 34
Plymouth Brethren 27
P.O.D. (band) 16, 39
Poland 38–39, 96, 98
popular culture
    definition of 24–25
    mass-mediated 25
    and religion 23–26
popular music
    and discourse 128–129
    and religion 21–23, 84–85, 88–89, 91, 94
Possessed (band) 15
Post Momentary Affliction (album) 64
post-structuralism 123
post-subcultural theory 85–87
praise pose 76–77, 80
Prayer Warriors 107
'Primed and Ready' (song) 55
Psalms, Book of 50, 142
punk rock 6, 12, 14, 103
Pure Metal Records 37, 100

Rad Rockers.com 102
Rage of Angels (band) 35
rapture 27, 55
re-aesthetization 63, 77
rebellion 14, 17, 38, 47–49, 59–61, 75, 142–143, 148, 151
Recon (band) 35, 59
Refinery Rock Radio 111
Reign Radio 111
religion, definition of 20–21
religious
    experience 4, 20–22, 27, 29, 67-69, 74, 77–78, 152, 155
    expression 4, 29, 36, 50–51, 115, 118, 121, 133–137, 140–141, 143–144, 146, 151–155
Resurrection Band (band) 34

Retroactive Records 101
Revelation, Book of 16, 27, 54–55, 63
R.E.X. Records 37, 100
Rowe, Steve 44–45, 101, 117, 135–136
Roxx Productions 101
Rugged Cross Music 102
Rugged Records 101

sacred-profane binary 20–21
Sacred Warrior (band) 35, 54
Saint (band) 35, 54–55, 57, 63
'Salvation' (song) 60
Sanctifica (band) 38, 54
Sanctified Steel 109
Sanctuary International 36, 97, 111–113, 117, 136
Sanctuary-movement 35–36, 49–50, 98, 113, 140
Satan 14, 19, 39, 49, 58, 63
satanic 15, 17, 19, 37–38, 76, 94, 105, 146
Satanism 6, 14–17, 19, 46, 48, 50–51, 91, 94, 110, 115
Saviour Machine (band) 38, 54
Saxon (band) 12
scene, concept of 84–85
scenic
    capital 89, 91–92, 116–117
    construction 92–95
    infrastructure 89–90
    institutions 89–90
    production and consumption 92
    stability 90
    structure 89–92
Screams of Abel 105
Scrolls of the Megilloth (album) 38
Second Coming of Christ 27–28, 54
sensational forms 74–75, 78–81
Seventh Avenue (band) 38
Shaver Audio and Video 102
Sherlock, Jayson 116
Show no Mercy (album) 63
Slayer (band) 14
Slechtvalk (band) 38
Slipknot (band) 16
social constructionism 122–127
Soldiers under Command (album) 59
Solid State Records 101

Soundmass.com 103
spiritual warfare 37, 42, 48, 54, 57–61, 81, 105, 151
Stryper (band) 2, 35, 39, 59, 64, 117
subculture 6, 21, 29, 84–87
sui generis (theoretical term) 20–22
Swaggart, Jimmy 49
Sweden 5, 34–36, 38, 42, 95, 97, 101, 103–104, 106, 113–114, 117, 140
Sweet, Michael 117
Switzerland 98, 113
Sylvan, Robin 21–22
Sympathy (band) 38

testimonies 27, 106–107, 114–115
Theocracy (band) 38
Theocracy Ministry 99
There will be Violence (album) 64–65
'There will be Violence' (song) 59
thrash metal 14–15, 37, 50, 62–63, 101, 116
Time's End (album) 63
Timothy (Epistle) 58
To Hell with the Devil (album) 35
Tooth & Nail Records 101
Total Armageddon Fest 113
Tourniquet (band) 37, 54, 116
transcendence 67–71, 73–74, 81, 152
transgression 3, 7, 14, 16–18, 48, 67, 69–73, 81, 92, 152
tribulation 27
'Turn or Burn!' 39
Twisted Sister (band) 48

Ukraine 113
unblack metal 38–39, 51, 54, 62, 97, 101, 116, 139, 148
Unblack Noise 142
Unblack.com 98
Underground Festival 112
Underground Outreach 99
unDark Webstore 103
Underoath (band) 39
Undish (band) 39
United Kingdom 113
United States 16–17, 29–30, 33–39, 47, 61, 94–96, 98, 100–101, 104, 113, 116–118, 147
Usvart Zine 38

Vaakevandring (band) 38
Vengeance Rising (band) 37, 63
Veni Domine (band) 38
Venom (band) 15, 37
Victory Zine 104
'Violence and Bloodshed' (song) 60
Vomitorial Corpulence (band) 38

Walser, Robert 6–7, 11, 14, 18, 128
War of Ages (band) 39, 64
Weapons of our Warfare (album) 59
Weinstein, Deena 6–7, 10–14, 16, 18, 20–22, 34, 47
Whipping Post, The 104
white metal 34, 37
White Throne 37
Wikipedia 34

Yellow and Black Attack (album) 64

www.ingramcontent.com/pod-product-compliance
Ingram Content Group UK Ltd.
Pitfield, Milton Keynes, MK11 3LW, UK
UKHW021048160426
470027UK00007B/136